HACKING
THE
GOD CODE

Classic Works by Patricia Cori

The Cosmos of Soul: A Wake-up Call for Humanity

Atlantis Rising: The Struggle of Darkness and Light

No More Secrets, No More Lies: A Handbook to Starseed Awakening

The Starseed Dialogues: Soul Searching the Universe

Beyond the Matrix: Daring Conversations with the Brilliant Minds of Our Times

Where Pharaohs Dwell: One Mystic's Journey Through the Gates of Immortality

Before We Leave You: Messages From the Great Whales and the Mighty Dolphin Beings

The Emissary — A Novel

The Sirian Starseed Tarot

The Sirian Seal: A Starseed Tool of Transformation

The New Sirian Revelations: Galactic Prophecies for the Ascending Human Collective

Heaven is Here Beneath the Tree—A Book of Poems

HACKING
THE
GOD CODE

PATRICIA CORI

HACKING THE GOD CODE is published by Patricia Cori

Cover art: shutterstock.com/ Cover design: Onyx Tikal Sermet
Interior layout and design: Michael Boalch

Library of Congress Cataloging-in-Publication Data

Cori, Patricia.
Hacking the God Code: The Conspiracy to Steal the Human Soul / Patricia Cori.

Summary: "Describes how our society is careening into a dystopian rewrite of global society and the future of humanity, penned by a tyrannical New World Order: the Great Reset. With the onset of Covid-19 and all that has played out since early 2020, Big Pharma and High Tech have seized our lives in the most evil of ways. They do not intend to let go, until their nightmare agenda to merge human beings with Artificial Intelligence—Human 2.0—has revolutionized everything about our lives, enslaved us and possessed our world."—Provided by author

ISBN: 978-989-53812-2-7

Disclaimer

I am a metaphysician—not a physician.
The information in this book is for general information purposes
and nothing contained within it is intended to be construed as medical advice.
It does not pretend to provide expertise in the field of medicine and therefore
cannot claim to serve as a substitute for medical attention, examination, advice,
treatment of existing conditions or diagnosis.
It is up to you, the individual, to determine what is the most appropriate and
desirable course of treatment and or prevention from what is available to you and
what you believe is right for your individual situation and health needs.
Choose Wisely.

Acknowledgements

I am so blessed to have such wonderful support from friends and from my international community. You know who you are! Heartfelt thanks to all of you for loving me, and for supporting my work over the decades. To all in service to Spirit, truth seekers, it is for you all that I march forward, sharing what I can to speak my truth, to whomever is ready to hear it. My umbrella got blown away a long time ago and I learned to walk between the raindrops. It is for you that I stand tall, collar to the wind, as the storm tries to push me back and away.

Sacha Stone, you are always an inspiration. Thank you for your beautiful words and all that you contribute to the world.

Shout out to Onyx Tikal Sermet for her powerful design for the cover of this book and to Michael Boach, who did the layout. Gratitude to my dear friend and publicist, Dea Shandera-Hunter, for all she is doing to help me get this out to the world; to my loving friend Peter B., who has shared a lot of my process and listened to endless pages and versions of the manuscript, in varying stages of the book's evolution, over many months. You are an endless source of strength and I am so grateful that you are in my life. And big love to my dear cosmic daughter, Jess Tyas, who is always there, showering love across the wires. You are my angel.

My beloved mother will forever be my inspiration, wherever she is in the heavens. Thank you, mother of mothers, for teaching me to always strive to be the best that I can be, to seek the diamond in the coal, and to never forget to laugh and celebrate life, no matter where my journey takes me.

And last but never least, my fur babies, Pepper and Scootch. They lie long hours, curled up by my chair, patiently waiting for me to finish the day's writing, so that we can play. They fill my world with laughter and remind me that love is all that matters in this life.

To the Sirian High Council,
My teachers, beloved guides and eternal inspiration . . .
You have given me wings
and shown me the brilliance beyond the clouds.
And now, for just this moment on the forever,
I must be brave
and fly this storm on my own . . .

"First they came for the Communists
and I did not speak out
because I was not a Communist.
Then they came for the Socialists
and I did not speak out
because I was not a Socialist.
Then they came for the trade unionists
and I did not speak out
because I was not a trade unionist.
Then they came for the Jews
and I did not speak out
because I was not a Jew.
Then they came for me
and there was no one left
to speak out for me."

First They Came
—Martin Niemöller

Table of Contents

Foreword by Sacha Stone .... *xv*

Introduction .... *xvii*

Part One

Secrets Revealed

1. Playing God With Creation 1
2. The Sirian Experiment...7
3. They Walk Amongst Us 21
4. The Strident March of Transhumanism................................31
5. Designing "Human 2.0"...41
6. Our "Type Zero" Planet..59
7. DNA: The Divine Blueprint 73
8. Battle Station: Earth...83
9. Biowarfare: Plain and Simple...95
10. The Messenger RNA Injection 107
11. Souls in Shut Down..127
12. The Great Disconnect...141
13. Honor the God Code Within..157
14. YHWH Deciphering the God Code 181
15. CRISPR The Cut and Paste Gene Disrupter.........................193
16. Lucifer In...203
17. Microsoft Patent WO2020060606A1 209

Part Two

Light Upon Darkness

18. The Light Strings of the Universe..229

19. Manifestation and the Sovereign Spirit 243

20. Reclaim Your Mind..253

21. Sacred Designs, Perfect Ratios...271

22. The "Shattered Glass"...277

Visualization Clearing the Pathways..285

Visualization Scanning the Double Helix................................293

Meditation The Primary Tetrahedron.......................................299

Meditation The Star Tetrahedron..305

Epilogue..311

About the Channel..315

The Divine Blueprint – On-Line Course in DNA Activation 317

Foreword

by

Sacha Stone

The wholesale elevation of humanity from its torpor, within an ancient galactic sleep-cycle, has been the cross borne by Patricia Cori for many years. The zenith of her great task of heroic authorship is exemplified by this axiomatic work: *Hacking the God Code: The Conspiracy to Steal the Human Soul.*

Demarcating the epochal departure of seeded Angelic Humans from an arcane thrall of the Lords of Time . . . this latter-day gospel of ascensionist strategy is the truest gift of a fully realized Mother of our age.

We are invited to review our individual and collective journey from cosmogenesis to the status quo, and from here to depart the linear and binary cage-matrix into the quantum realm of immanence. Threading the curve of collective destiny far beyond the galactic conspiracy of a draconian dragnet, Cori offers universal redemption to those with the eyes to see and the will to manifest "be-ing," not only as sparks of divinity, but as the roaring inferno of the Creator we truly are. This is the hallowed Christed message—the truest orientation of Buddhism—and the atom-seed of Sufic enigma.

Humanity is not only the Krystic octave of universal expression now standing at the threshold of the spiral of ascension; we are, in true-fact, the Gods of auld seeing the world through the eyes of a child—the Child of ages—bearing witness to the emergence of patterns of perfection in the mortal realm: in abeyance to the eternal principle of prior unity to which we claim birthright, and to which we salute one another in fellowship of remembrance.

For it is within the remembrance of our divinity that we reclaim ownership of the geometry of Now and accede within that quanta, that we never departed angelic source. We only laid it to the side, in a cosmic act of self-sacrifice, in order to ultimately remember ourselves to ourselves once adherence to the Lords of Time had fulfilled purpose: the forging of the fabric of soul in the cauldron of a temporal universe.

This sojourn within remembrance to re-genesis is the true hero's journey: a return to the still-point of Creation, armed with our cornucopia of stories, as we reconcile Alpha to Omega. This is our collective raison d'être and cornerstone to galactic ascendancy.

We bow to the Lords of Time, as they kneel before us. By this sacrament we bid them adieu, and take up our staff, to close the cycle.

What greater gift, than this.

Arise Homo sapiens.

Introduction

"Never be bullied into silence.
Never allow yourself to be made a victim.
Accept no one's definition of your life: define yourself."
- Robert Frost

My wise and blessed mother—my guiding light—always told me: "You never really know what you believe in until you have something to lose by defending it."

No greater lesson have I ever learned in life than what I gleaned from those immortal words. In times of tyranny, such as these, it becomes a truly noble commitment for any of us to pursue truth and to share what we perceive it to be, in service to others . . . especially in the wake of condemnation that comes of challenging the status quo. Faced with the tightening screw of censorship and a very real threat of persecution for those of us who choose to swim against the tide of conformism, we find the strength to own who we really are, to examine our values and morality, and to hold firm to our mission to serve as warriors of light, as we travel the path of self-discovery and enlightenment.

It demands of us a state of fearlessness and courage . . . and immense determination. It requires peering into the darkness and dredging up the accumulated debris of many lifetimes—shadows that cloud the tenebrous lagoon of the subconscious—into the radiance of conscious awareness, where we can sift through all the garbage we have collected along the way and examine it all with objectivity. We must be willing to sail the seas of those uncharted waters of subconscious mind, where our resolve pushes us to peer into the deep—there, where ancient phantoms, specters of our own making, wait to be brought up into the light and set free.

At this time of incredible upheaval and radical change from the world we knew a few short years ago, we are most empowered and liberated when we confront those irrational, inexplicable fears, in the full light of awakening mind. Anchored deep within the Earth, we need to be strong enough to hold our ground—like a lighthouse—when ceaseless storms flood our shores, eroding the fiber of our earthly existence. Only from that place of immutable strength can we reverse the destructive course set for us by a global political class comprised of swarms of minions, dedicated to those who rule over them, as they do us, as the "New World Order."

Theirs is a corrupt cabal that we can only describe, at this point, as ruthless, criminally insane and toxic beyond measure.

If we are truly to liberate ourselves from its grip, we are going to have to bring the proverbial hammer down on any persistent sense of powerlessness that still deters us. With every ounce of force and determination we can muster . . . overcoming all obstruction and the inertia born of fear and doubt, we must find the strength to crack the emotional encrustation that encases the gem—**TRUTH**—hidden within it, and hold it up to the sun. Bathed in the brilliance, it refracts, like a faceted diamond, into rainbows—revealing the full spectrum of visible light; it nurtures the heart and spirit of all awakened souls who have eyes to see past the smoke screen that has been placed before their lens on reality.

The act of seeking truth, and sharing what we understand it to be, empowers us all to go deep within ourselves to examine the existential dilemma that has so overwhelmed us with terror over anything that threatens our physical lives that we no longer recognize how that irrational fear has been manipulated and utilized as a precision weapon against not only our mortal bodies, but our very souls. Angst over what the ubiquitous shadow can provoke in our world dulls our reason, numbs our hearts, and brings so many people to their knees, in submission and obedience.

Where there is fear, the bogeyman never sleeps.

Damage to the physical body from a prolonged state of living in fear is immense and can be long-lasting, even permanent, as is the case with the debilitating mind/body condition psychologists have named "post-traumatic syndrome." Beyond the emotional disruption triggered by a traumatic event, the survival fear, and the resulting chronic anxiety it brings about, weaken the immune system. They can cause all manner of physical impairment, including permanent cardiovascular damage.

Let us not confuse a perpetual state of being always afraid and terrified of life, each other, and the world around us with how our exquisite mind/body mechanism responds to what the brain specifically perceives as an "immediate threat" to survival. These are two very different matters. An imminent threat or danger, such as being stalked by a wild animal in the woods, or hearing someone break into your house when you are in bed, activates a response in the region of the brain known as the "amygdala"; that is the part of the brain that triggers the release of stress hormones and activates the sympathetic nervous system, in preparation for fight or flight. The physical body automatically moves into emergency mode; adrenal glands start pumping, pupils dilate, breathing accelerates. The muscles instantly swell up with blood, prepared to react with Herculean physical strength to whatever is threatening the body's survival. The heart rate increases and blood pressure rises, as the body systems determine the proper response: to stay and fight, with that exceptional strength, or to run ... with superhuman speed and the stamina needed to escape.

These are just some of the built-in bodily responses designed to help us deal with the rare occurrence when we find ourselves in real danger to our survival, or when we perceive an immediate threat to our safety. It is why a mother can lift a car with her own two hands, when she sees that her baby is about to be crushed under its weight; it is how we exhibit heroic strength we never knew we possessed, and access the primordial instinct that triggers our fight or flight response to extreme and present danger.

Like all animals who flourish in Earth's embrace, we, electromagnetic biological units of Divine Creation, were designed to thrive, in good health, and to have the innate wisdom and strength—the unconscious and automatic body response—to survive any immediate threat to our own being, or to those we love . . . even to help a stranger in trouble. In those rare instances, we don't have to think about what to do. We simply move into automatic pilot mode to react and respond, as we have been designed to do. Once the danger has passed, all body systems return to normal.

What we are **not** designed for, however, is a constant, never-ending attack on our emotional and mental bodies. It comes from being bombarded, daily, with terrifying messaging from the media, the dysfunctional, emotional exchange between people, near and far, and a world government that dangles us—deliberately—over the precipice, holding us in a state of perpetual survival fear on every level. Whether it is war, crime, health, poverty, famine, or, most recently, the forced isolation we have been under with the "pandemic" that holds us in that state of anxiety and terror, most of the human race today live in constant anxiety and fear for their safety and their very lives. They worry about their children, terrified of what world awaits them, if we continue down this path of destruction and blind obedience to the purveyors of fear. That perpetual apprehension and feelings of rage and helplessness over the devolution of our social order cause them to live in a state of constant adrenal overload—the overproduction of the stress hormone—which, in turn, affects the brain's ability to assess the perceived danger, release from it when it has subsided, and then return to a calm, restored state of mental, emotional and physical relaxation.

For people who follow the propaganda being pumped out across the waves and who vibrate to its bandwidth, there is no release, because the perceived danger never subsides. It is designed to create perpetual anxiety and trepidation in the population. Jacked up on their body's own excess production of adrenaline, the cabal-owned media's captive audience lacks the discernment to separate reasonable perceptions of danger from reality, and so people eventually lose the ability to dial back their emotions altogether.

We are seeing human beings everywhere stuck in this state of chronic angst and acute adrenal stress. It is a direct result of what has been coined "the new normal."

*

Fear is a wild animal that preys on lost souls in haunted forests; love is the meadow . . . a wildflower . . . the sun. And it is that diamond—truth—and how, like Archangel Michael's sword, it glistens in that light that truly frees us. We must never stop seeking truth. We must never stop speaking it, whatever we understand truth to be, no matter how crushingly the loveless force that stands in obdurate opposition to Light tries to suppress and silence us.

Recognizing that unveiling truth is the only way forward and following it—past fear, obstruction, and doubt—sharpens our intellect and strengthens our inner warrior, freeing us of fear's grip upon our hearts and souls, so that we may bring the mind/body/spirit back into balance. From a place of mental and emotional quietude—the stilling of the pendulum—we are able to return to calm, restful states of conscious awareness, and finally to walk, once again, as we were meant to: as free and loving men, women and innocent children of Planet Earth.

We are ready for the truth of what is really going on to be revealed: in space, on other dimensions and most importantly, right here, on our own planet. Let there be no more secrets . . . no more lies. The more we understand any given reality, rather than accepting what is being portrayed to us by perpetrators of targeted agendas—fomenters of our base emotions—the less we fear its unfolding. We realize how our perception affects the outcome, and so we become more responsible for our thoughts, words and actions. Whether small or great, local or global, those thoughts, and more importantly our voice, contributes to the collective: asleep, awake or somewhere in between. It doesn't matter. Truth eventually seeps in.

What does matter is that we penetrate the barriers between us, ideological and behavioral walls that are being mounted to divide us, perhaps as we have never been divided before, and that we remain mindful of the rights of others, to walk as close to freedom as we possibly can. That is a far more difficult state to achieve today than it was a few years ago, before the New World Order moved into high gear, stripping our rights, silencing our voice and holding us in the forced isolation of their terror campaigns.

We are our most empowered to break free of the shackles placed upon us when we shake off the fear, and commit to bringing truth forward, as we understand it. But we can never achieve that if we remain locked up in emotionalism, hysteria and obedient group mind-think. If we are to reverse the course set for us by petty tyrants and their puppet masters, what is required of us now is that we question the narrative across the board. We need to remember how to observe with objectivity, to think critically and, above all, to seek peace, over war . . . respect, over condemnation . . . and acceptance, over dismissal of the other.

Politicians, media and the "mob mind" are actually calling for nuclear war with Russia today, in our contemporary crisis. They **want** it. Have they learned nothing from the destruction of the past and present? How anyone would ask for his own annihilation—a thermonuclear war that has the power to destroy the planet thousands of times over—is utterly beyond my comprehension. That, alone, is a sign that absolute ignorance and the stupidity born of it are becoming endemic in certain communities of our troubled societies and in the ruling political class.

We must use our divine intellect to reason and reunite, refusing to allow the rising New World Order leaders, perched on their thrones of power, to stir antagonizing behaviors or victim consciousness within us, dragging people down into mindsets of hateful opposition, helplessness and resignation. Such emotion-based states of awareness provide the energy those power mongers feed on to instigate war, disparity and destruction on every level—and so, their shadow grows.

We can only overcome this oppression if we join together, in fearless unity. We have a long way to go before enough of us achieve that state of being, but we are getting there. It may not look like it from where you are watching, especially if it's coming at you from mainstream media. But, people are waking up at last.

This **is** the Great Awakening.

Let us never forget that every piece of the jigsaw puzzle, each as important to the outcome as the next, locks into another. All the colors and artistry of the design take us, step-by-step, through the process of rebuilding, through focused thought, attention to detail and the vision of a spectrum of colors and nuance that guides us through the process until, finally, the big picture becomes clear. We snap that very last piece into place, observe, and celebrate all we have done, together, to co-create a new perspective on the landscape of our shifting reality.

May our highest intentions to shine light and compassion through the realm of matter that is born of them break through any and all imposed barriers, to touch the lives of the one and the many, and may what I share with you in this missive reawaken the power within all who have elected to read these words—mirrors of my soul—to share my thoughts and the intent behind them. My hope is that, through them, you will feel my love for humanity, and all the living beings of our world. It is love that emanates from my very core . . . heart and soul.

*

Many times during the writing of this book, I experienced the dreaded "writer's block," and had to step away for days, weeks . . . even a month of crucial writing time—as the clock master, that relentless timekeeper, ticked away the hours, charting my progress toward the fast-approaching deadline for submission to the editors, only to end up publishing it myself. In this increasingly troublesome four-dimensional mutation of time in which we find ourselves now, the hour hand seemed to be forever racing around the dial with such unbridled momentum it felt as if it would simply lift right off the clock and disappear into some obscure portal to other realms. It didn't help that through every phase of the book's evolution, I felt time slipping altogether, like a hazardously loose belt on a treadmill, throwing me out of step, to where it seemed I was constantly out of pace and falling backwards, losing my grip. So clear to me was the fact that the "no-time" of the fourth dimension had begun manifesting in the "right now" of my experience.

As I write these very words, we are in the thick of it, tumbling round and round like threadbare clothes in an electric dryer, slowly pulling out of the third dimension, wondering where we will end up, and what will happen when we get there, when this difficult cycle is finally behind us.

My last book, *The New Sirian Revelations, Prophecies for the Ascending Human Collective*, foretold of how this shift from the third to fourth dimension would be happening now, and how it would be difficult, at first, for us to recognize the subtle shifts that would quickly become so glaringly obvious that they would smash into our conscious perception like a rogue asteroid crashing into the Earth! It is my impression, at this portentous hour—one minute to midnight—that we are bang on that phase of transition, in the thick of it . . . still believing we are in the third, but recognizing, with every new day, that we are dealing, among other things, with the absolute transmutation of time, as we have never known it before.

We find we simply cannot keep pace with the rhythm of day . . . a month . . . a year.

Time, as we have understood it until now, is fast becoming a four-dimensional blur.

Ours is an experience no other civilization has known before us, one in which we find ourselves bizarrely entangled between two dimensions: knowing we cannot go back, while experiencing trepidation and mind-boggling uncertainty over what actually awaits us, as we find ourselves catapulted forward into a strange and eerie future, already playing out in our lives—one that reads like a science fiction novel. It is a struggle to make sense of it, and to find a context from which we know how to deal with these changes.

Beyond the rather limited understanding we possess of our complex energy body, and how it interacts with the quantum field in the tireless operation of human biogenesis, we are capable of applying our exquisite minds to affect, alter and manifest all that appears as matter in the elusive physical realm we still perceive as the third dimension. Mind over matter, or "manifestation," as we prefer to call it, is happening with such immediacy now that we are in this new frequency band. We have yet to grasp how this time warp, which so many of us are currently experiencing, affects the very projections that we understand as reality, but which—as we move forward—we recognize more and more are mere illusion. It is still too young, this 4D consciousness, and we have much to learn, as we travel the timeline of the no-time—a deliberate contradiction in terms.

It is not unlike having one leg in two separate row boats, straddling the open sea, as you watch a massive storm moving in on you.

*

As the dreaded deadline for delivery of the manuscript loomed ever closer, I kept faltering, and stopping . . . and then starting again. What was it that would block me so unwaveringly that I could go for days on end without being able to bear to even glance at the computer screen? Over the entirety of my writing experience, spanning almost thirty years, this had never happened to me before. It was only when I finally penned the very last word that I understood how it had been the nature of this, possibly the most controversial material I have ever written, that had challenged me. This time, I did not have my team, the Sirian High Council, dictating through my brain to the keyboard, as I have in former books, so there was no other choice but to dig down into my gut and pull out everything I had to share, without questioning myself . . . without worrying who might be offended, or why.

In today's world, that is a revolutionary act.

Given the overall mood of humanity now, and the unprecedented acceleration of totalitarian censorship and mass mind control around the globe, it became clear to me that my writer's block had never been about a lack of inspiration, nor the task of writing, per se, and I have never lacked the discipline to meet a deadline. It was the act of daring to delve into the highly polarized field of discussion upon which I have embarked in this work, of refusing to yield to the dictates of the new political correctness, and of being well aware of what challenges and eventual criticism lay before me, by the new censors, that I had grappled with for months on end.

It is clear to all of us now that we simply are no longer free to communicate openly with one another, neither in print, through social media, nor in open dialogue. Red flags are snapping against the masts, blowing wild on the winds of change, and signaling real danger for those who are speaking this truth at a time such as this—a time of Communist-style censorship: the new McCarthyism. I had to keep re-examining my own fear and trepidation—emotions I rarely experience. Was my dedication to being in service to Spirit worth subjecting my peaceful existence (as peaceful as it can be in the dystopia of our new world) to the risks posed by an unrelenting "cancel culture" society and the rising tyranny of the New World government? I was forced to weigh the value of honoring my mission, against protecting my privacy and my life, and declaring my truth, at a time when truth, usurped by endless distortions and lies, is being choked into oblivion.

Truth tipped the scales.

In a world where dark soldiers of a pervasive army lurk in and out of the dimensions, demanding our silence, speaking that truth is seen as a treacherous, even treasonous act against the state . . . or rather, against the global governance at the highest levels, and against any and all of its minions, one step down.

There, where shadows veil the light, suppressors of freedom lie in waiting, scrutinizing every word, disallowing free thought and dialogue, and threatening . . . eager to leap out and grab us by the throat, should we so much as dare to challenge their intolerable, dehumanizing narrative.

But I hold to my conviction that we must speak it anyway.

Let the bells ring, and may the voice of truth peal through the village squares.

*

And then there is this great divide between people, and the extreme polarization of ideologies, perceptions and convictions. Driven by overtly controlling mainstream media, so many human beings have become mentally rigid and emotionally frozen, locked into positions of righteousness—believing what they are told to believe and nothing else. First, they are taught to be "offended" by whatever does not fit into the acceptable collective paradigm, next they are driven to irrational fear and rage against the other. They cling to this newly acquired, immutable world view that has been drummed into their consciousness, in just a few years, through the strident, militant march of the New World Order.

An agenda that has been fomenting in the globalists' cauldron for centuries, its virulent brew has been served up to the global populace via the Covid-19 "pandemic," and the highly dangerous and deadly inoculation experiment of men, women and children worldwide. It is the harbinger of a totalitarian, transhumanist agenda laid out for decades, delivered through the sentinels commanded by those who, for far too long, have ruled over the Earth.

We appear to be nearing the apex point of their doomsday timeline with the launch and progression of the Covid-19 "virus."

And yet, whilst so many people succumb to fear and all the lower emotions stirred within them by the extreme propaganda and outright lies surrounding whatever this "virus" actually is, others, forced out of their comfort zones by the overt abuse of power exercised throughout the roll-out of the so-called pandemic, are awakening. Once they access the undeniable truth of what this thing really is, they cannot help but reshape their view of a global reality . . . one they had never even imagined before. Many others of us, which probably includes those of you who have chosen to read this book, have been awake a very long time, waiting for humanity to finally shake off its slumber, to look reality in the face and to arise . . . at last.

We have been labelled "conspiracy theorists" for so long we can barely remember the time or the catalyst that "red-pilled" us out of the matrix mindset.

Whatever time it is in anyone's personal appointment with the reality of our unfolding drama on the earth plane, one thing is certain: almost no one on this little blue sphere in space is indifferent to the questions I pose in this work, even if a vast number of them is still unwilling to even consider anything that challenges the status quo, which this book does, unabashedly, from cover to cover.

At this critical juncture of our planetary evolution, everything that is unfolding at the global and local levels triggers us all, in one way or another. With very few exceptions, the mainstream media, which has become nothing more than a constant propaganda machine pushing the globalist agenda, no longer reports any factual news, whatsoever. It is whipping up our frenzied societies to such a froth that we barely think anything through anymore. What we have, instead of critical thinking, is a perpetual knee-jerk reaction, twenty-four/seven—and that is deliberate. It is essential to the suppression of the human spirit, and the subsequent take-over of our global society. We are being rocked to the very core—slammed into survival mode—watching the quality of our lives erode and wondering, from the observation decks where we now stand, what a future earth reality can possibly hold, especially for the children, and what legacy we will personally leave behind.

Unfortunately, there are those who act upon those emotions in extreme and dangerous ways—whether turning them inward, against themselves, or striking out against everyone else. We all have seen how violently people stand in opposition to each other now, with families and friendships torn apart over manufactured doctrines and the life-altering choices they are being forced to make because of them, and where opposition to anything that does not fit one person's conviction results in dismissal, alienation . . . even outright hatred of the other.

Who of us has not lost a family member or friend because we do not embrace their survival codes?

With that in mind, I am highly aware that plenty of people, particularly those who embrace the narrative being fed them through from those mainstream talking heads, will most probably be upset by what I propose as the "bigger picture" view of the spiritual war underway at this time on Mother Earth.

It is never easy to expose evil and destruction, especially when one seeks to find a spiritual framework from whence it can be examined objectively. I knew I had to be willing to rattle some cages, to face the repercussions that come of challenging people's convictions, and then to help whomever I can to look the beast straight in the eye.

I was, thank God. And I have done so.

"Damn the torpedoes. Full speed ahead!"

*

War is everywhere—people against people, nations against nations—and with the churning of the lowest emotions in so much of the global population, these escalating divisions serve as energetic fodder for the tyrants who are attempting to turn our beautiful Earth into a lifeless, miserable prison planet. They relish in and are fueled by perpetual war, dis-ease and suffering, and lust for destruction. Vampiric creatures, they feed on fear, which they suck from the adrenalized ethos of all species—especially ours. Sadly, as many of you are all too aware, they have a predilection for that of the children: the younger, the better.

They need to tether us to a perpetual battle against each other, for they believe that, as long as we are engaged in what appears to be irreversible division on every level, we will never find our way back to unity, from whence we are emboldened and empowered to rise up against them.

How wrong they are!

We are beginning to witness their power waning. Their machinations are not going according to plan, because they have made one enormous, strategic error in their war against the free men, women and children of the living soil. They have made the crucial mistake of underestimating the greatness of the human spirit.

Spirit? It is imponderable for them; they do not walk with God, and they do not believe in the immortality of the soul. As for the greatness and potential of the human being, it is something they cannot begin to comprehend, because they perceive us as inferior, mindless cattle. They have chosen to stand in opposition to love, for that is all they know: the cold, dark cave ... the conjuring ... enslavement to the demon.

And they curse the light. Like the bad witch of Oz, the demon shrivels and turns to dust when a focused beam of love permeates its shadowy walls. They believe that light will burn and destroy them, and they are determined to put it out, before it spreads through the prisons of their lost souls.

Ours is a flame they can only extinguish if they find a way to eclipse the radiance of the God Code within us—to blow out the candle of our collective spirit, subverting everything that makes us human.

That is their work-in-progress. And that, my fellow warriors, is their ultimate goal.

At no other time in recorded history has the dictator Julius Caesar's "divide et impera" (divide and conquer) strategy been more flagrant than it is now, for this is an on-going world war. It is not merely about territorial expansion and conquest, for in the end, these globalists believe they already own the entire planet. No, this is Armageddon—the battle of darkness and light—being waged by a cabal of Luciferian overlords, possessed imposters and their demons, against the One Heart of Spirit.

It is your soul they're after, and they are coming for it.

Our 21ˢᵗ century problem has nothing to do with the intention of one despotic leader or another to invade a neighboring country, or to suffocate the life force out of its own. That is all camouflage, wherever it is playing out. It is not about a Hitler, or a Stalin or any other omnipotent dictator ... nor the newly trained puppets in positions of power in government. For us to rise against any one of these actors alone is effectively useless and, eventually, self-defeating, because, like the mythical Greek monster, Hydra, for every one that goes down, two more will rise. We need to understand that we are fighting a multi-headed beast, whose tentacles reach around the entire globe.

To liberate ourselves from the monstrosity that has assumed rulership over the planet, we need to strike at the root—at the absolute core of evil—or we will never be free of it. Never. To do that, we must absolutely understand this beast: what is the fire in its belly, what feeds its insatiable hunger, and what is its ultimate objective.

The roots of evil remain an obscure and unfathomable mystery. We ask ourselves: "Why must polarity define the physical plane in this seemingly endless battle of darkness and light, and when will we truly be released from its grip?" As we contemplate the wisdom of an all-knowing God who created the abyss so that we, sparks of His divine light, may know free will to choose, we can only question why it has to be so intense, this malevolence, that so many souls and innocent beings must suffer such unbearable pain and misery—only to perish under its ubiquitous shroud.

How do we truly reconcile the evil force—for, if it is a godly creation, rather than a separate, opposing power, must it be so all-encompassing, and so impenetrably dark? The obvious answer, ringing over and over again in our souls is, "Yes, it must!" until we honor our soul purpose, fear not, and step into the full illumination of our own godliness. It must be so tremendously powerful that it leaves us no other choice but to rise up together, at last, and surge, as an immeasurable tidal wave, against it. It must be so omnipotent that we know no other recourse but to hold our ground in the God light—the almighty force of unending, unconditional love—and then, fearless in that brilliance, to flood the dark halls of evil in the infinite radiance of eternal light.

Only then will we truly know and embrace the immensity of our galactic mission here on Earth today, and beyond tomorrow.

*

In the end, the great chasm of separateness that defines the true social divide on Planet Earth lies between the ultra-rich and the growing poor: the elite and the hardworking, or disenfranchised. Isn't it amazing how the ruling class has managed to redirect our perception to fixate on the ideological and social "differences" between us—to destroy each other over them—when it is the super wealthy and powerful, the puppeteers, whom we should be challenging? They keep us fighting, drugging us with their poisons, killing one other, while, all the while, we continue to tithe a third or more of everything we earn to governance, through an arbitrary taxation structure—one of their design, of course. The never-ending story of abusive power inevitably banks on the blood, sweat and tears of the working class, and coasts on the privilege of the ones who write the laws to make themselves increasingly richer, while we, the people, become unceasingly poorer.

This corrupt system siphons off those funds that allow the super-rich to buy up all the land, sail the mega yachts, fly their private jets and play in gated neighborhoods of ostentatious luxury—knowing that if we, the 'great unwashed' and 'useless feeders' (as they like to call us) were ever rise against them, united, those gates would come crashing down . . . and so, their obscene power and abuse.

We need to understand that mechanism, in order to grasp how we are being partitioned into opposing camps through exacerbation of all that has kept us divided throughout history—race, religion, wealth, nationalism and unfounded, mostly uneducated political ideologies—to newly-created ones, such as: gender identity, pronoun classifications, exacerbation of irrational racist hate and the latest, dogmatically divisive pro- or anti-vaccine positions.

Pick your poison.

Always, the aphorism, "If you aren't with us, you're with the terrorists," widens the chasm that divides us. "If you aren't vaccinated, it means you want to kill me," and "If you are for Putin, you are a Nazi extremist," are the latest judgment calls to carry that same threat—and they serve the same purpose: divide to conquer.

In this post-2020 world, where, daily, we feel the vise of suppression tightening on the whole of civilization, almost no one—especially those of us who refuse to comply—has escaped the yoke of those crushing restraints, being put into place by this autocratic New World Order, reining us in with its sweeping controls, corralling our minds, and whipping the life out of our civil liberties.

Everywhere in the world, the voice of freedom is being intimidated, stifled, and rapidly silenced, usurped by scripted narratives and distortions of reality, relayed through the globalists' mainstream media pawns, whom they own and control. You may not be aware that a whopping ninety-percent of the media that feeds propaganda into the minds of the global citizenry is owned by six mega-media giants: General Electric, News Corp, Disney, ViaCom, Time Warner and CBS. So, if you still believe you have a diversity of choice and opinion coming from this consolidation of programming-disguised-as news, forget it. You have no choice. Six corrupt media giants control just about everything you read, everything you watch, and everything you are told is a "true and balanced" representation of "what goes" on the world stage.

Those of us who represent an alternative to the mainstream propaganda are struggling to keep the voice of freedom alive, but the channels of communication are closing down, rapidly. Our bridges are being bombed, crumbling into raging rivers, one by one. It is a daily battle just managing not to be "cancel-cultured." I know exactly how that feels—I have experienced in personally—and I know the ignorance that propels it forward.

That is how things appear to be done these days. It is a sad state of affairs . . . testimony to the extreme polarity that now divides us. You fall in line and embrace the narrative, or you're done.

But I am not done—far from it. Here I stand, all the better for it, stronger in my resolve, knowing that truth eventually finds its way around obstruction, denial and lies.

We must never forget that.

We must never give in to the schoolyard bullies' ignorance and be forced to turn our backs on what we believe, or our right to speak it, because somebody demands your silence.

From the flames, smoke and ash, the phoenix rises.

*

We have now a much clearer picture of the centralized globalist power that is intent upon owning the entire planet, and classifying every biological unit that inhabits it. Steadfast in their manipulation of any and all avenues of public discourse, and convinced of their invincibility, they are coming out of hiding, dropping the masquerade of their pretentious philanthropic masks to reveal the shape-shifting fiends behind the façade.

Their stronghold over the High Tech industry has been massively successful in its mission to control our access and freedom to speak on social media, silencing our questions and answers, and preventing just about any and all discussion or debate about anything in the socio-political arena—which is just about everything these days, given how absolutely politicized is our experience of contemporary society. We are not supposed to reveal what those who lord over our world do not want the hypnotized masses to see. We are not allowed to offer alternatives to raise people out of despair and powerlessness, to lift their spirits higher, closer to their own connection to the Divine. God forbid we suggest an antidote to Big Pharma's poisons, or alternative healing for what they do not intend to be healed.

And yet, still we find our way, like a blade of grass, wending its way through a crack in the pavement, knowing no other destiny than to reach for the sun . . . knowing no other purpose but to live and to grow, and to seek the light.

Isn't it time we set our sights on the stars? For however many years we have left here on this beauteous Planet Earth, and no matter what unfolds in the illusionary 3D/4D transitional field in which we find ourselves now, we are meant to celebrate life, not to fear it. That is not what we came here for.

The morphogenesis of life on this planet defines how we grow. It reminds us of the divine wisdom within us all—exactly what we are capable of—from abstractions of thought and perception, right down to the incredible wisdom within our microscopic DNA, whose role it is to birth the new, to let go of what no longer serves, to weave the sacred tapestry of our cellular memory, and to maintain the body electric in vibrant health and optimum performance mode.

It is inherent in our cellular make-up that we strive to live in harmony with the Earth, to prosper, and, then, to co-create our world—working our way past obstruction, like that blade of grass . . . simple and pure, guided by and connected to the God Source, whatever we perceive that to be. It is all written out in the language of our DNA, the Divine Blueprint of all living beings, which requires no artificial correction (by injection or any other means), no imposed interference or redirection.

If only we remember that we are the God light. It is within, not outside of us. And when we own that divinity, and know what immense power we truly possess, none of the opposition forces intent upon our destruction can ever manage to obscure the sun within and around us enough to block the infinite light: no matter what they do . . . no matter how desperately they try.

The Oligarchs intent upon depopulation of the planet—those who program us to think what they want us to think, and inevitably to do what they want us to do—are more than happy to "take us out" for daring to challenge them, for human life is of no significance to them whatsoever. From their distorted perspective, the fewer we are, the better. We are merely an obstruction to their ultimate objective to possess the entire planet: below the surface, in well-stocked, luxury bunker cities that line their underworld, and above ground, with us "surface dwellers," where they intend to cleanse every square mile of the surface—oceans too—of any and all remaining biological humans and natural life forms in their way.

It is no surprise that this class of individuals, whose perverted desire it is to abort the natural, evolutionary progression of living beings on this planet, always manages to find the financing to push their agendas. They have an endless supply of wealth and infinite resources, and they control the global monetary system. In the foreground, in nearly every case, is a communal intention to take humanity into a control grid, whereby everyone is connected to what they have coined the "Internet of Bodies," as we are turned into robotic, soulless beings that respond, like automatons, to AI orders. They have the power and the money to corrupt and persuade anyone and anything they require to push that agenda forward.

There's no denying that these individuals march to a different drummer. One could argue that it is simply because they are so locked into their left-brain genius that they do not know how to communicate emotion, and so, they appear rigid and very uncomfortable in their (human?) skin. Perhaps they are an alien species—reptoids—intent upon taking the planet as their own. Can we really rule that out, knowing what we know today? Or it might just be that they are human robots, some strange new form of Cyborg entity resembling human form. It could very well be that they, themselves, are plugged into the central computer, and it is artificial intelligence that is directing them to implant the human brain with a miniature hard drive, or an RFID tracking device in the arm or forehead, in order to redirect the public into surveillance, unreality mind . . . or altering us at the cellular level—in the DNA—all the while preparing us to relinquish our biology to the hive mind of the "Borg."

We are in a reality that defies science fiction, where anything is possible! So, it is high time we ask the difficult questions, despite the ridicule and defamation that comes from challenging what appears to be reality. Moreover, it is the very now of our existence that we are duty-bound to find the answers, and to act upon them with all the power and force of our unified determination and vision.

It is time to step up to our divine heritage, and climb the ascension spiral to our destiny. We either stand in our human sovereignty, owning our power to heal ourselves and our world, or we lose both.

We are diverse beings, each with unique ideas and opinions, however thwarted and homogenized they have become, by means of hypnotic mind control and group-think. Still, we are all human—at least for now. We must be free to use our innate intellect to express those ideas, to question others, and, bouncing those ideas off each other in free forums—in town halls and across the internet waves—to find real-time solutions. From there, we will be enabled to pave new ways of experiencing and understanding the world that we perpetually co-create through our very existence.

Fundamental freedom begins there, in our free expression and our exchange. Without it, we are one step away from being interred indefinitely, caged animals in concentration camps and dungeons, such as those being built and already operative in Australia, Canada, China, and FEMA camps in the United States. Supposedly, they are intended as isolation centers for the "contagious," but it appears their real purpose is to "re-educate" those who dare to question the narrow bandwidth of "accepted," thought, and to crush those who challenge the narrative that has forever coerced billions of people who have given their freedom away to story after story, lie after lie . . .

Will the administrators of those prisons be using implants to alter the minds of their captives, so that they never remember who they were and what they once were free to believe? It is absolutely possible.

To this end, we are constantly being threatened. Our "unacceptable thoughts" and the words we use are being censored in every possible way, right down to the annihilation of language itself. Every day, we lose words to the cloaked judges of that self-declared language patrol that has, as its mission, the total destruction of what once we believed was our inalienable right: freedom of speech, through dialogue and artistic expression.

How could we have been so careless as to take freedom—as vital as the air we breathe—for granted?

Alas, that right is disintegrating, at an incredible rate, before our eyes. Dissenting thoughts are being stricken from all media forms; classic films and books are being banned and burned in effigy; libraries are slowly being transformed into pornography shops for the youth; history and culture are being wiped from the record; even words—innocent words—are being declared "illegal."

If this is not mind control, intent upon destroying our culture, and crushing our humanity, then do tell me—what is?

And so it is that we are being groomed to be voiceless, obedient and willing slaves—far more subservient than we have ever been—tethered to a global agenda that is far worse than we ever could have imagined possible. They want us to believe that we are powerless against them, so that we will either bow down, unquestioningly, before the master, or submit to their degrees of punishment, through which we will be metaphorically (for the time being) whipped into submission. They have the tools to do that, and they are actively using them against us, all the while letting us know that whatever atrocities they inflict upon us all—the end justifies their means.

Those who dare expose the truth and reveal the dirty secrets, like our brother, Julian Assange, have already suffered some level of defamation, extreme mental abuse, physical torture, and imprisonment—all to the absolute destruction of their lives, simply because they have given those lives to standing in that truth, so that we may regain our freedom . . . so that the human race has a chance to survive.

It seems daily we hear new pronouncements, warning us of a two-tiered global society: one for the obedient, another for the dissenting—the noncompliant. They keep pushing the end zone further and further down the field, studying human resistance each time they move the goal post, and measuring how far they can go before we finally rebel . . . before it is game over.

Despite the obvious overreach of government on every level, the majority of people still comply willingly. Many are innocent, trying to do what they believe is right for themselves, their loved ones and for the community—to protect themselves from the conjured bogeyman. Others are complicit, all with a different price tag on their ethics and morality, and their very souls.

We are witness to a violent mob mentality emerging, whereby reasonable people are now losing their handle on reality, calling upon the very crushing, self-imposed ruling class that has them in its manipulative grip to execute the cruelest punishment on those in opposition to their mass mind—friends and family alike! No one is spared. Who could have ever imagined, for example, that millions of people would consent and comply to such a point that they would willingly empower their governments to imprison or even execute people who would choose not to accept the experimental chemical/synthetic injections rolled out upon the global population?

Did we learn nothing from Nuremburg and the Nazis?

How far we have fallen from grace, and how quickly. It is as if we are reliving the days of Ancient Rome—of ruthless emperors and slaves—where desensitized spectators in the Colosseum, foregoing their humanity, called for brutalized gladiators to fight to the death: never even acknowledging that those unwilling warrior-slaves were human beings, like them . . . never thinking that they, the good citizens of the Roman Empire, were one mistake away from being thrown to the lions, too, for the entertainment, empowerment and sheer bloodlust of their overlords.

It was, shall we say, life-preserving, for the citizenry to adhere to the dictates of Emperors and to tithe to Caesar then, in the class system of Roman society and its imposed lordship over significant lands that it raped, pillaged and conquered. However, today the "Empire" is the entire planet. It consumes everything, everywhere: earth, sea and sky. Not even the great oceans, nor the life forms that once thrived there, are exempt from their power grab. The omnipotent administrators of this ruthless power are intent upon controlling all life on the globe, with particular focus on the human race, and to own all territories as their personal playgrounds, where they are determined that a greatly reduced human population still will not be allowed to trespass, and certainly not to prosper.

We are almost eight billion people, caught in the clutches of a few thousand bluebloods whose origins are, at the very best, questionable. We still bow and curtsey to these kings and queens—imagine?

Somebody remind me why we still do that, and why we still finance their empires.

It is becoming increasingly clear that those who have assumed power in this system—the New World Order—have initiated an extermination timeline on this planet, slated to reach its apex in the year 2030. It is intent upon dramatically reducing the population, and the broad scale transmutation of biological human beings into technologically controlled transhumanist robots.

If we do not break free now from the claws of the oppressors, the light of human consciousness will be dimmed and eventually go out altogether, subsumed into the Borg of artificial intelligence.

We cannot let that happen.

The fissure in the dike that has restrained the flow of human freedom for millennia is splintering in every direction. Those cement walls are crumbling against the weight of growing segments of humanity pushing back, standing in unity against the oppressor.

The minority will soon become the majority.

The Great Awakening is underway.

And once those walls fall, there will be no reconstructing them. Never again.

So immense will be the flood of humanity's liberation, washing away the old, cleansing the Earth to seed the new, that we will at last liberate our beloved planet from their constructs of perverse reality, and get on with the divine decree that brought us here: to assist in the re-birthing Gaia into the higher dimensions, out of the density and the exacerbation of polar extremes.

It is so difficult for us to truly grasp what we are up against, because we cannot fathom the immense loathing that drives their hatred. However, what we do know is that it is going to take unprecedented courage, determination and heroism from as many of us as possible to finally shine the light of godliness into the "battlefield," and to stand down the dark warriors.

"The evil that men do is oft interred in their bones. So is it with Caesar," wrote Shakespeare. How much bad karma these perverse beings have accrued and will eventually face is staggering. How many spins on the perpetual wheel of reincarnation will it take for them to finally complete the seemingly never-ending cycle that has them tethered to an obscure dream spell of their own making, until such point that they are ready, at last, to initiate their climb up the spiral, back to Source?

Their pace as individuals, whereby the karmic debt of their actions affects them alone, is theirs to determine. It is not our problem, in many ways, although we know that compassion helps dissolve the darkness. Our response to their destructive actions against us, however, is our responsibility … and it is our right, as individuals and as a global society.

The Caesars of our contemporary world do yield immensely destructive power—we certainly cannot deny it and we are wise not to.

We have ignored it long enough. No good has come of that ignorance, for, in the end, we only delayed the inevitable. Rather, we need to examine and scrutinize the force of their hatred: to know its strength, to anticipate its strategic moves and to stand tall, in our divine and blessed light, wherever hatred pushes up against us . . . wherever darkness attempts to obliterate the light of love.

If that means war, so be it. There are many ways to win a war.

Let us raise our light sabers and divine shields in fearless, peaceful opposition and in unity, committed to truth and justice.

Most of us are heart-centered, peaceful souls who cannot imagine the aridity of life with no love . . . no joy. We do possess the capacity to feel compassion for lost souls—even the darkest ones, no matter how hateful they are . . . no matter how contemptuous. We must be capable of forgiveness if we are ever to heal this divide between us, and to dissolve the great cloak of darkness that attempts to block the brilliance of the star that feeds us—a force of immense evil that desires nothing less than to blanket our world in gloom and misery.

Deep down inside us all—more difficult for some to access than others—we know that truth, love and integrity are the only things that truly matter; they are the only things that make sense of our passage here on Earth and beyond. Even those caught up in the drama of this passing hour in earth reality—those who have chosen fear, anger and hate—still, in their humanness, eventually rise to the loftier aspects of their own existence. In this four-dimensional field of timelessness, that can feel like eternity or an instant—a flash—if the conscious mind wills it.

It is my hope that all beings—even the darkest ones—can accelerate that process and find their way back to the love of All-That-Is, That-Ever-Was, and That-Always-Will-Be.

*

I admit that I am a rebel of sorts. I have never been obedient to anyone or anything, and I do not intend to start now. From as far back as I can remember, I have lived my life protesting injustice and questioning authority. It has always defined who I am and why I am here, and it will to my dying day.

So, I do indeed dare to share, as I always have, the biting truth of what is unfolding on our planet now: the decades long, progressive spiritual war whose mission it is to steal the human soul, one that is determined to dim the God light within us all. It is a war that has already subverted the course of civilization and it appears to be hindering our progression to higher ground, but, ironically, it is bringing about the Great Awakening. It is a war that has been waged against the entire global population and all living creatures of our beloved planet: the war of wars . . . the biblical Apocalypse.

Whether you have yet to recognize it or not, we are in it. It is upon us all, bearing down upon our global civilization.

We are living Armageddon.

Weighing all these considerations, I came to realize that if I were to continue to serve as a warrior for the Light, not only could I never choose my private life over my mission to serve humankind, but neither could I water down the information I wanted to divulge in this missive, for the sake of somehow distracting the demon and hopefully to move on, undetected, under the radar. It is too late for that anyway. Years later—a dozen "controversial" published books, countless interviews and a substantial presence on social media—it is way past the time where I can sidestep the steamrollers, as they crush down upon our free societies, mercilessly bulldozing anyone and anything that stands in their way.

All I know to do is to stand boldly in front of them, like the unknown protester in Tiananmen Square, and to hold my ground. It is the only thing that makes sense anymore.

It is the only way I know how to be.

Such omnipotent suppression is no longer limited to the ideas and opinions expressed through one's words. No, it is the very words themselves that are under fire now. Even our words are at war! At this fragile time in human interaction, almost every form of communication has been beaten down by "political correctness," censorship and the resulting cancel culture punishment for those who dare to express their ideas freely. It is becoming so very difficult to even speak, much less to write, using proper, grammatical English, so much so that we are being forced to mutilate the language to conform to imposed ideologies and subsequent banned thoughts, words and expression.

Politicians demand the use of "politically correct" words of their choosing; academia enforces it: the imprisoned word, the programmed thoughts of hive mind. So many people today are psyched up, antagonistic . . . just waiting to ambush that pronoun or word that they have suddenly deemed offensive to their belief system, life style, race, religion, and gender. It is because of that hyper and sometimes irrational sensitivity that all too many voices and the wisdom of their words have been silenced and lost forever—and that is deliberate.

It seems we spend more time defending our use of language of late, or attacking another's, than we do communicating openly and without concern over being misunderstood or condemned, for daring to use a word that doesn't fit into the confines of contrived acceptability, circa 2022. People have been programmed to be offended for just about anything—the great division strategy—enforced by a self-serving political class that has everything to gain from accelerating distrust and intolerance amongst us all.

That is a great travesty for humanity-at-large, and an even greater danger to the prospect of the evolution of free societies around the world.

As I watch the drama unfold, I cannot help but ask myself, "How will we find our way back to sanity? How in the world will we win back our freedom to speak without being censored, to communicate ideas without recrimination, and to accept, rather than to condemn?"

In an Orwellian era of AI computer bots, trolls and arbitrary language police, that dictate new socio-political norms by which we must abide or be marginalized, we find walls and fences everywhere. They render expression and a fluid, readable style nearly impossible. Take the example of the innocuous pronoun, which today can provoke such rage in another that it has become a common practice to have to declare which pronouns are "acceptable" before daring to engage in conversation. It is even being embedded in the AI commands of social media.

Identify your pronouns—or be damned!

It is unimaginable to me that our orchestrated division has become so profound and so deep that even the lowly pronoun can trigger the irrational, and separate us from each other. Once a writer is no longer free to use simple pronouns correctly, without being burdened by those newly-imposed constraints that have us choking on pseudo-language and alternative meanings, the flow of thought and free expression becomes hindered and stilted. Therefore, I beg your tolerance where, throughout this text, my use of pronouns reflects the literary rules of the English language, rather than adherence to the evolving laws of political correctness. Despite attempts to invent a new third-person, gender-free pronoun, the rule in English is still to use the word "him" or "his" to fill that gap. That is my education in the use of grammar, and that is how I choose to express myself in my writing.

My use of proper English is not a socio-political statement; it does not reflect a gender preference, or bias—at least not to me.

In reference to God, or the Creator, where I use the capitalized pronouns "His" or "Him," I do also ask that you recognize how this serves, again, as a literary device—not a statement of gender superiority, or bias. Personally, I understand such a force as a Prime Creator to be completely free of any gender identity for, as we evolve beyond the confines of our three-dimensional understanding of reality, we **become** the unified field: male/female, electric/magnetic merged.

In my years of metaphysical studies, experience and teaching, I have always understood the male energy to be the "electric" and so, the God Force—the spark, the electrical impulse—I represent as "Him." The female, the great and infinite cosmic womb, I celebrate and honor as the "magnetic" that, together with that electrical impulse, birthed all existence—all Creation—and which perpetually births anew, through the metaphorical *Vesica piscis*, across the multiverse.

Neither is superior to the other, nor can either exist without its divine counterpart: not separately—as it appears to do in the physical context of our 3D perceived framework—nor refined in the higher dimensions, and clearly not at the Godhead, where all is merged in the Oneness.

To overcome all this obstruction is to commit entirely to the pursuit of freedom and the unbridled human spirit. Please do not allow yourself to misconstrue meanings from my choice of literary ease, simply because of word jails and nuances, such as those imposed by our modern-day perceptions of what makes a pronoun acceptable or objectionable. Do not choose to be offended where there is no intent to do so—it only separates us as human beings. Rather, feel the energy behind the words, and know that my purpose is never to offend. My goal is to share what I understand to be truth, to be free to express it as best I can, and to embrace any and all individuals who are eager, or at least willing, to hear it.

We used to talk to each other, not so very long ago. When did we lose that . . . and why? Differences of opinion were motives for dialogue, not mutual destruction.

Not war.

Let us open our hearts and minds. We do not have to agree, and certainly not blindly. No conscious, thinking human being wants that. But we do need to be free to share and exchange our thoughts, our dreams, and life experience with each other—our "humanness"—without having to walk on egg shells all the time, tiptoeing over appropriately defined "politically incorrect" words and all the misconstrued meanings people are programmed to take from them. We do need to understand that these newly-imposed language controls have been put in place systematically, for reasons that are politically motivated, and how, inherent in that kind of control, is a blatant form of political incorrectness!

May we all be keen pioneers in our mutual search for new visions of the world around us and beyond. Let us give meaning, not take offense . . . and be open to new ideas, whether we agree with them or not, as humankind has been free to do in the forums of great civilizations: in the halls of Ancient Atlantis, Egypt, the Greek Parthenon and universities the world over, from time immemorial.

This is the way of the New Aquarian.

One day, not so very far away, we will have ascended, at last, well past divisiveness, greed and corruption at every level, and words will not be needed to unify what still today is our experience of separateness, for we will have arrived. We will simply communicate heart to heart, soul to soul.

And then, my friends, we will truly be free . . . at long last.

In the meantime, I stand tall in my decision to speak my truth, as I have in this book and those that came before it (when the world was a gentler place and people were more embracing), because bowing down to a fear of the ubiquitous monster that lurks in the darkness, endlessly shapeshifting, like putrid sludge on the waters of human emotion, is a luxury none of us can afford—not when the future of humanity and all life forms on this planet is at stake.

This is my very personal Declaration of Independence.

Part One
Secrets Revealed

"After this, there is no turning back.
You take the blue pill—the story ends,
you wake up in your bed and believe whatever you want to believe.
You take the red pill—you stay in Wonderland
and I show you how deep the rabbit hole goes."
From the Movie
The Matrix

Chapter 1

Playing God With Creation

"For everything there is a season,
and a time for every purpose under heaven:
a time to be born, and a time to die;
a time to plant, and a time to pluck up that which is planted;
a time to kill, and a time to heal;
a time to break down, and a time to build up;
a time to weep, and a time to laugh;
a time to mourn, and a time to dance;
a time to cast away stones, and a time to gather stones together;
a time to embrace, and a time to refrain from embracing;
a time to seek, and a time to lose;
a time to keep, and a time to cast away;
a time to rend, and a time to sew;
a time to keep silence, and a time to speak;
a time to love, and a time to hate;
a time for war, and a time for peace."
—Ecclesiastes 3:1-8

We are in that time of war—a war against Earth and humanity—believing, trusting, knowing **peace will follow**.

At the core of this war is a formidably diabolical agenda, centered around the extermination of ninety-percent of the entire global population. The ultimate goal of a group of powerfully positioned eugenicists, this dire depopulation program is engraved in eight different languages upon four mysterious nineteen-foot-tall monolithic structures, known as the "Georgia Guidestones," that appeared, overnight, in the fields of Georgia forty years ago.

In tandem with the decimation of the population is the transhumanist plan for those who survive any and all of the cataclysms they are currently rolling out over the planet—estimated to be anywhere from ten percent of us to a mere one million—to have our human genome altered and reconstructed in such a way as to turn us into a new "hackable" semi-human, robotic species, controlled and operated through the "cloud" of computer central.

What kind of mind would desire that I cannot remotely fathom, but I imagine it would not be one that is human. No matter how distorted a person can become as a consequence of life's challenges, I cannot imagine any human being, unless possessed by demons, ever desiring such a fate for his own kind. Perhaps, as I have already intimated, an AI robot civilization is behind this, one that is already well-imbedded in our civilization.

Surely, some of the individuals pushing the transhumanist agenda are trying to let us know they are not human. However, for the most part, people ignore their signaling, because they do not understand what that could possibly look like, behind the subterfuge, and what it would mean to our understanding of life on our planet and beyond.

I am referring to a multi-layered technological control system over the autonomy of human mind/body/spirit that they have been putting into place for decades, which they intend to have up and running, fully operative, by 2030. That technology includes "wearable" body sensors, brain and body implants, ingestible pills containing tracking devices, tracking apps for the smart phone, spy cameras in televisions, AI devices such as Amazon's "Alexa," and much more transhumanist evil than we can even begin to imagine—and yet, it's already here. The ultimate of these invasive devices will have robot surgeons drilling right through the top of our skulls (disrupting the crown chakra in the process, as a matter of course) to insert hardware that will link us directly to the new "Internet of Bodies." This brain-to-computer link, known as "Neurolink," will supposedly be ready for launch on humans by 2023—basically, **now**. In the meantime, it appears the mad scientists are at work cleaving the God Code out of our Divine Blueprint via intrusive software, delivered via mRNA injections—whereby they can, theoretically, replace it with whatever "code" or signature they wish to install in its place, as is the case with their synthetic mRNA's command to continually produce multitudes of spike proteins, which are so deleterious to the organism, as we are seeing in the horrific adverse reactions in alarmingly growing numbers of people.

We get a glimpse from time to time of what futuristic technologies are already being used to affect the mutation of the very essence of our humanness and the ensuing take-over of humanity, but we still are not privy to most of the laboratory aberrations and electronic surveillance warfare that, supposedly, are at least forty years ahead of our existing knowledge and collective awareness.

I think most of us agree it has to be some form of futuristic extraterrestrial technology being used against our species, and rolled out under the guise of controlling this pandemic of a "virus," whose origins are questionable at best. But for now, while people are being distracted with an unrelenting string of issues and hyped-up events designed to push their emotional buttons, most of that information remains **above** "Above Top Secret."

What we are learning, however, and what I intend to expose in more depth in this work, is that biogenetics experimentation upon the human genome, for reasons that have them stripping out of us the very essence of our godliness, is proliferating in underground biolabs around the world, and that—alongside of every unimaginable freak by-product of their experimentation on helpless, tortured living beings—a new species of human being, the "cyborg," is being prepared for launch into 21st century Earth civilization. It is the modification of human DNA, the re-writing of our God-given architectural design, and the disconnect from Source that will come of it, that has the New World Order all aflutter.

This disturbing reality cannot be dismissed as sci-fi fantasy or "misinformation." The science is out of the box. We, who are bringing that truth forward, can no longer be laughed off as "conspiracy theorists"—not when "theory" has given way to a "reality" that is visible and tangible, unfolding everywhere around us.

It would have been so much more helpful to have exposed the bio-engineers' intentions on a massive scale, decades ago, when their progress was still somewhat contained, as I and several of my peers tried to do, but minds were much more closed then, and the horror of what this secret government was up to was too evil for most of the global population to contemplate—much less to accept. It had to show its ugly head, belching smoke and terror out of the black clouds, like the terrifying Typhon, father of all monsters, considered the most powerful and deadliest of all creatures in Greek mythology. And it has.

But, let us not forget that everything has its season. And this is the season of Revelation.

More and more people are lifting the veil every day. They are able to see the underpinnings of the New World Order's twisted drama being played out now. Paradoxically, the tighter the tentacles of power attempt to squeeze the life force out of us—the greater their evil—the freer we become. That evil is palpable now, and the science through which its venom slithers through our life force is actually visible . . . in the petri dish, and in the sunken eyes of those who are possessed by it.

We can sense it everywhere around us.

The push is on to pervert human nature: our innate ability to love, to dream, to grow. We are perceived by the transhumanist demagogues as soulless, hackable animals, whose humanity can and must be suppressed by the AI god they worship. They want us to believe that the idea of a soul, or a Prime Creator, is mere illusion and that we, biological humans, are a species in extinction.

Apparently, in their new-improved version of future humans, AI will tell us everything we need to know, what to think and how to feel about pretty much everything. Their vision is that we be rewritten, plugged into AI central: obedient, submissive, soulless bio-technological units. No mystery, no wonder, no free will... no dreams.

No God.

Transhumanists are eager to classify the future selves of those one out of ten robotoid humans they expect will survive the die-off. They refer to them as *Homo sapiens 2.0*, and have already pinned the acronym, *GMH* (Genetically Modified Humans), on this developing class of genetically altered, techno-implanted, semi-biological units. Unapologetic, mad scientists, they're telling us exactly what they have planned for our species, and what they have set in motion—gloating over what they perceive as our powerlessness to stop them.

They are convinced that they have taken us to the point of no return.

There is no doubt that our response to what they are projecting into human consciousness is being scrutinized, classified and stored in their AI computer matrix. Therefore, it is of the utmost importance that we hold firm to our resolve and that absolute, unshakeable "knowing" that, above and beyond whatever they believe they can do to mutate our species, we are sovereign beings. Our souls are immortal.

We know how to affect change and to deflect transgression.

We, who are not lost in the narrative being doled out by the mainstream fear mongers, refuse interference of any kind to penetrate our multi-layered, multi-dimensional bodies and to play with our minds.

We are mysterious, complex beings, sparks of the God light. We are emotional, searching, growing (and sometimes falling) souls, new and old, who came here to experience everything we can as free will beings, and to take part in the expulsion of the leviathan insect that feeds on the bloom—all living beings—of Planet Earth.

What these transhumanist radicals have yet to get their AI heads around is that we will be here long after they've disappeared forever.

We will survive them . . . and we will thrive.

Chapter 2

The Sirian Experiment

Before I delve into the use and abuse of modern-day genetic experimentation that has been focused, for decades, on the mutation of our DNA in secret laboratories around the world, with particular emphasis on what can only be described as the globalists' unbridled corporate/pharmaceutical interventionism on human health and our sovereignty of mind/body/spirit, I feel it is essential to re-examine the question of our own starseeded heritage. Information I have brought forward over the years, with which you may or may not resonate, describes what a growing number of alternative thinkers understand to be our "alien origins," rooted in a bioengineering feat undertaken by participants from several star systems beyond our own galaxy.

There are buried references to extraterrestrial involvement in our emergence in so many holy books as well, including the Old Testament. My earlier books, particularly *No More Secrets, No More Lies*, describe how our species, Homo sapiens, is just that: the "product" of a genetic experiment of universal, multidimensional scope and otherworldly proportion: *The Sirian Experiment*.

Those of us who identify with being part of a collective of starseed beings from beyond this Earth often overlook the idea that, in actuality, we are not merely a select group of migrating interstellar souls, as we so often identify ourselves. Perhaps it is because we are fortunate to hold distinct memories of distant lifetimes in several layers of our conscious-ness . . . perhaps because we are recovering salient memories, as we walk through our current lifetime here. With what we observe in the decline of certain segments of humanity at this moment, it is very challenging to embrace the idea that we all are starseed . . . every last one of us. That can be a very difficult thing to accept, seeing how far from Spirit so many souls have wandered. We seem to want to believe that only en-lightened souls can be starseed voyagers, and that is not necessarily the case.

Our perception, and one with which we identify as souls in transit, is that we came to Earth with a noble purpose, one that was born of one or many lifetimes from more highly evolved planetary civilizations and distant stars. But, we must remember that whatever we perceive as souls traversing the universe, we must keep in mind that all Homo sapiens possess the DNA material that responds to those ten scattered strands of which we are endowed—still today identified as "junk DNA."

Like the Egyptian goddess, Isis, who collected the parts of her slain husband, Osiris, and breathed life back into him that he might bear her a son, so do we know, at the soul level, that we have the col-lective power to breathe life back into those who are willing to cast off their resignation and despair, and step back into the Light. We sim-ply need to remember who we really are, how these temples—the body electric—were built, to know what we are capable of achieving for our-selves, our loved ones, and the community.

Let us do what we can to understand that if we are, indeed, the ge-netic "seed" of ancient off-world geneticists, then **all** human beings are descendants of "extra-galactic" star beings, from beyond our own galaxy, the Milky Way, and from higher dimensions as well. And if that is too way out for you to digest, ask yourself how hybrid cyborgs of the future will look back at their seeding—the transhumanist mutation of human biology to machine—and if they will ever be able to embrace the idea that once they were simply "human."

It is not easy to embrace these creationist paradigms and science fiction parallels; the very idea can boggle the mind. Or that we were all designed to be luminous light beings, especially seeing what little light some people are carrying in their troubled souls. But we need to reclaim that heritage now—for ourselves, and for the human collective. One day, in the not-so-distant future, aliens will openly walk among us uncloaked. Then, at last, we, Homo sapiens, will honor the history, the heritage and soul of our stellar seeds, as one species, undivided, and strive to embrace what benevolent ETs have made their home here alongside us: Earth beings all.

The primary overseers of the genetic experiment, for whom I have been honored to serve as a scribe for nearly three decades, are Ascended Masters—no longer in physical form, no longer bound to the confines of time and matter. They hold frequency in a six-dimensional vibrational field within which Sirius B, Sothis, a star system that ascended to the sixth-dimension hundreds of thousands of years ago, holds resonance still today. Hence, it was originally referred to as the "Sirian Experiment," and later as the "Great Experiment" (with various translations relevant to the languages of all participants) since the project embraced experts, and their DNA, from not only Sirius, but from a notable expanse of the universe.

I should make note here that all developing, intelligent species—from our world, to the farthest reaches of the universe—eventually develop an understanding of the microbiology of biological life, in all its magnificent shapes and forms, chemistry, mathematical proportions and expressions of consciousness. All beings evolve from sparks of divine light that take that leap into the dark abyss, to then slowly find their way out of it: from fearing the unknown—worshipping and offering up sacrifice to placate "vengeful" gods—to seeking an understanding of the mechanics of Creation . . . recognizing, within its perfection, their own divinity.

It is inherent to the nature of all conscious beings that, as we evolve, we strive to understand the origins of life, and why we exist. What is the purpose of it all? Seeking that is the motivation that pushes sentient beings forward—in fact, it is the driving force of civilizations. What they do with the knowledge, however, once they decipher the genetic code of life in their domain and what, then, is their intent and purpose in meddling with it, is what determines the impact of their interference with the Divine Blueprint will have upon the evolution of their re-design, and the karmic liabilities that result from it.

The designers of Homo Sapiens—whom I understand to be the extradimensional Sirian beings and their adroit team of stellar geneticists, biologists and environmentalists—came to the project divinely inspired. They possessed the knowledge and capabilities that allowed them to utilize Creator's Divine Blueprint to co-create what they intended would be a superior race of Christed beings, walking in physical bodies, to anchor light in this quadrant of our galaxy. They designated bountiful Earth, the ultimate Garden of Eden, as the idyllic, unblemished biosphere in which to nest their seed.

To accomplish their mission, participants in the seeding of Homo sapiens collected genetic material from contributing off-planet species, whose common attributes were applied to successfully splicing genetic sequences that they then wove into complex light strands, merged into a twelve-stranded, dodecahedral matrix. Utilizing complex mathematics and equations, geometric form, sound and light as their scientific and spiritual measure, they created what they believed would be a species of light beings embodied in human form, on a planet that would serve as a beacon to the light forces of the Milky Way galaxy and beyond.

Their metaphorical petri dish was the material universe; the growth medium, in which the cells were cultured, was pure love, made manifest through extraordinary vision, unity of purpose, and a commitment to the highest outcome for all concerned.

There were many false starts, several of which revolved around genetic incompatibilities, before, finally, the blueprint was cast. The super race took seed in the wombs of thousands of surrogate mothers, volunteers from the *Alliance for Intergalactic Commerce and Cultural Exchange*, who laid down in the warm embrace of the Earth Goddess and birthed our ancient ancestors, progenitors of our species: Homo sapiens.

The light of the heavens, and the frequencies of love that poured from the heart collective of so many light beings, shone down on the Earth then, bathing the planet in hope and anticipation.

*

Woven into that complex, multi-species biological matrix, the cellular memory of every human being alive today still contains all the genetic material of four primary off-planetary species, from a total of twelve participating ET races, who contributed their genetic codes into the matrix. If you believe that to be impossible, just remember that our genetic engineers are doing similar work in their secret laboratories, blending the DNA of countless species, and they have been at it for decades.

Unfortunately, soon after its inception, the experiment was disrupted by antagonistic ET aggressors, who utilized advanced electromagnetic frequencies, beamed into the Earth, to scramble ten of those strands—so that only two, which we know today as the "double helix," remained intact and activated.

That additional DNA material is within us still, all these millennia of generations later, awaiting the disengagement of the electromagnetic grid that surrounds the planet, and the merging of multidimensional coordinates that will allow the reunification of every fragment, every microscopic bit, back into its geometric, vibrational design: the original blueprint. The activation of this DNA material, and the restructuring of complex geometric templates within every cell, will serve to awaken corresponding neural structures in the brain, and to then turn on the master switch of our true heritage as Homo sapiens: "light beings walking."

I often wonder if the enduring story of the Virgin Mary and the so-called "immaculate conception" of the Christ is, in actuality, a vestige of that pre-historic, colossal event—the seeding of our species. Could it be that she was a walk-in from a far more ancient past, an extra-galactic, divine surrogate mother from that time, and is it just possible that the Christ was an exalted twelve-stranded being, born, over one hundred thousand years later, of that original blueprint, to an enslaved Earth population that had been socially re-engineered by aliens?

What of the goddess, Isis? According to historians' interpretations of chiseled hieroglyphs that still remain, she roamed the breadth of ancient Egypt, in search of the scattered parts of her husband, Osiris, who had been viciously murdered and cut into pieces by the envious and evil Set. The gruesome myth describes how the vengeful god scattered fourteen of Osiris's body parts all along the length of the sacred Nile, to ensure that they could never be retrieved, so that Osiris could never be resurrected in the afterlife.

Thus, with Osiris out of the way, Set became King of Egypt. But the love of Isis was so immense, and her magical powers so great, that she managed, with the help of her sister, Nephthys, to find the pieces of her husband's body and reassemble them, after which she molded a penis out of the soil and "breathed life back into him," resuscitating him long enough to bear her a son, Horus.

Is the myth of the strewn pieces of Osiris an allegory for the scattered strands of DNA within us? And are we able to breathe life back into them, by reconstructing the electrical impulse of focused mind that will birth the dormant Christ within us?

So much of our true history is hidden in parables of ancient lore and myth. No doubt it is from the Akashic Record, not written history, that we are most likely to retrieve the true story behind the legends and religious accounts of our distant past ... a story etched on the forever, in the ethos and the stars. But we do have clues that have been left for us by ancient wisdom keepers. They are sculpted on the walls and statues of ancient temples in so many sacred domains, and written on the tattered scrolls and papyrus of ancient texts, if only we can figure out how to decipher them correctly, and to glean from them what true wisdom those ancient record keepers meant to carve into the collective memory of countless generations that would follow.

*

Dispelling Darwinism, a theory of biological evolutionism that has yet to uncover that unscientific "missing link" of transitional morphologies, so necessary to proving the theory of evolution, and to establishing that Homo sapiens is genetically descended from primates, my Sirian sources have always insisted that, although we do share DNA similar to that of the hominids of our planet, we are not indigenous to Earth.

Neither are we descendants or relatives of the apes, although we share similar essential elements of DNA material.

As we are all too aware, ninety-percent or more of our DNA has been dismissed as "junk," by today's "experts" in scientific fields related to the genetics industry ... as if there were ever a superfluous aspect to Creation. How do those who still claim to own the science and empirical knowledge of our ancestry get away with it? I never stop being stupefied by how so much of the human race continues to buy the story that only ten percent of human DNA—our very essence—is utilized, and that the rest is simply superfluous "junk." Or that we use only ten percent of our brain and the rest, the ninety-percent, is "grey matter." Because researchers in the field of bioengineering—the "scientists"—

have been unable to reassemble the trillions of microscopic pieces of our genetic puzzle, it must be, in terms that evolve from their ignorance of our Divine Blueprint, and the spirit that defines the essence of what it truly means to be human, that we have an ocean of "junk" aimlessly floating around in our cells, and a superfluous mass of "grey matter," sitting idle, in our otherwise remarkable brains.

Missing links, junk DNA and grey matter, I'm afraid, are mere vagaries of men who claim to know the science and biology of human beings—but obviously do not. That cannot be called "science." They have been getting away with their missing links for way too long, while the purpose of ninety-percent of our DNA, which today they refer to as "non-coded genetic material," appears to have escaped them entirely. Futuristic technology notwithstanding, it appears that all the king's horses and all the king's men have yet to put Humpty Dumpty together again.

Obviously, the true function of the ninety-percent "unknown" in our DNA and our brains has a very specific purpose, which, undoubtedly, links us to other dimensions, frequencies and Spirit. Once that DNA is reassembled, and those neural highways of our complex brains are plugged back into the pineal gland, our cellular circuitry is going to be lighting up like a floodlight. We shall step into the embodiment of the Christ light of our original design, rewired to effortlessly access higher dimensions, the core knowledge of our ancient ancestors, and our direct and immutable connection to Source.

But for now, much of that information lies dormant, although we do have the means to activate more of that genetic information if we so desire, and if we possess the spiritual clarity to utilize highly-focused mind over matter. Some of us do actually have additional strands already lit up. But to modern-day geneticists and related researchers, the non-coded DNA remains scrambled and unintelligible—and we are wise to consider how, paradoxically, that may just be a godsend . . . for the moment, at least.

It may actually serve as our species' salvation.

It is imperative that the incredible wisdom and stellar records contained in our "grey matter" and our deconstructed DNA not fall into the hands of the transhumanists, who, judging from their plans thus far, would inevitably use it for the most nefarious reasons imaginable, starting with connecting us to the mechanical grid of the new so-called "quantum" computers—and the fourth-generation world-wide web. If they are indeed intent upon stealing the God code from our DNA, as I believe is the case, then it is essential that they not access that ninety-percent. Suffice to say that within that "junk" lies the roadmap to all our stellar and multidimensional bridges and highways, which we are learning to access, via factors that include our star's highly active transmissions, Earth's heightened resonance, and our immense evolutionary leap from the third to fourth dimension. And above all, within its fragments, lies the signature, the name, and the divine language of Creator, awaiting reassembly.

That must come from our own conscious and determined manifestation of mind over matter, not from the cold hands of a desensitized laboratory materialist.

Information that describes the scrambling of our original twelve-stranded blueprint is not unique to the Sirian works that I have been honored to bring to light, however my very first book, *The Cosmos of Soul: A Wake-up Call for Humanity*, channeled in 1997, was one of the earliest sources proposing this idea to the community of awakening souls on our planet. It offers the seeker a theory of species co-creation, that today has become far more widely embraced by spiritual communities as our true heritage.

From the chapter, DNA and the Great Experiment[1], we read:
"You are not the evolutionary brood of the gorilla, nor are you cousin to the chimpanzee, as you have been taught in the

---

1 The Cosmos of Soul, Patricia Cori, 2022 edition, pgs. 184-187

Darwinian context. You are a species unto your own, Homo Sapiens, seeded from many other systems and parallel galaxies ... star beings of the Earth Project.

As you were the hybrids of many species in the universe, your race was a multidimensional experiment in the extreme polar consciousness of physical reality. Originally, you were engineered with twelve strands of DNA, light codes of intelligence that would allow you all the gifts and potential of your stellar heritage—the genetic assemblage of some of the more evolved beings of the universe. You were designed to be the greatest of all intelligent life forms in the material universe, to master 3D like no other species had ever done before. In essence, we thought we could create a super race of light-bodied beings who would be capable of anchoring the higher frequencies, while crystallizing form in the third dimension. That was our challenge. We believed it to be a light quest of noble intention.

Our Elders took part in the Earth Project, along with the Light Emissaries of many other dimensions and star systems. Never was there celebrated a greater victory than the seeding of Gaia—the successful genetic splicing of many species' DNA codes—which utilized a select strain of bacteria as the base structure, into which snips of diverse genetic material were implanted, creating strands of what your scientists refer to as "recombinant DNA." Beings from many galaxies were united in that effort and your planet became, in many ways, the center of the universe, as all eyes were upon you—the emerging super race of human beings. Earth energies vibrated golden across the Web, as expectation of the Great Race resounded through the Cosmos.

Gaia was to become the clearest light of the galaxy, the greatest communication station in the universe. The human being would be known as the golden child of creation: a flaw-less physical entity of supreme intelligence, Spirit, and light.

There was another significance to the Earth Project, which we feel you have a right to know. You are most likely aware from your history and that of your animals that the genetic make-up of a species weakens with interbreeding. With time, defects in a genetically isolated species develop into weaknesses in the strain, which eventually dies out com-pletely. This was an aspect of consideration in the seeding of Earth, for we believed that, through the creation of the re-combinant DNA, we were assuring the survival of many re-mote civilizations, which did not have access to other races with which to cross-breed. By creating the four master pro-totypes of the human race, each bearing genetic material of different species, we were assuring the survival of the genetic pool on Earth as well.

Soon after the gestation of these four master races, the polar forces of darkness moved in and took control of the planet in every sense of the word. You were left with only two active strands, the incomplete matrix, and that is how they have controlled you ever since. If they could have unplugged those as well, they would have, stripping you completely of all intelligence and the ancestral memory of your true origins. Fortunately, your existence depended upon the double helix, so they had no choice but to leave the two vital strands. The memory, you see, lies in those codes, for they form the nucle-us of every single cell of your body and the controlling lords wanted you to forget forever the Family of Light.

This is why the core belief that yours is the only life in the universe was formed and implanted in your consciousness. It is why religions refuse to contemplate life on other planets, and why your governments hide their contact with beings of other worlds from the people of Earth. The antecedents of the power elite feared that, one day, you would be reactivated, and that day has finally arrived. Now is the time to remember.

We learned from the Experiment that, like your current genetic engineers, we were playing God to the extreme—overstepping our boundaries—and that such genetic tampering denied you the process of self-discovery and the journey of Spirit. It denied you the choice of which we have spoken with such emphasis and interfered with the Master Plan of the Creator. As infants of an evolving third-dimensional planet, you were never meant to hold that kind of super genetic wiring, for it was inharmonious with the very nature of evolution within your reality. Indeed, you were meant to populate Gaia in her physical stage of evolution and to awaken, as a race, along with her. It was meant to occur at this time, foreseen by Prime Creator, for your reaching the limits of physical reality and exacerbating the extremes of its polarity were all part of the very design of Gaia's evolution.

Do you comprehend the significance of what we are telling you here? We hope that you understand that the dark forces were allowed to disturb the process of your incubation because, like all other sentient species, you had to travel the road of soul ascension: no short cuts then, and none now.

Think back. Do you recall the thrill of diligently saving your money to buy your first used cars and the pride and sense of achievement that you derived from purchasing them yourselves? Surely you have remarked upon how much greater was your satisfaction than that of today's children, who demand your gifts of the flashy and new just out in the showrooms. Values, you see, are very much determined by your personal commitment, motivation, and need. As free-will beings, you came in to create your own experience, make your own choices, and know the focus of dedicating yourselves to an ideal. Quite simply, you came to do the work.

It was our intention to create a race of Super Gods on Earth. How could we have overlooked the obvious—that it is the spark of divinity within every life form that knows such title. It is the soul essence which creates the form and descends into matter and that is the creation of Prime Creator leaving itself; it is Divinity crystallizing in matter to know the process of its return to the light. That is the purpose of the soul essence. No other architect but the Creator is capable of such design.

In our misguided enthusiasm, our ego-centered creativity, we believed a master race could be genetically constructed, forgetting that the very purpose of life is to become masters through the process of descending into the darkness and then returning to Source. Otherwise, there would be no reason to separate out as co-creators. Like Adam and Eve in paradise, everything would have been done for you. There would have been no motivation or reason for such a race of giants to exist at all.

We were humbled by the lesson of the Great Experiment, for Prime Creator allowed the darkness to destroy our masterpiece in order to teach us karmic debt, right action, and a fundamental understanding of the free-will process. In a sense, we are just as responsible for your enslavement as are the lords of your subjugation. Having experienced divine intervention, we know now that it is against universal law to intervene in the karma of any sentient being."

Before the great sabotage that stripped all but two of these light strands from Homo sapiens, reducing us to the double helix (the minimum necessary for our biological survival), these Christed beings—our true ancestors—walked, briefly, in the ancient world of their creation, the early civilization of Atlantis, before it, too, was destroyed by dark forces. That same breed troubles us to this day: dark marauders who wish that no light permeate this corner of the galaxy, and that any biological life form that does not slither and crawl be cast off our planet forever.

Whether we are blessed to have retained conscious awareness of our true human ancestry—starseed from ancient, bio-engineering progenitors of other worlds—or whether we are so locked into the polarized sensate world of 21st century Earth that we cannot see beyond our fingertips, to reach for the stars, we are all, according to what I have brought through from my Sirian connection, descendants of that original experiment.

Like hopeful children, we eagerly await the return of our cosmic creators, wondering why they do not come to help guide us, beings of their genetic design, out of the drama playing out on Planet Earth. All too often, we forget that **we** are the aliens we've been waiting for and that we, and countless other souls, elected to come to this precise pinpoint on the screen of the universe for this very particular moment.

We are here to remove the dark stain of the Order's mark on our precious Earth and to restore light to this quadrant of space, just as those ancient star beings intended at our seeding, in order to bring joy, love and prosperity, as we take our giant leaps up the ascension timeline.

Think of that, when you are drowning in moments of despair, feeling like you can no longer bear the evil attempting to take over this breathtakingly beautiful orb in the heavens, nor the insanity that diabolical imprint is searing onto the subconscious fiber of people's minds, everywhere around you. Strive to remember why you embarked on a lifetime as a 21st century human, and what you have come to learn and accomplish from the upheaval and eventual resolution of Earth, ascending.

Close your eyes and listen . . . to the music of your soul.

Can you hear the divine melody of Spirit, strumming your heartstrings?

Chapter 3

They Walk Amongst Us

In the meantime, there are sentient, non-human extraterrestrial life forms visiting or currently residing on our planet, which has been rife with alien intervention from our inception, and well before.

Extraterrestrials do walk amongst us. This will be revealed, in most of our lifetimes. It already has been, in mine.

We have traipsed along for decades through a slow-moving, suppressed disclosure process that has seen undeniable evidence be quashed and "debunked," from countless whistleblowers: from government, military, researchers, contactees and experiencers. We have seen NASA's blurred and photoshopped images, supposedly of Martian and Lunar terrains. There are obviously structures there and even amateur astronomers are able to identify artificial constructs on the Moon, and in the region known as "Cydonia" on Mars—with its Sphinx-like structure and pyramid, which NASA dismisses as "a trick of light and shadow." And for over a half a century, we've had sightings of unidentified craft whizzing over and around our planet, hovering over strategic military sites, and reportedly abducting humans, who claim to have been subjected to terrifying experimentation that, in most cases, has to do with retrieval of sperm and ova by alien beings—or our own secret government. Some, as in the case of Roswell, have crashed, but of course these events have been covered up and denied by the secret government and their military militias.

But what the media is pushing now, supported by NASA and related government agencies, is a widescale, global "reveal" that will see fleets of alien craft arrive in key locations around the world, simultaneously, undeniably announcing that we can at last put aside the notion that we are the "orphans" of an uninhabited galaxy, and wake up to the fact that we are being officially inducted into a universe teeming with life.

What that will look like no one knows. Will it be the "real deal," as prophesized by the Sirian High Council, or will it be a staged false flag event, an "ET invasion," orchestrated by the Cabal? Imagine, if they have control over that drama, the kind of fear it could generate. And will we be faced with aggressive alien forces of the dark persuasion, intent upon total domination and the final destruction of our world, or will we finally meet illuminated beings who come in peace, as representatives of an interplanetary alliance for the advancement of galactic civilizations?

What concerns me most is the first option, whereby the guys pulling our strings fake a series of events that include initial communications, supported by images proving some form of life on Mars and the Moon, then, craft over the White House and the Kremlin and, finally, the appearance of some strange-looking life forms (possibly actual ETs from the underground ... possibly deep state actors, costumed and masked) taking center stage in the world arena. They have the technology, the media and all manner of control systems to put a scenario like that into place—and they certainly have the motivation, so science-no-longer-fiction is very possible, in a moment not too terribly far away.

Some of us believe this is the last card the cabal intends to play.

All we know with any amount of certainty, at this point, is that an actual, global ET encounter is going to catapult our civilization into a paradigm so foreign to our current understanding of the universe and our mortal existence within it that we will be forced to perceive life and our role in the galactic order of things in a very different light than we do now. We want to believe it will be positive . . . but we do not know that yet. We simply do not know who or what we are going to encounter when this actually comes down, so let us remain cautiously optimistic that what will be presented to us will be real, above all, and if any off-planetary beings decide it is time to show themselves en masse to the human race, that they be at the very least benign, and, hopefully, from the light side of the galaxy.

Aside from the many years of sightings I have experienced personally, I have had my own encounter with tall Nordics, supposed "space brothers," in the crop circles of Wiltshire, and in Rome, Italy, where they originally sought me out, several years ago, disguised as intelligence officers from the NATO base in Naples. Something about my work as a channel for the Sirian High Council intrigued them, they told me, and from what they projected as a purely scientific perspective, they were intent upon understanding just how I received the Sirians' messages: on what bandwidth, and in what state of consciousness I would find myself before, during and after transmissions.

I knew something was "off" about them from the first minute they stepped out of their car, at our meeting point in Rome. It was an intimidating, uncomfortable encounter. I felt no "brotherly" love energy from those two—no symbiosis—and my gut told me to beware, and to hold my ground. They did not emanate an auric field that I could perceive, at least not one I could recognize, and there was no light in their eyes. Rather, it was as if there was a camera behind the lens of those unnaturally blue eyes—the right eye specifically—and I was sure everything I said was being recorded.

It was one of the more uncomfortable of my supernatural, eerie life experiences.

That constant and pervading presence of my exquisite guides, and the communications I receive from them, told me not to look the two of them in the eyes, to stay shut down psychically in their presence, and to get away as quickly as possible—which I did.

After that first meeting in Rome, this alien-duo-posing-as-intelligence-officers mysteriously appeared to me several times in England, year after year, to where I traveled every summer to explore the crop circles, or to lead spiritual groups through sacred sites. Having these two strangers pop in, out of nowhere, was always an invasive, uncomfortable experience. I would be lying in a crop circle, experiencing deep altered states, and then suddenly, boom! I would feel their presence pull me back into my body way too abruptly, and activate the fight or flight response within me. They would step into the formation precisely where I was lying, with no regard for whatever I was experiencing, and peer into me, like cold, detached scientists in a laboratory, staring down a microscope at an unsuspecting microbe.

Still today, I get the "creeps" just thinking about it. In fact, I do everything I can not to draw them back into my consciousness, to be sure there is no opening in my etheric sheath for their telepathic, remote viewing probes to reach me.

Another encounter occurred when I was guiding a group of spirit travelers in meditation at the mystical Glastonbury Tor. There again, these two appeared out of nowhere and stepped right into our circle, uninvited. Most of the people were too blissed out to notice that I had interrupted the meditation rather abruptly, for their safety. I did not reconvene our circle, until the two aliens disappeared, but I admit, it shook me. And once again, they had broken the energy around me.

In yet another occasion, they emerged through a dimensional portal of their own making and materialized behind me on a small walking bridge in Marlborough, England, where I was standing, with a friend, peacefully watching the mallard ducks in the creek below. She was looking straight at me when they appeared out of nowhere, behind me, on a bridge where only she and I were standing. I thought her eyes were going to pop out of her head! I am so grateful that she was there to see it happen in real time, and to have had a witness to how these persistent intruders were capable of walking into my space through some kind of tear in the universe. A third-party observer helps me keep my wits about me in bizarre moments such as those, and also helps prevent me from going full paranoia in the face of otherworldly manifestations—being stalked by aliens, for example—that perpetually test and sometimes play with my sanity.

It is not the kind of thing you can discuss with just anyone. In fact, I have never written about it before now, for reasons that are obvious—and others, not so much. All I can say is that I did not enjoy these "close encounters" in any way. I could not break through my own resistance to the two beings to explore who they really were, where they were from, and what they really wanted from me. I only know those were not the kind of aliens I was looking forward to encountering in this lifetime, and I was more than relieved when their impromptu appearances in my sacred moments in the crop fields and temples of England, which continued over a period of five or six years, finally ended.

Perhaps if those encounters had happened now that I have almost thirty years more experience under my belt, I might have handled it very differently than I did back in the day. I realize that there was an opportunity to learn so much from those episodes that I did not take advantage of. But my guidance and my instinctive response to them told me to get away, and that is how I chose to deal with it at the time.

And so, when I hear people longing for ET to finally come "help us" on Planet Earth, I am always reminded of the two Nordics (if that is what they were), and how, when it comes to extraterrestrials, we really haven't a clue what we are dealing with. We have our fantasies, reports from "insiders," whistleblowers, military reports, "truthers," channels (myself included), remote viewers and mystics and sightings and the mostly terrifying accounts from abductees—but, by and large, we still do not know, at all, what we are really up against.

Experience tells me that, at the very least, we should be circumspect about who or what it is we are calling in, before addressing the even bigger question of why we believe we need help to manage our lightworks on our own.

Isn't it time we put the "savior" myth to bed, once and for all . . . and get on with the work of saving ourselves . . . if "saving" need be?

ETs do walk in plain sight for those with eyes to see them, as in my case with the two ETs, who looked human enough, and who could easily have passed as very tall Swedes—except for those strange, mechanical eyes. They walk freely in the top floor halls of several corporations and military command centers, where they are known, by the higher echelons, to be directing above top-secret government enclaves with whom they interact, and to whom they regularly give orders. They penetrate several layers of the underground as well, burrowed deep down below us, as far from the light as they can possibly get. Others, like those Nordics, traverse the dimensions effortlessly and materialize, apparently at will, as physical beings, pseudo-humans, in 3D. Some—the reptilians and the insectoids—can shape shift into approximate replicas of the human form (or animals) like otherworldly chameleons, but they are not human. Far from it. There is never any light in their eyes. And if you can read energy psychically, you are very aware, in their presence, that they do not have a familiar electromagnetic biosystem.

Such was the case with the two Nordics. There was no familiar roadmap in their auric fields and they were impossible for me to read. For all I know, they may very well have been non-biological life forms: synthetics, robots or cyborgs.

As featured in my novel, *The Emissary*, ET races reside in deep-sea colonies, and they have, in fact, been here since hundreds of thousands of years before us. They perceive humans as the true aliens to Earth—

hostile ones at that—and for good reason, if we are objective enough to recognize our species' inharmonious rapport with the ecology of our Earth and the great oceans, manifest in the military and industry's behaviors towards the great whales and the dolphin beings . . . and all ocean life.

Some are benevolent; others, like the elongated skull beings, the greys, insectoids and the reptilians are most definitely not. Neither were the two I encountered.

Through the masquerade, we are beginning to see how effortlessly they ooze in and out of the dimensions, as the veil over our collective third eye lifts, and the four-dimensional framework of our shifting consciousness reveals.

These creatures, who believe Earth is their dominion and theirs alone, are determined to annihilate Homo sapiens and get us out of their way, once and for all. But it is not enough for them to take us to extinction, which they could have done a long time ago. No, they want to drastically diminish our numbers, to make us more manageable, and then to take over our bodies and minds to utterly control all biological life on the planet, and to usher in the Star Trek inspired Borg Central Command—the "Internet of Bodies."

To see the light of Homo sapiens finally extinguished, and to lord over us by extracting the God Code within our DNA and replacing it with AI technology, are their ultimate ambitions. They are after our soul essence: the complete denial of light, of God and Spirit, and make no mistake about it: they are coming for that light within you . . . and your children.

It is so utterly important to know how to mediate any and all interference that attempts to penetrate your energy field, to possess the knowledge of how to protect your bioelectrical energy body, and to exert extremely focused mind power to override all programming, such as that being pushed into the populace now. Moreover, given the ramped-up agenda playing out since the onset of the current decade, it is a matter of absolute self-preservation that we all know how to heal, replenish and activate our biological DNA, through mental, emotional and spiritual alignment with the quantum light field, utilizing the infinite resources of energy, abundantly available to us, to maintain our mental, emotional and physical integrity and the sovereign experience of soul in transition.

*

Even those of us who are blessed to retain memory of lifetimes lived at other points in the time-space continuum and who, traversing the quantum field of universal being, determined that we wished to incarnate as humans on this planet now, still crystallize as human beings with the biological DNA template of those ancient geneticists. It is still the blueprint of how we construct and manifest human form, albeit with ninety-percent of that information still scattered and "non-coded." Immigrants from beyond, millions of souls who have never before walked the good soil of our bountiful Earth are choosing to do just that—to crystallize in this physical field of matter—pouring into our slice of reality in droves. They are drawn to this karmic school of learning, incarnating as human beings, to take part in the Great Shift that is revolutionizing our planet: whether to serve as light warriors, or simply to watch, from up close, the greatest reality show ever broadcast . . . in real time.

The convergence of so many souls drawn here, from realms near and far, is a significant and relatively rare cosmic event. They are called, at the soul level, to participate in the battle of darkness and light, unfolding on a planet that is contemporaneously struggling to ascend from third to fourth to fifth dimensions and higher, while dealing with a full-force, global Armageddon.

We are those souls.

We just arrived a bit ahead of the crowd.

It is important to recognize that, in our climb up the spiral of light, we, starseed, have billions of options from which to choose to work out our karmic lessons, that define the passage of the soul's journey, as we wind our way back to Source. Although our embattled 21st century Earth may look like a last resort to some, to those who understand the mechanics of karma it actually serves as a higher institute of learning, where the lessons are excruciatingly challenging and the tests are unending—but where, nonetheless, souls in transit are provided an amazing, invaluable education.

We chose to come here. Never forget that.

Sadly, since the "experimental" injections first began, a growing number of new souls attempting to enter now become consciously aware, during gestation, that something is grievously wrong. Something has altered the architectural blueprint of the species they had evolved to, following their last lifetime. They walk away from the suspect fetus and never look back, rather than to be born into a lifetime not fully human . . . into a lifetime devoid of the God light. How those who do choose to come in, despite the ominous biological warning signs and how these new transhumanist babies will develop, now that they are being born with graphene, human and animal fetal cells and synthetic mRNA acquired, in the womb, through their "vaccinated" parents, is cause for immense concern.

Even though the censorship program that continues to deny truth to the global population does not allow us to acknowledge what is really happening to these babies, or what is really in those needles, there are people in the medical profession leaking out images of black-eyed babies, and newborns with extremely bizarre behaviors, and malformations. Some very frightened medical professionals are telling us that these newborns are not fully human.

Are they, in fact, the new, genetically modified humans of transhumanist design?

We may not all agree that we have proof of this aberration appearing in newborns, or that it is the cause, in 2022, for a shocking increase in miscarriages and stillbirths. Unfortunately, alleged reports from reliable sources, that indicated shocking spontaneous abortion rates in expectant mothers vaccinated in the first and second trimesters, have been obfuscated or eliminated altogether. Sadly, some of us know people who have had to live through this tragedy.

Let us pay close attention and do everything we can to educate pregnant women to the dangers of taking those injections, while they are carrying a life within them, or soon after, when they will be passing the poison through their milk, if they nurse their young.

The near and distant futures of not only our individual lives, but of our entire species' survival, depend upon it.

Chapter 4

The Strident March of Transhumanism

The concept of a genetic experiment performed by off-world beings, which led to the birthing of the multi-racial, hybrid super species, Homo sapiens, is certainly not new to those of you who are familiar with my work, for it is a recurring theme that I have shared from that very first book of the classic Sirian Revelations trilogy, first published around twenty-five years ago.

Our own scientists are performing gene-altering experiments all the time in underground laboratories, creating bioweapons out of genetically-enhanced or mutated viruses and bacteria, experimenting with freakish chimeras from the DNA of animals, and mixing their DNA with snippets of the human genome. We mostly ignore it, because if we were to acknowledge what is going on there, we would have to question the ethics, the morality and the outright evil of what is being done to living beings—innocent victims of such cruel and indifferent scientists. The truth is, we don't want to feel that pain. And most people do not feel empowered to do anything about it. So, by and large, we ignore what goes on behind those secret walls, and the mad scientists get away with just about anything they want to do.

At least, they have until now.

That said, is it so hard to imagine that ETs light years ahead of our contemporary bioengineers would have mastered the technology required to create a hybrid humanoid from the DNA of several contributing extraterrestrial species?

Is that the real "missing link?"

No doubt, as I have previously stated, others of you have sourced knowledge of the great genetic experiment elsewhere, for, there are other channels and luminaries who have brought forward very similar information. But the question of our true stellar ancestry, and how our species emerged from the Sirian Experiment (undertaken with the highest of intentions) still needs to be re-examined, over and over again, until we really understand how universal the practice of genetic engineering truly is. Moreover, scientists across the universe need to learn—no matter how pure the intention of those souls who try . . . no matter how noble their vision—that tampering with the perfection of divine design, which will always remain beyond the scope of any of God's conscious creations, can never lead to improving on it.

In the end, how can any conscious being pretend to know better than his own Creator?

Alas. It appears to be a lesson that must be learned the "hard way."

Funded by a collective of eugenicists, many of today's earth-grown geneticists and bioengineers appear to be willing conspirators in the globalists' transhumanist agenda, as they come to the task with a completely opposite intention to the one brought by distant beings of the Sirian star team. It is far from "pure," and certainly not noble. I speak, primarily, of the all-out war being waged upon our DNA, and the implantation of nano-technology within our cells that has, as its goal, the ultimate mutation of biological human beings (and animals) into chimeras, clones, alien hybrids, and, ultimately, into semi-human, robotic life forms: cyborgs.

Don't be fooled by altruistic rhetoric coming from their public relations outlets and the misdirect that expounds on the wonders of what such technology will provide a "needy" humanity. They are telling us that more mRNA "vaccines" are coming down the pike, and that the new revolutionary medicine of our present and near future will be delivered directly into our cells, via laboratory-created mRNA, to repair our "broken" DNA, for all manner of health issues and diseases. Racing to the foreground of our individual and societal awareness, that transhumanist agenda is intent upon mutating the human genome for its human 2.0 version of Homo sapiens: first, by implanting software that can strip the God code out of us entirely—the Great Disconnect—and then merging what is left of us into a vast techno-mechanical matrix as emotionless, robotic beings . . . like mindless tools, controlled and manipulated by artificial intelligence.

We do not "need" that. And I, for one, will not allow synthetic devices to be implanted into the sacred temple of my being.

The race to transhumanism is on a fast track to hell—let there be no mistake about it. The technocracy left the gate a long time ago. We just were not paying attention. While we were being beguiled by tricks and illusions from the magician's left hand, the right was setting up all the necessary systems that would eventually plug us into their ultimate matrix.

And then came Covid-19.

There is a whole field of investigation into the real origins of this "virus," which proves that it was in play years before it "leaped out of a bat cave" to infect the entire globe. Despite all efforts to obscure the history, that information—including several patents that have to do with the genetic design of various bioweapons labelled "viruses"—is on file with the U.S. Patent Office. If you are willing to do the research, you will find it readily available to you. It is no coincidence that names of people who are directing the entire "emergency vaccination program" are on those patents, but then . . . we are not supposed to know such things, even though they are public record.

You can follow the trail of evidence to the truth, if you seek the scientific proof . . . and if you are ready for it. We have very courageous lawyers, doctors and senators joining together to reveal what has been done by the perpetrators of the "vaccine" campaign against the people, pushing past the barriers, challenging governments and the health organizations to come clean—and then, to be held responsible. Law suits against these individuals and the corporations behind them are emerging from the fog of their failing narrative. Citizens around the world are standing in defiance of the greatest crime ever perpetrated against the entirety of humanity. And we have alternative media, publishers, and authors, such as I, bringing that information forward.

The Covid-19 agenda was rushed out in February, 2020, with the evolution of the abruptly-named "pandemic," and the untested emergency "vaccine" campaign that immediately followed—a global never-before-tried experiment that continues, two years hence, to inject billions of people with DNA-altering, synthetic mRNA, over and over again, demonstrating that what they are putting into people is not a vaccine at all.

If it is, it certainly is not an effective one.

And no, the idea that whatever poisons and software they are injecting into people alters their human genome is not a "conspiracy theory." Despite the controversy as to whether or not the "vaccine's" synthetic mRNA mechanism alters the DNA, scientific proof from qualified researchers is available, and more is surfacing every day.

Of course it affects the DNA!

We have synthetic mRNA implanted into the body unnaturally, blocking the body's natural messenger RNA, designed to create the necessary biological response to any viral or bacterial invader. The synthetic, laboratory-produced mRNA in the injection sends a new message to the body systems—to constantly produce a dangerous "spike protein," which appears to take over the entire organism with no "off" valve, instead of what the body is naturally designed to do, in order to fight infection and maintain the natural balance.

Your body knows what to do. It was designed to protect itself and to maintain a state of health and well-being.

Anyone with the slightest understanding of how vaccines and immunology really work would immediately recognize that what is being put into people cannot be classified a vaccine. It is something very different . . . something Big Pharma itself admits has never before been used on human beings . . . hence, the term: "experimental program."

The lab rats of the Covid-19 "vaccine" are human beings, and the laboratory is the entire globe.

Surely people can see this by now . . . can't they?

We can identify a pre-meditated roll-out between the explosion of the pandemic, the shut-down of societies around the world, the strong New World Order rhetoric, the deliberate destruction of the global economy, and the peddling of a whole new way of "treating disease" through mRNA vaccines.

Big Pharma and the global health organizations are telling us that there are plenty more mRNA vaccines on the way, and that gene therapy is the future of medicine. Lest we forget, the mRNA injection is **not** a vaccine! Still, the masses refuse to ask the glaring question of what this new, invasive technology means to our human genome and our future. They still trust what they are told and believe what they are sold. Many are in a state of mass hypnosis, entrained to the narrative.

After all the death, all the adverse reactions and destroyed lives, they still believe that what is being put into their arm, several times over—a substance that reportedly contains poisons, graphene, gene-altering synthetic mRNA, and still unidentified biological matter—is a vaccine, for a virus that, allegedly, has never been identified.

These people refuse to accept irrefutable proof that their own governments, backed by global health organizations that are supposed to be caring for the health of the populace, are injecting them with gene-altering, synthetic nano-technology. After all, their trusted media and health organizations insist the mRNA shots do not alter the DNA . . . or that it does, but only "temporarily." And, after all, they have the "fact checkers" confirming what they want us to accept as "the science."

So, what's to worry?

Researchers at Lund University in Malmö, Sweden, found that the mRNA vaccine enters human liver cells and triggers the cell's DNA in the nucleus to increase the production of the LINE-1 gene expression to make mRNA. Apparently, the whole process occurred rapidly in the laboratory, within six hours, their study concluded.

Published on the website of the prestigious medical journal, MDPI, the actual article from Lund University[2], entitled: *Intracellular Reverse Transcription of Pfizer BioNTech Covid-19 mRNA Vaccine BNT162b2 In Vitro in Human Liver Cell Line,* mostly a jumble of medical terminology, clearly states: "A recent study showed that the SARS-CoV-2 RNA can be reverse-transcribed and **integrated into the genome of human cells.**"

MDPI (Multidisciplinary Digital Publishing Institute) is a publisher of open access scientific journals, based in Switzerland. It claims to have published research from over 330,000 contributing authors, and that their journals receive more than twenty-five million monthly web page views. So, perhaps we should, at the very least, be giving equal time to what they bring forward, as to what we allow to seep in from the mass media, from spokespeople who represent the pharmaceutical corporations that produce these "vaccines," and from global health organizations that categorically deny that mRNA nano-technology in those vials does, in fact, alter the DNA.

Dr. Peter McCullough, a highly respected and established internist, cardiologist and epidemiologist, one of the leading critics of what is being into injected into people as Covid-19 vaccines, said the Lund

---

2   https://www.mdpi.com/1467-3045/44/3/73/htm

University findings have "enormous implications of permanent chromosomal change that could drive a whole new genre of chronic disease."

If they can alter the chromosomal nature of our body electric, they can alter every aspect of our biology: thoughts, emotions, and physical forms. This growing body of influential transhumanists is pushing world governments to adopt AI technology that can fuse human consciousness with computer central, to be used, whether we want it or not, to that end. They are openly talking about altering the same DNA that pharmaceutical corporations say they are not altering. It is about stealing our souls, hooking us up to a robotized AI control center that alters the mind, the emotional body and the operation of our physical being.

This is our final wake-up call. There is no more time to roll over and go back to sleep, hoping this is all a bad dream and that it will fade away with the morning coffee and an egg McMuffin. With the excuse of Covid-19, they have jettisoned us into a dystopian mutation of the world we knew, when, in so many ways, we felt so much more human than we do now ... so much freer to live our lives, whereas now people are still hiding behind their plastic face covers and dirty masks, locking themselves into their own cages of paranoia and fear.

It is insane that anyone walking on this planet still believes that this conspiracy against humanity is mere theory ... not when they are putting it out there for all to see that they are intent upon redesigning the old version of Homo sapiens (the natural one) to a genetically restructured, AI-controlled new edition: Homo sapiens 2.0. And they are openly discussing this, driving the agenda, mutating human consciousness on the way to their goal.

In the sterile mind of the devoted transhumanist, there is no future, there is no soul, and there is nothing beyond the physical lifetime, unless consciousness can be captured as and redefined in terabytes, finding a false technological immortality in the hive mind of artificial intelligence. How terribly difficult it must be to never find any peace, and how impossible to make sense of existence, if one believes, as they do, that nothing exists beyond these limited years of physical life.

To have no vision of eternity, the soul immortal, is something I cannot imagine. That would have to be such a painful state of mind, such a hollow feeling, no matter how many mansions, Bentleys, and gold bars one might acquire. No matter how much we accumulate in the world of matter, no matter how voraciously we live our lives, it is meaningless if we perceive nothing else, when that appointment with our maker finally arrives, and we pass over the life-death barrier, to journey as spirit to our next destination.

How utterly terrifying it would be to believe you cease to exist in that moment . . . and all that remains is dust.

The curtain falls. The lights go out.

You're over.

It is no wonder that so many people lose themselves to addiction, trying to numb the pain that stems from fear of a future of nothingness. I feel for those who perceive that these few years of physical life on Earth, many spent in suffering and unfulfilled desire, are all they have, and that, when they take that final bow, nothing follows; no trace remains, like footsteps on a sandy beach . . . washed away with the waves.

Or worse, perhaps because they know they sold their soul, to fear so profoundly what darkness awaits at the hour of death, that they are desperate to preserve their mortality by all means . . . no matter what the cost. To freeze the body via cryonics until a cure can be found for the disease that has taken their life, or to willingly merge with AI in order to project their consciousness into a cloud in a computer network, are desperate acts of beings who have no understanding whatsoever of their own immortality.

Apart from the rewards that come to them in their short journey through the material realm, do they think, when they sign off their souls, that the "devil" gives merit points for how many souls they can deliver to the dark side? Do they believe, I wonder, that by selling out as many people as they can, they may somehow free themselves from the tormentor's hook? Is it that fear of non-existence after this physical life that drives the transhumanist to seek immortality in a bunch of neural impulses, pulsing frequencies through the mechanical brain of a mega-computer?

Or is it more likely that the fear of a devil-in-waiting, eager to administer retribution, is what drives them to do everything they can to lure people into the twilight of their interminable gloom?

It really makes you wonder, doesn't it?

It certainly does me.

Chapter 5

Designing "Human 2.0"

So, how do you build a human robot—one that you re-design from its self- and species-perpetuating, biological template—to be systemically linked into the monstrous "cloud" at computer central, through which it will be managed, controlled and enslaved by artificial intelligence? And then, once your deviate techno-lackies and funded bioengineering teams have acquired the know-how and the capability to rewrite the Divine Blueprint, deleting the God Code within the DNA, and replacing it with your coded messenger of choice, how do you achieve the task of reconstructing what you describe as the outdated, imperfect "human 1.0," without your unsuspecting test subjects ever knowing that they are being mutated into a new, improved version of their former selves—man merged with machine—the updated "human 2.0" model?

What do you need to put in place, before you activate your plan to alter the essence of being human, in order to change the course of an entire civilization's evolutionary future? It's simple. You create the perception of an existential threat to people's very survival, pumped out of media you basically own, and you slam the propaganda into their brains, every minute of every day, creating such a terrifying group mindset that those who are entrained to it blindly agree to whatever you decree is the antidote to the projected danger.

So, in essence, you own the problem. It's patented, and you own the solution, which you've also patented. That is what you call a tight sphere of omnipotent influence.

Those who do not cower and adhere to your plan you designate as dangerous insurgents and extremists, who must be isolated from the flock, cut off from society, interred in "re-education centers," and eventually disposed of. You silence any and all logic and real science; you eliminate all expert testimony, and blackball anyone questioning anything that could expose your position or reveal your master plan, until such time that people are so anesthetized they won't care when they are confronted with the truth, anyway.

You destroy the credibility, careers and lives of the opposition.

Like a page from an Orwellian playbook, you convince your hypnotized public that these "other" people—the renegades—pose a grave danger to their survival, so that it will suspect them, and reject whatever truth they are trying to share, in their quest to help awaken those who have been so blinded by your endless campaign of terror that they still cannot see what is being perpetrated on the human race.

You convince your subjects that you have the means to protect them from any and all danger, because you are, in fact, their savior. They must trust you, because you have everything under control. You and only you know what to do to keep them "safe." Everything your noble soul does is for their safety, after all.

You distort people's perception until they come to believe that serving as a slave to a central master is a good thing. They will be rewarded for it, earning merit in your social credit system, whereas the free thinkers will be ostracized and punished. And then, once that is accomplished, and you've completely captured the minds of a large enough segment of the world population, you deliver your Trojan Horse.

You show the people, through financial manipulation and the destruction of the economy, that material things are not important and that they can live without them, because, in the end, only your Order—

the control system—can save them. Squeezing them until they lose their jobs, their homes, cars, and all they have acquired, you take them down to survival, carnal mind where they will agree to just about anything to survive.

You even tell them they should start adding insects to their diet, and learn to eat weeds, while you deliberately destroy the food supply and prepare to starve billions of people to death.

You veil the plan to steal their free will, their independent thoughts, and their capacity to love and feel compassion, by tricking them into believing that the message, "You will have nothing and you will be happy," is intended to mean material possessions, while the real message behind those chilling words is that they will have no sense of "self" anymore, no more free will—nothing—and that they will be unresistingly, happily obedient to you, self-proclaimed keepers of their safety: the overlords of the Borg.

Your task, as a mastermind, technology-worshipping transhumanist, is to find the most effective method of delivery, one that allows you to secretly build cyborg technology from within your target population's fully functioning bodies, without any of them even realizing it—until, of course, it is too late to do anything about it and until the will to save their very souls has been supplanted by the hard drive and software, embedded in their brains, organs, cells and blood.

You develop the devious means to deliver the fundamental building blocks, structural, self-organizing materials, such as graphene oxide, to build your intra-cellular nano-technology systems, designed and operated by artificial intelligence, into their unsuspecting bodies—technology that has the capacity to deliver the payload, bit by evil bit, in order to lay down a self-assembling, nano-computing drive at the cellular level. You engineer it to override the former "software"—the God-given DNA architecture—cutting Creator's signature out of the blueprint and stealing the soul out of your test subjects, by building synthetic genetic "hardware" to overwrite the original.

Once you have cleaved the DNA, disrupting the sacred language of its design, you then insert a program of your choosing, supplanting the God Code with a new signature, all the while massaging your new subjects, through controlled and almost inescapable propaganda, which convinces them that your turning them, their children and the entire human race (an outdated, inferior design) into a hive-feeding, robotized version of their former individual selves, is simply an inevitable progression of their species.

That is how you do it.

And no, what I am describing here is not a watered-down script from a sci-fi horror movie, or a page out of Orwell's *1984*. It is exactly the way things are on our way to 2030, the target date for conversion of Homo Sapiens to the "new, improved" model of the transhumanists' design: human 2.0.

You may think I'm being facetious here, but I assure you I am not. I have watched this roll out for decades, sharing what I could all these years to help awaken as many people as possible. And here it is. As the Sirian High Council stated twenty-five years ago, "The New World Order is upon you."

We either accept this horror as our future, or we say "no," loud and triumphant, and retain the purity of our sovereign souls. The destiny of our lives, our families and communities and the future of our species is in our hands—not theirs.

We have the power to say "no" to Homo sapiens 2.0.

With all our flaws, weaknesses and shortcomings, we are still a magnificent species. We have the capacity to love beyond measure; we have laughter, joy and a purpose for being here. We are souls in school, learning how to climb higher.

We are the Light Brigades.

So, shields up, beloved. There is no turning back now.

We must prevent the architects of the New World Order from meeting their fast-approaching deadline of 2030 with success. They know that a rebellion is surging and that they cannot suppress us for very much longer. They must disconnect as many of us as possible from Source, and remove the God light altogether, or their agenda will not move forward as planned. You can understand why they have mounted an all-out campaign against those of us who simply refuse to drink of the poison chalice.

The plan they have set in motion for 2030 is to kill off as many people as possible, and for the rest—to deconstruct human DNA entirely, by replacing the God Code with a Luciferian override. Before our biological bodies are turned completely over to the Borg, to be absorbed into the AI matrix, they want to be sure that nothing remains of our soul connection to Source: no divine signature, no God Code, no light written into the software of their newly designed human/Borg hybrid. It is the express intent of those dark overlords that that they remove Creator's signature from within that Code, to obscure the path back to God, so that nothing can ever guide us back to the light, and so that only a synthetic replacement "overwrite" that does not speak the word of God in any way remains.

That, my friends, is the Mark of the Beast. Do not be afraid to look it in the face.

There is no place for love and the expanse of human emotion in that equation. There is no place for light . . . unless it is the illusive, false light of the Luciferian idol.

It is not difficult to understand why they hate us for being the light bearers of this relatively remote place in our galactic space—on a planet their ancient ancestors intended to claim as their own real estate, before we were birthed here. Obviously, they want it back, as if they ever held title to it to begin with, and they want us out of the way.

Their objective is the obfuscation of all light, all warmth, all love, within and around us all. They are diminishing the sun's brilliance—not, as they would have us believe, to fulfill some mock-up "green energy plan," designed to line their pockets even more, but because they loathe the sun for nourishing our inner light, illuminating the highways of life within our body systems, and transforming the cholesterol in our skin into Vitamin D, so essential to the immune system and healthy bones. It gives us so much essential energy on every level, warming the heart and evoking joy, which then manifests as the exaltation of sacred geometrical form, within every cell of our being.

They do not want that.

They want us unwell, from the cradle to the grave, so that we will continue to ingest their pharmaceuticals and be weak, unhealthy and dependent.

Remember this: they need huge numbers of us to die off as quickly as possible. Those who will survive the eugenics program they have already sprung upon us, they want to feed into their system, zombified new versions of Homo sapiens, to walk the Earth as soulless units of the Borg.

*

I cannot help but ask myself, over and over again: "How can human beings who work in these laboratories demonstrate so little concern for ethics and the consequence of their actions?" Are any of them even human anymore? Do they have children, and if they do—do they love them? Don't they realize the enormous impact their actions will have on the entirety of living beings on this planet, including themselves?

The obvious answer is no, they simply do not. They could not proceed against us so ruthlessly if they did. These clinicians appear to have no awareness of the karmic debt they are taking on, most likely for an immense swathe of their eternity, given the enormity of their transgressions. Then again, I must remind myself that most of them do not believe in the soul, nor can they perceive eternity. Not at all. So, they obviously do not care. And, in the case of intervention on live animals, they clearly feel no compassion for those innocent victims of their bizarre experiments and torturous protocols. If they did, they could never do what they do.

Eager interventionists, they have been given free rein to take their experimentation to the next level—directly to the human population—under orders from globalists, who have clearly charted the course. I understand that to be the separation of all human beings from each other (particularly children from their parents), from the life force of the goddess, Gaia, and, above all, from the Light of Source, by means of deconstructing the God Code within the DNA.

They have acquired the capability to alter, splice and rewrite our divine blueprint—the same basic principles utilized by our star ancestors, who joined together to birth us. And when I say "joined together," I refer not only to the consolidated effort of participating exoplanetary scientists, biologists and geneticists, united with Sirian overseers of the experiment. I refer more specifically to the "joining together" and amalgamation of DNA material from twelve distinct species, from within and beyond our own Milky Way galaxy.

Homo sapiens, the Sirians' brainchild, is actually the genetically-enhanced, merged lineage of these extraordinarily intelligent, deeply compassionate off-planet beings—representatives of the *Alliance for Intergalactic Commerce and Cultural Exchange*. Depicted as the "Star Fleet Command" in the sci-fi series, the original *Star Trek*, the AICCE (pronounced "ace") was shown to us through that wonderful vision of our future, courtesy of the time traveler, Gene Roddenberry. It was so ahead of its time in the 60s, when we still had so far to go before we could envision a very real possibility of interactive cultures beyond our planetary boundaries, and the workings of the greater universe. And yet, *Star Trek* titillated our imagination.

It certainly did mine.

That delicious fiction charted our course to *boldly go where we had never gone before.*

What a legacy Roddenberry and his heroic characters left behind—one, I believe, that has truly impacted our vision of the future. The series had so very much to do with our awakening to the fact that we are not orphans in what so many perceived then, beyond our own backyard, as a lifeless, motiveless universe beyond Earth's borders. It teased us into contemplating a universe of conscious, vibrant life, and showed us that integration between civilizations across the universe was a very near and probably reality.

In essence, *Star Trek* taught us how to dream.

And here we are in 2022, struggling between the dimensions, living a science fiction scenario far more unbelievable than the Starship Enterprise could ever have depicted for us, from those early Hollywood studio days, to the "final frontier."

*

In order to fully comprehend our true ancestry, and to apply to our current genetic "dilemma," what we glean from that knowledge, we need to understand how and why star beings from beyond took it upon themselves to bioengineer a sophisticated, genetically enhanced super race of light beings to take seed and proliferate upon Planet Earth . . . and how that has affected our respective karma. Those who contributed understood and revered the God Code within themselves and throughout all Creation. Their mutual intention was to offer Planet Earth an evolutionary head start out of its primitive state—a giant leap—to bring light to a comparatively dark place in space, at a remote location in our Milky Way Galaxy, which, in turn, is located in a relatively small cluster of galaxies . . . in a particularly remote place in space.

Bodhisattvas of the universe, those who contributed to the Great Experiment knew enough about karmic retribution to understand that they would be entraining their karma to ours, but they did what they believed was needed to anchor the light here, just as all lightworkers attempt to do, there where we perceive darkness.

If we are to understand what it truly means to intervene in the Divine Blueprint, Prime Creator's architectural roadmap, then we cannot ignore that, despite the highest intentions, the Sirians and their team do recognize how their ancestors have caused them to be karmically bound to our species. In effect, there exists a cord between them, our human race, and Earth herself, for their intervention in Gaia's own evolution bound them to her as well. Whatever that means to their advancement is difficult for us and probably for them to know, but we can only consider ourselves blessed for it—for they do have a vested interest in our liberation and illumination as individuals, and as an entire race of beings. They do have a karmic purpose for assisting us in our evolution. And that is a good thing.

In this hour of untold disruption of our planet's harmonics, it is reassuring, as it is empowering, to know that we are not alone in our struggle against the great antagonist. And, although we know better than to await a savior to set things right for us, we can find comfort in knowing that those star beings have every interest in seeing light reign over darkness—within us, in our electromagnetic biological life forms, and surrounding this precious gem of a planet.

Now that the powerful, dark force they undoubtedly foresaw attempting to consume our realm has initiated its all-out campaign to strip the very light out of our DNA matrix, to overwrite it with a dominatrix-styled artificial intelligence control system over all life on our planet, and, finally, to dim Gaia's own light forever, it is, indeed, a very good thing to know.

*

There **is** a backdoor here. Consider how software developers manage computer data storage. When a file is deleted, it does not mean that it is gone. The file system in the disk updates the database to indicate that the file is no longer active, or in use, so it gets buried. But it is still there, and unless the space it held gets overwritten with other information, that data can eventually be recovered.

I am suggesting that when we proceed with the DNA healing visualization later in this book, we bear in mind that, like any software writer, we are capable of retrieving what may have been sent to the background, and restoring it. Then, using the same principles of data overwriting used by computer experts, we shall peer into the sacred coil, as if we were looking into an electron microscope, to see if there exists an invasive code, or "rewrite" in the double helix of the body system. If so, we will overwrite it with the sacred letters of the Divine Blueprint, and remove any invasive data, by assuring that the space it filled in the altered genome has been totally erased.

All is written into the Akashic Record, the quantum field that serves as a cosmic library, of sorts, for the whole of Creation: all beings, all universes, all consciousness. As long as we are not cut off from the God Code within us all, we perpetually interface with and are receptive to that resource at the cellular level, accessing whatever we need to restructure, renew and accelerate our genetic memory—both at the biological and conscious levels, which of course are never separate.

This is of the utmost importance to our ability to heal and activate our DNA construct, and the sacred form that embodies it—through acute focus of thought and intent—which I will elaborate in Part Two of this work.

*

Drunk on their perceived power and control, these "rulers" are out of the closet: they do not care anymore if we know what they have in store for us—in fact, they revel at how we give our power to their tech-no-world. All of these developments are in our face, as Silicon Valley and the mainstream media massage the mass mind into acceptance of what they want us to believe is an inevitable non-human future.

It is the right now of their horror show.

Combine the ability to interfere and alter the human genome with the immense data processing capacity of super computers and what you get is a bunch of insane transhumanist masterminds holding the keys to altering human behavior, and the capability to recode the basic oper-ational system—the DNA—of the human organism, so that it is simply not human anymore. Their dark vision for the future of Homo sapiens involves disrupting our natural biorhythms to such an extent that, with the implantation of sensors, chips and wearable sensors, our thoughts will be reduced to electronic signals, received, stored and analyzed by computers. Those same technologies will also be structured so that AI not only receives information and data from our monitored bodies, but it will send commands as well: instructions to manipulate our thoughts, and commands that tell the body how to move, how to feel, and who the controlled version of our former selves has become.

*

It is not enough for these modern-day purveyors of the transhuman-ist techno-god that those ancient alien disrupters stripped us down to two-stranded consciousness, reducing our brilliance and subverting our trajectory, where we walked in Christ light. We survived that "hack," and still we rose, knowing ourselves, and still learning more, with every moment, about who we really are and where we fit in the universe. Through the peaks and valleys of our existence, and despite the unre-lenting, perpetual interference in human evolution, our God light still shone through.

We are capable of greatness they never imagined, so brilliant is the Divine Blueprint. Despite every attempt to dissect and destroy us, there are growing numbers of creative human beings who remain free-thinking, love-seeking sparks of that divine and inextinguishable fire. More are awakening every hour, every day.

We, **sovereign** human souls of Earth, shall not be lost in the techno-cloud. We refuse to be reduced to algorithms, to be merged into a concocted matrix of simulated information and biotechnology. You will not tell us who we are. You will never have us, because you cannot hack the light of divine consciousness within us—unless we let you in. You may be successful in controlling a swathe of the population, to feed your AI beast, but you will never succeed in transforming the human race to your desired end. You will never kill the spirit of the awakened, for we will never sign the contract, accept the needle, eat the poison willingly—and you need that resignation to achieve your goal. We know that.

With all your algorithms and biometrics and computer data processors, you keep underestimating the human being. We will find our way around you, trust me. Whatever you throw at our civilization, your time will soon be over on Planet Earth.

You may have stolen some souls along the way. God help them . . . they did let you in. But we will do what we can to free them, and to help them heal.

We sovereigns will never bow down to you.

We do not consent.

You have no entry here, so move away.

*

If we are to release ourselves and our human family from the clutches of these adversarial forces, to overturn the transhumanist agenda in time to preserve our fundamental human biology, present and future, we must begin with an all-out campaign to unplug from the technology grid as many people as we can, starting with ourselves, with particular emphasis on the cell phone, television and the home computer. Detoxification from those programs is difficult, for they are designed to be more addictive than any available substance on Earth, and so many vital activities, involving banking, sourcing materials and information, and on-line commerce, make us dependent upon them. Why do you think they call them "programs? However, liberating ourselves from that dependency and electromagnetic entrainment is essential to our clarity of mind, emotional independence, and, it now appears, to our very survival.

These tools of the techno-lords entrain the mind and the emotional body to accept and absorb whatever programming, filled with subliminal messages, that they cook up for their global audience. It is absorbed at various levels of hypnotic mind and fed deep down into the subconscious pool, which constantly reflects back as behavioral response mechanisms.

For as long as I have been a public figure, I have been appealing to people to avoid the lure of AI and to turn off their devices—or, at the very least, to limit access to them.

When I am not typing away at the computer, writing a book or recording an interview, I limit access to technology—especially social media. I have never played a computer game in my life, and have no desire, nor intent, to ever start. And I have never even had a GPS system in my car, simply because I prefer to use my mind to get me where I want to go, in every sense of those words. Learning how to read maps and paying attention to the signs to watch out for develops cognitive function. Why would I want to give that away?

I think it is insane to introduce an AI device into the home, such as Alexa, the latest Big Brother technology, supposedly designed to supply people with any information their heart desires at the drop of a hat. Its real purpose is to spy on people in the sanctity of their own homes. It is recording you.

Why in the world would anyone willingly embrace this intrusion? Is "convenience" so much more valuable than privacy and mastery over one's own thoughts? Apparently these proud "Alexians" are so naïve that they do not understand how their private information, habits and intimacies are being fed into computer central—as if the AI is only for information in . . . not out.

Who knows? Perhaps they simply do not care. They most probably have yet to learn about the social credit system, tested and operating in Communist China, where every step and movement, every deed, every spoken word and quite possibly every thought is monitored by the government. All behavior is evaluated by AI systems that constantly determine your real-time "social rating," which provides rewards, or credits, for good conduct, and doles out punishment and restrictions for what the government determines is "unacceptable."

All of this is coming to a country near you.

And, while Alexa is proliferating in homes across the world, selling in the billions, the tech business is making a fortune on it. I'm sure whoever, or whatever, is behind the technology is grateful to their growing customer base for the business, making the work of controlling citizens so much easier and so profitable. I imagine we are nearing the time foreseen in Orwell's book, when these spy devices and much more sophisticated and pervasive ones will be mandated by the government, in every room of every house: no longer sold as a convenience, but as a requirement of the one world government.

These are just a few of the reasons why simulations, virtual reality and artificial intelligence do not entice me whatsoever.

And what of the youth? There is no question that overexposure to technology leads to addiction, and limits children's abilities to create, to enjoy physical activity and being in nature. It stunts their intellectual, social, and emotional growth. There must be a reason why people like Steve Jobs and Bill Gates restricted their kids' use of computers, iPhones and other devices, even into their teenage years. Jobs was known to say that limiting his daughters' usage of computers was important to their creative development. Bill Gates and his wife reportedly limited their children's time on-line at home to forty-five minutes per day. Unfortunately, the wisdom and safety precautions they imposed on their own clearly did not apply to the rest of the children in the world.

The physical body suffers as a result of sitting before a screen, for hours on end, in states of accelerated adrenaline stress. The U.S. Department of Health and Human Services recommends limiting screen time to less than two hours a day to protect against deterioration in vision. Obesity, lethargy and nervous disorders—even heart attacks and strokes in children—are becoming more common manifestations of those who are glued to the screen.

So, at the risk of sounding like an overprotective parent, let me reiterate that now is the time to find the strength to turn off the television—Big Brother's primary control mechanism—and free ourselves and our children of its hypnotic, mind-numbing controls. We must drastically reduce our use of the cell phone, the power's obedience and tracking tool par excellence. We must limit our dependence on computers, gadgets and all manner of technology that distracts us from tuning back into the natural, beautiful world around us, while it holds us glued to the matrix.

Only then can we ever find our way to the restoration of true independence on this planet.

*

In our struggle to take back our power from all of this intrusion and manipulation of the human psyche, we need to forgive the darkness in ourselves, and in everyone—for that is surely one of the greatest lessons attached to this drama and, I believe, it is the ultimate roadblock to our ascension.

God knows it isn't easy. These are monstrous beings we are up against and they revel in their evil: the more malevolent . . . the better. But then, paraphrasing the words of the late, great President John F. Kennedy, "We didn't come because it was easy, we came because it was hard."

"Easy" does not teach. It doesn't inspire. It doesn't challenge us to reach for the moon and the stars. It doesn't move us to greatness, to seek Creator, so that we will forever spark the light . . . the light . . . the light . . . re-igniting the Christ within.

As for the karmic bond that ties us to the Sirians, I am grateful, at a very deep, very personal level, to have been given the glorious opportunity to serve as their scribe all these years. Clearly, if we are to believe, as I do, that the soul knows exactly what it is doing, before it agrees to manifest in the physical, then I surely took part in that experiment willingly, many lifetimes ago, as soul essence and as a galactic traveler. Many are we, starseed, who made that choice now, when we decided to incarnate here on Earth, in order to be part of this revolution. We signed on to take part in a collective soul contract. We do honor that, for we know, on some level, that we are here, hundreds of thousands of years later, to stand in the light of Spirit and anchor it in the earth, no matter how difficult it is to hold our balance against such fierce galactic winds as those that are pushing us hard through this shifting Age.

There are others, who are willing participants in the genocide experiment currently underway, eagerly taking what the government dishes up without question, without a doubt in their minds. That, too, can only be considered a soul contract, to which they chose to adhere in this lifetime. When I grieve for those who have already suffered so much, and for those who still will perish, I do my best to always remember that it is not for me, or any one of us, to judge another. And I remind myself to honor each and every soul's choice and process, however painful it is, knowing what karma they are creating for themselves, and how those choices affect the entirety of conscious reality.

As for the perpetrators of so much evil, I seek to find compassion for even the darkest souls, to forgive their grievous acts upon us all, and to pray that others will find that compassion, so that we will not be bound to them in perpetuity . . . and so that we always resonate to frequencies that emanate from the heart and elevated mind.

We are in our utmost power when we walk the talk of being sovereign beings, children of Creation, the stars and the Earth, and celebrate that no matter what unfolds around or within us, we are always a blessed manifestation of the God light.

In my personal experience, I have died twice and come back—and so I am privileged, as others who have gone through the near-death experience, to know, without question, that **we do not die**.

I know the immortality of the soul and I will never allow anything to interfere with the natural unfolding of my eternal being. No matter what transpires in the outer world, or within, I know that my passing here is a mere drop in the cosmic sea of "I am" experience.

Sovereign I shall always remain. So did I enter this world of matter, cradled in the immense and loving vibrational embrace of my extraordinary, beloved mother, who birthed me into this physical test tube of earthly life, and so will I remain, when I take that final curtain call. There, back in the bright light of the cosmic flame, I will re-unite with her and all my ancestors (of the Earth and stars) once again, one step higher on the spiral of light that leads me home . . . back to where my memory of form dissipates and sets my spirit soaring.

What an immense gift to have been given that brief glimpse of eternity: dying and coming back to life. I returned from that experience with a picture of "heaven," etched, indelibly, on my soul . . . alongside of all the beauty of this magnificent Mother Earth, and all the love I have known in this life and others.

As my essence traverses the Cosmos, I carry it all in my karmic satchel—even the pain and difficult memories—with a sense of joy and wonder: lifetime to lifetime; star to star.

Chapter 6

Our "Type Zero" Planet

Over the course of my many years exploring that quintessential question of existence—the meaning of life and our place in the universe and beyond (for there is always a beyond . . . from any vantage point)—I have been privileged to meet and converse with some of the great thinkers of our times: philosophers, explorers, scientists, visionaries, futurists. What I have gleaned from them all is that, no matter our field of expertise or experience, we conscious, aware beings share a common goal: to understand where or what we come from, to discover our purpose for incarnating here and now, and to know where we, caretakers of Planet Earth, are headed as individuals and as a global civilization.

Scientists and engineers are determined to get to the nuts and bolts of it all, so that our civilization can be catapulted forward into a new age of off-planet exploration, as a new "manifest destiny" mindset projects our species into the future. Metaphysicians and spiritualists, on the other hand, come from the perspective of how we, units of universal consciousness, recognize and understand that we are co-creators of all reality, and that the immense expanse of Creation lies within us—within every cell—and even further beyond, in the minutia of the subatomic world.

From that microcosmic wonderland that is the subatomic universe, to the macrocosmic multiverse, all that is infinite eludes those of us who believe in eternity, as much as it befuddles the AI-engineering mind. Telescopes that penetrate space and electron microscopes that allow us to peer into the subatomic world give us glimpses—bits and pieces—of the boundlessness of existence, yet still today, the vast and impenetrable reaches of the universe, and the complexity of multidimensional reality, remain unknowable. We share countless theories, clues and riddles and a whole lot of conviction, but in the end, all that makes sense to me, personally, in my indefatigable spirit quest to somehow define the unknowable, is that some incredible mathematician, a lover of artistry—music, color and vibration—had to have cooked up the cosmic soup that triggered a precise and pre-determined number of atoms, protons and neutrons to create all life, and to replicate those same dynamic and spatial relationships in the planets, moons and the stars.

Where we merge these two systems—science and spirit—is where we come closest to unraveling the mysteries of existence and the proliferation of life itself.

As we observe how our advancing knowledge of hyper-dimensional physics, must, by its very nature, merge with a broader acceptance of the metaphysical, it becomes very clear that, in the end, we are all searching for the same thing: to know Prime Creator, to have proof that God exists. Even the die-hard atheist stumbles when questioned about the trigger that sparks life. If not from a Prime Creator, then from where, how, why and when does everything originate? And for what purpose?

Physicists, struggling with conundrum posed by the "Big Bang" theory, search in vain for the explanation of what came before it; religious leaders can never convincingly answer the unresolvable question: "Who created God?" Quantum physicists, who study matter and energy at that fundamental, microcosmic level, tell us they are discovering aspects of matter and energy that are not yet fully understood by science, and that they are uncovering new keys to the actual evolution of the Cosmos. They are excited about their breakthroughs, as are we devoted spiritualists, for we are accessing, from two different "on ramps," the highways of a multidimensional universe that beckon all galactic explorers to reach higher, and to raise our frequencies to meet the dawn of our true awakening: the Age of Aquarius, when humankind is meant to evolve to a higher understanding of truth and reality, and finally take its destiny into its own hands.

We have another two thousand or so years to see that play out, before we take that next cosmic leap into the Age of Capricorn. I do not plan to be coming back around for that one.

To know what lies beyond what we believe we know . . . what we see . . . what we experience in the sensate world, and to challenge those perceptions in search of a greater, more universal truth: that is the challenge of the true Aquarian—spiritualists and scientists alike.

Of those illuminating encounters, one of the most memorable was with the co-founder of String Theory, Dr. Michio Kaku, described by many as the "Einstein of our times." He is arguably one of the most renowned theoretical physicists of this century and many others. Unquestionably, Dr. Kaku has proven himself to be one of the great contributors to a field of science intent upon understanding how universes interact, co-exist and share in the greater multiverse of parallel worlds, simultaneous realities and multidimensional vibrational fields.

In an effort, wherever possible, to bridge science and spirit, empirical knowledge and innate wisdom, I was thrilled to have the opportunity to interview him on my BBS Radio show, *Beyond the Matrix*, many years ago. Speaking with him directly, trusting that my intuitive sense of reality and a very basic understanding of quantum physics (provided me from my work with my extradimensional guides and teachers) could keep pace with his genius, I was pleased to be able to follow and grasp his scientific analysis of the forever unknowable Cosmos of Soul.

I did not resonate with everything he had to say, especially when his political persuasion seemed to want to redirect the conversation to where we would surely hit an impasse, but I did listen intently to every word, running his perceptions through my mind, and gleaning what I could from the science—a field diametrically opposed to my own intuitive process.

For the most part, there were many synchronicities between our two fields of thought, where physics meets metaphysics. Dr. Kaku was raised a Buddhist, and so he was introduced at an early age to the philosophical precept that there are no beginnings, nor endings, to existence. Yet, as a physicist, who believes we exist "in a multiverse of universes," the science compelled him and his peers to search the realm of the possible to seek and eventually discover proof as to the true beginnings of the physical universe!

In our fascinating exchange, during which we discussed several unproven theories surrounding that yet undetermined "beginning"—the perpetuation of the expanding universe, and our role in it as conscious beings on this tiny marble in space—he elucidated a system for measuring the advancement of any given planetary body by its energy development and consumption, first classified, in 1964, by Soviet astronomer Nikolai Kardashev, into three primary categories:

Type One – defined as a *planetary* civilization, which uses and stores the energy available on its own planet.

Type Two – described as a *stellar* civilization, one that derives all its energy needs from its own central star.

Type Three – known as a *galactic* civilization, capable of controlling its energy consumption on the grand scale of its entire host galaxy.

I asked Dr. Kaku where Earth fit into this rather simplistic, energy-based rating scale for celestial evolution. He replied that our planet had not yet advanced to a Type One civilization status, as we are still primarily exploiting the planet's resources, consuming fossil fuels and mismanaging nuclear fission and that, overall, we might not achieve Type One status for another one to two hundred years or more.

Earth, according to Dr. Kaku, is simply a "Type Zero" planet.

Could our beleaguered planet, with its blood-thirsty global leaders, ecologically negligent human populations and dwindling resources, sustain another two hundred years before evolving to its next stage? "Interesting," I thought, contemplating all the far more resounding reasons why we were still at zero than energy alone and that, as we were entering the Age of Aquarius, we would have to first circumvent some extremely treacherous evolutionary barriers, before we could take that giant leap forward into the Golden Age, prophesized by the science of astrology, esoteric masters and indigenous wisdom keepers of old.

And then there was the question of planetary ascension, and whether we were, in fact, on our way through the fourth dimension (as it appears to so many of us who are experiencing it psychically and viscerally), as the Sirian High Council prophesized as our solar and planetary trajectory. Were we really ascending—accelerating our resonant vibrational frequencies to higher "ground"—and would that process of releasing ourselves from the density of our three-dimensional world be somehow less painful than what we are currently experiencing, in the chaos we have seen unfolding, since the onset of this decade?

How monumental in scope it is, this Great Shift of Ages. How powerful, and painful, and at the same time extraordinary it is to be alive for this immense shift from the Age of Pisces and into this next 2,160-year cycle of the Age of Aquarius, as we contemplate Earth's trajectory into the yet unknowable multidimensional future. Some noted astrologers believe that this is the Golden Age, where humanity finally takes back its power and steps into its destiny, to walk once again as Christed beings and guardians of the physical realms—as was intended when we were seeded here, in this Garden of Eden.

We certainly have a way to go, considering the traumatic world in which we find ourselves at the moment. And yet, despite the obstacles before us, we are being catapulted from those ambivalent days of our comfortable armchairs and late-night television, where so much of our "Western" civilization only observed the suffering of great swathes of humanity from afar . . . where it did not touch us personally . . . to the front lines of our current global war for human sovereignty.

The war that has been waged by the ruling elite against all of civilization is devastating. It is frightening and infuriating on so many levels, but, to those of us who understand what is at stake here, it is very empowering. It is the impetus that has yanked us out of our comfort zones and thrust us into a battlefield that is unquestionably driving us to save a world being driven into extinction. It is calling us to wake up, shake ourselves out of the brain fog, raise our light sabers, and stand for all the living creatures of this good Earth.

Every single human being on this planet is now faced with the choice between obedience and resistance. There is no escaping it, no matter how removed or distracted we are from unfolding events. There is a revolution in progress, all around the world, and it has reached our doorsteps now. We either stand in our power, or bow down, perhaps never to rise again.

Through the spiritual Armageddon underway in our little corner of the galaxy, a great clashing between evil and love is playing out in the global arena. And, despite our despair over what we have to pass through to get to the other side of it, we feel an immense sense of urgency to move into action, for this stain upon our liberty is spreading fast, clouding the waters. For those of us who can see, every day brings the face of evil closer, pushing up against ours as if to say, "Resistance is futile. You cannot escape me . . ." and, for so many of us, this overt malevolence serves not to weaken us, as it is designed and delivered to do, but rather, to empower us, strengthening our resolve. We are finally coming to understand what it is that we are actually dealing with, perhaps more than we ever have recognized it before—as individuals, and as the collective consciousness of our awake and awakening species.

We do not seek to escape, for we know we are here to face down the demon . . . for once, and for all. It is the only way to restore freedom. And that is what we must do, no matter where it takes us: no matter how long . . . no matter how widespread the malignancy appears to us. We must blanch its darkness in our God light, where it withers, shrinks down to no more than a tiny spot in our peripheral vision, and eventually evaporates in the etheric dust.

We, who choose to stand up against the venomous fire breath of the dragon, are more alive, in so many ways, than we even thought imaginable. Through this palingenesis, I believe, we are feeling the growing pains of sprouting our metaphorical wings . . . as we prepare to take flight and soar beyond the extremes of Earth's polarities and opposition altogether: beyond good and evil, beyond light and dark, beyond all the suffering to which we bear witness, when we observe the world through a dark lens.

With these thoughts swirling around in my head, I came away from that conversation with the illustrious Dr. Kaku thinking that what really determined a civilization's evolutionary pace was not at all the issue of energy consumption, although I agree that reverting to star power would unquestionably reflect a greater respect and synergistic relationship with its corresponding planet. In the case of our own Mother Earth, there is no doubt that the planet would benefit from our advancement to an ecologically-sound use of solar energy (which we have yet to design effectively), and an end to poisonous fossil fuel consumption, which has so stripped the Earth of its resources, and wreaked such damage upon the environment.

Ironically, we do already possess the technological savvy to do just that, if only this dastardly ruling class, made disgustingly wealthy by the very petroleum products they currently claim to disdain, would put humanity and the planet first—and if only they would allow, rather than to suppress, the proliferation of solar power, which they have been doing for decades, while they block the sun's light with their ubiquitous, perennial sheath of chemical particulates, dispersed in the atmosphere through deadly aerosol chemtrails.

The Deep State has been spraying the planet for thirty years or more, dimming the sun's light, altering micro and global climates, and dousing us with whatever poisons their twisted minions and obedient slaves within the military-corporate complex wish: relentlessly raining down deadly chemical cocktails laced with toxins of their choosing. It is an assault on the entire planet: above the Himalayas, over the Andes, the oceans, over population-dense cities worldwide and everywhere in between. Most humans, blind to the visible chemical lattices laid into the atmosphere day after day, remain in their "ignorance is bliss" denial of the daily bombardment of unmistakable and unnatural checker-boards and grids that coalesce overhead, giving credence to the motto: "The best place to hide a secret is right out in the open."

It is a chilling thought that those aerosol trails, engulfing Earth's atmosphere from the North to South Poles, can be observed clearly, from over two hundred and thirty miles above our planet, from the international space station. Yet, billions of human beings, who merely need to peel off their blinders and just look up at the sky a moment—really look—cannot, or simply will not see what is right over their heads, dripping dangerous chemicals and metal particulates down upon them.

It is a "conspiracy theory," after all. Only a conspiracy theory . . .

Information is widely available for those who are at least willing to consider that a coordinated aero-chemical attack is being waged perpetually, and has been on-going for decades. The United States government spells it out very clearly in a 363-page document entitled, *Geoengineering: Parts I, II and III*,[3] presented over ten years ago in the House

---

3   https://www.govinfo.gov/content/pkg/CHRG-111hhrg53007/pdf/CHRG-111hhrg53007.pdf

of Representatives, in a hearing before the Committee on Science and Technology. It describes, in chilling detail, how the world government planned to alter the planet's climate, supposedly to reduce greenhouse emanations, by "solar radiation management methods that reflect a portion of the sun's radiation back into space," and injecting aerosol chemicals into the atmosphere: chemicals, they admit, "present fundamentally different challenges of governance, ethics, economics and ecological impacts."

These self-appointed managers of our energy communion with the sun, and any eventual exchange with neighboring planets, have taken it upon themselves to block our central star's radiance from the living fields of Earth, altering the self-correcting capabilities of nature's own balancing act to repair and rejuvenate herself in alignment with the galactic field. How the sun interacts with us as individuals, feeding our very souls, activating the physical cellular structure through light and joy itself, and amplifying the energetic sheath, within which the physical holds presence, is something that we dare not overlook as well.

If bouncing the sun's energy back, away from the planet, is the plan, how, one can only wonder, is the Earth supposed to progress from our primitive Type Zero status to the more galactically progressive Type Two planetary civilization? It doesn't take an aero-engineering genius to figure out that these two approaches to managing the problem of a given planet's energy system—ours, for example—are at opposite ends of the solution spectrum.

I wondered if Dr. Kaku and his fellow physicists were taking **that** into consideration—the deliberate obfuscation of the sun's energy by the cabal running that operation—in their evaluation of our ranking in the hierarchy of planetary evolution. Were the astrophysicists and engineers at NASA and in his greater scientific community blind to aerosol spraying as well? That certainly did not sound scientific to me. And if not, if they were well aware of the global aerosol spraying agenda that for years the military has perpetrated on the planet in weather wars operations, would Dr. Kaku and friends have even dared discuss it in any open forum? Would knowing that make them complicit in one of the greatest crimes ever committed against humanity . . . and Mother Earth herself?

But yes, of course it would make absolute sense that a civilization utilizing solar or galactic energy, rather than stripping the planet of its life blood, would be more aligned with the universal energies—and hence, it would be significantly more aware of its role in planetary and galactic dynamics. But did that necessarily speak to the greater question of societal evolution? Did it answer the question of spiritual progression and the ascension of individuals and their planet alike?

Perhaps Kardashev's rating system, as simplistic and limited in scope as it is, made 3D sense to the scientific world . . . for the engineers and physicists seeking physical answers to celestial problems. But it did not to me.

What was the greater design? Did some planets in a solar system evolve faster than others? And why? And if our sun is indeed ascending through the fourth dimension, as themed in my earlier works, how does that affect all the planetary bodies and moons that perennially orbit the star, in the galactic synergy we know as "the solar system?"

How do biological life forms of any given planet affect its evolution—or is it the other way around, and can one be separated from the other? And how, by nature of that galactic relationship between planets in any given solar system, can or does one evolve at a different pace than another?

Genius minds such as that of Dr. Kaku are determined to decipher the mechanics of it all, in order that our civilization be catapulted forward, into a new age of off-planet exploration, bringing with our future galactic explorers a far more complex understanding of the nature of the physical universe than that which we possess today—or shall I say one that they "admit" to today. However, there are far more pressing questions that need be addressed by our scientific communities, and those surely must include the question of ethics involving every field of thought and experimentation that affect the planet and the living beings that inhabit it, to include:

- biochemical and genetic experimentation of all life forms
- the push for genetically-controlled and modified organisms in the food supply
- the creation of hybrids, clones and synthetic beings for reasons that speak of the diabolical abuse of all natural life forms, particularly Homo sapiens
- ghoulish experimentation with genome blending intent upon the creation of chimeras and other mutations
- the race to transhumanism and the increasingly apparent take-over of artificial intelligence over human mind, body and soul
- the deliberate alteration of the atmosphere, and its ecological consequences for the entire planet.

Where, in the greater scheme of Creation, bridging everything we know about science and Spirit, does it all lead? What happens if these wayward scientists abort the Divine Plan, and is that even possible, if a Supreme Consciousness created it all: darkness and light? What was the causal impetus that triggered everything that exists, and what is the purpose of its creation? From whence does the spring flow into the great ocean of our sensate reality, and the greater consciousness that lies beyond it? And within that immense framework, where do we, mere mortals, ever find and know that Source ... within and outside of what we understand as "self?"

We metaphysicians have long known that matter is nothing more than the coalescing of directed energy and its manifestation, focused through the intent of a prime mover.

A carpenter builds a table. It is his vision, intent, physical ability and acquired knowledge that sculpts raw wood into serving a specific function, based on principles established by rudimentary physics, a knowledge of form and structure, design, etc. But who designed the wood? Who breathed the spark of life into the seed, from whence it grew into a mighty tree, and who created the seed itself? And then .. . whose intent was it to design the biological architecture that would determine the perennial, cyclical lifetime from seed to tree, from whose substance is given another form and purpose—and back to seed again, to spring forth another?

Who is that Prime Creator?

Are we even meant to know?

*

The more we recognize how our advancing knowledge of hyper-dimensional physics, must, by its very nature, merge with a broader acceptance of the metaphysical, the clearer it becomes that, in the end, we are all searching for the same thing: to know Prime Creator: the trigger ... the spark ... the designer of all life. In their tireless search for a definitive answer to the question of what came before it, physicists have yet to resolve the obvious pre-bang conundrum with their "Big Bang" theory. Nor do religious leaders, set in their scriptures and holy books, ever convincingly answer the unresolvable question: "If God (Prime Creator) created everything that exists, then who created God?"

Physicist, priest, guru ... no one has yet to answer the glaring questions that surround the pre-God/pre-big bang conundrum. That is: if what we understand as the "All-That-Is" is not the design of a Prime Creator, a supra-intelligent architect, then from where, how, why and what did it spring forth? Who intended the Cosmos into being? When, if ever, will we finally know our Creator with certainty, rather than holding a conviction, a theory, or simple "blind faith?"

What I had been shown, in my first years of scribing such time-worn, multidimensional wisdom from the Sirian High Council, was that the ultimate advancement of individuals, and the collective consciousness of intelligent beings on any given planet, had to hold, as its core understanding of reality, an awareness of all life as the manifest biological creation formed from the artistic and architectural design of a Supreme Being, or consciousness.

How difficult it is to conceptualize that this flame of Creation has always existed, with no beginning or ending, and that everything springs from its perpetual artistry, mathematical genius and the love of its own wondrous works—and that, above all, it is designed to perpetuate an eternal light that can never be extinguished. Yes, indeed, Creation loves itself. It marvels at its endless beauty, for it is all love—every bit of it.

We, sparks of that love light, leap from the Godhead into the dark abyss that we, too, are capable of creating, or rather "co-creating," so that aspects of Source—sparks of the Divine Flame—can experience how far from the light they can travel, experiencing what that entails, and then slowly to find their way back, back to the infinitesimal light, to merge back into the Holy Fire.

For me, there is no other explanation that holds up to the complexity and wonder of existence. There simply is not.

And there is no darkness so profound and so cold that it cannot be reached, to find warmth and forgiveness in the Light.

Chapter 7

DNA: The Divine Blueprint

Creator's master design, the coalesced artistry of vibration, music, and an exquisite formulation of complex biological software—the genome from which all life is designed and constructed—is deoxyribonucleic acid: the DNA. Coiled within the nucleus of every cell, it is the absolute seed of life . . . the supra-intelligent architecture of all biology and inevitably all dimensional aspects that contribute to the complexity of any and every living being, anywhere and everywhere life is manifest in Creation. It defines every single aspect of all organic forms that exist in the Cosmos of Soul, and drives the evolutionary progression of all organic substances and beings.

As important as that is, we give so little thought to our own operating systems, and to the question of our survival as a species. Yet, Big Pharma is dedicated to little else. They want to own every living being, modify it at will, as suits their purpose, and to patent our genetically modified DNA so that, legally, they actually own us—right down to every single cell in our body.

This is a complex language, dictated from Supreme Intelligence which, transformed into matter, is a living software program of extraordinary complexity, wisdom and intent. Like some incredibly articulated owner's manual, our DNA defines, through code, everything of which every biological life form is made, with particular detail to all that regards the proteins that determine structure and function of the living being. And it tells every aspect of the cell what to do and when, how to operate, when to birth and when to die off—all for the optimum performance, well-being and longevity of the electromagnetic biological unit of life, through which each of us is given the wondrous opportunity to experience our place in the universe, this time around, as living, breathing beings of the Earth realm.

Within its chemical structure—within the nucleus of every cell of every living thing—is a very precise roadmap, a biological instruction manual interpreted by every single element of everything that bears life and consciousness. And within this incredible, complex language of light coding is embedded the God Code.

Let me say that again.

Coded within every single cell of our bodies, inside the nucleus, is coiled the DNA material that carries within its unfathomable wisdom the essence of Creator: His identity and His Word. I am speaking not only of the vibration, the light, the love. I am saying that, like any artist, He left his signature: buried within every single cell of our being, in over two meters of tightly wound microscopic codes that reveal an estimated sequence of over two billion "words." Right there in the genome, the DNA sequencing, identified in the TCAG nucleotide software of all biological life forms, God left an imprint of His coded identity, over and over again. How exciting to contemplate that! To seek to discover the God Code, the "I Am," written into the DNA, surely is a challenge, as much as it is a mind-expanding journey into the unknown.

Yet, think about it. Of course, His signature would be there—right there, woven into the DNA itself.

That oversoul, the God within us, is written into the Divine Blueprint.

*

I wish to emphasize that it is not my purpose here to prove or disprove the existence of God, to whom I prefer to refer as "Creator," nor a devil, which I consider the opposition to the God light: the "Lucifer" construct. Long ago I learned never to engage that discussion, and I was most certainly never interested in persuading anyone else to embrace any faith or belief system, for there is no specific path with which I, myself, have spiritually "fused." There just isn't any right way to connect with God, Creator ... whatever you perceive Him, Her or It to be. Therefore, arguing questions of faith, ingrained within individuals locked into a religion, is futile and, as we have seen throughout our history, it only leads to disharmony and distrust, and serves as a perpetual excuse to drive people into senseless, irresolvable wars and dissonance.

Finding one's way in this earthly world and experiencing a connection to Source is so personal, and there is no right answer, no matter how fervently any individual or culture attempts to impose it upon another. No matter how arduous is one's devotion to a belief system, it is only that—a system. Throughout time, with every civilization struggling to understand the forces of the universe and beyond, we have yet to uncover a right answer to the question that man has sought to know from our most primitive beginnings, to this very day.

In my experience, although I have found much truth and beauty in scriptures I have read, of many religions and faiths, I have chosen, respectfully, to sidestep religion. For all its wisdom, beauteous parables and profound ideologies, religion, inevitably, reflects someone else's interpretation of God. Inherent in that interpretation is the intent of the writer, preacher, teacher, priest. I do not want that filter to alter how it is that I perceive my direct connection with my Creator, whom I seek and find in the extraordinary beauty of nature ... in the innocence and grace of all beings who walk in the light of love.

There lies my temple: in the heart, in the interactive intricacy and beauty of all that surrounds me and there, where the inimitable manifestations of the living soil, sea and air reflect back to the miracle that is life—the exaltation that comes from one's very powerful connection to Spirit.

It calls me to know and explore the "I Am" within me.

I delight in the sacred form and geometry of a leaf; I feel the pull and sway of planets, the moon and our solar deity. I am forever mystified by the eternal vastness of the stars, knowing there is no end to the multiverse and, hence, there can be no beginning. I watch the tide roll in, sending me racing back up to the dunes, and then out again, revealing a magical universe of tiny creatures residing in-between the great sea and the sandy shore: each with its dignity . . . each with its reason and purpose . . . each with its godliness.

It is difficult, even for the devoted atheist, not to recognize or admit the inevitable fact that a force and intelligence beyond man's comprehension, beyond science and empirical knowledge, is behind the grand design. It is so undeniable, from both the scientific and spiritual points of view, that all living beings are divinely crafted, ultimately simple and miraculously complex organisms that contain, within the nucleus of every cell, a Master Plan, the blueprint of supreme intelligence and artistry. It underlies the physicality of all living beings—from the humble earthworm, to the mighty whales and dolphins . . . to the human being.

The core knowledge that opens souls to their self-awareness and connection to Source is gleaned not only from their personal search for the meaning of life, nor from the misdirected quest to know Creator through human-sculpted religions, and certainly not from limiting analytical systems within the scientific fields.

Only when these approaches to the great questions of existence, of Creation, are merged in balance and mutual recognition and respect, can any given civilization finally begin to know and discover that all living beings are sourced in the God light, and that knowing Source/ knowing self is coded right down to the essential core of their being.

There is a roadmap, a meticulously coded system, similar in many ways, yet infinitely greater than the complex software of the most unfathomably sophisticated computers. It defines every aspect of a given life form's being: all genetic qualities, aspects and functions, spelled out with scientific precision. Once that master design has been identified, it is then the use or abuse of that knowledge that determines the evolutionary or devolutionary pace of any given civilization: building or destroying, heightening or diminishing, ascending or descending the evolutionary spiral of all consciousness.

And we are there now.

What we, 21st century Homo sapiens, do with that knowledge will determine the progress or plight of our civilization. While dictators attempt to overtake and crush all semblance of true democracy and destroy civilization, we have reached the moral and technological crossroad, where once we watched and waited, but must now decide what direction humanity will choose.

The troubling question remains: does the government-funded, military-driven scientific governance possess enough moral and ethical substance that it should be allowed free access to experiment and manipulate the foundational blueprint of life on our planet? The answer is a resounding "No." Tools that are capable of altering evolution from the cellular level of all life forms are misplaced and highly dangerous in the hands of spiritually unevolved beings.

Will those scientists and bio-geneticists playing God with life respect and honor the secret that lies within that godly architectural design? Can they be entrusted with this knowledge?

Judging from what is unfolding in those secret laboratories, and in the proliferation of "gene therapy" mRNA inoculation programs, it most definitely appears not.

The bigger question is: "Who will stop them?"

*

Besides the geo-engineering, aerosol spraying program that has been underway for decades, the world government openly admits to a next-phase plan to diminish Earth's access to our central sun—the energy source that feeds all life in this galactic realm.

Isn't that diametrically opposed to Dr. Kaku's reach for our evolutionary giant leap?

One of many disturbing ventures, *SCoPEx* (The Stratospheric Controlled Perturbation Experiment), developed by Harvard University scientists funded by Bill Gates has, as its primary goal, the development and implementation of sun-dimming technology that would have the capacity to bounce even more sunlight away from our atmosphere, by spraying calcium carbonate dust into Earth's upper atmosphere.

The first three-million-dollar phase of the test by Mr. Gates and his Harvard team, which has been momentarily blocked, involves the launch of two steerable balloons into the stratosphere, where they would release calcium carbonate particles, so that the team could study how successfully they are dispersed. The idea behind this highly questionable experiment is that, as small particles injected into the stratosphere can spread quickly around the globe and remain in that layer for several years, strategically injected particles in both hemispheres could create an artificial shield against the sun's own light, and cool down a planet that they still have not proven is overheated (at least not naturally) to begin with—one that, conversely, several ecologists believe is about to enter into a new Ice Age!

And what about the on-going, extensive chemtrail program? Is that not enough obfuscation of vital sunlight for the globalists? And the proliferation of volcanic eruptions around the globe—what of that? Is it just not possible that they are being artificially triggered, to achieve that same end: to block the sun?

According to an article entitled *How Volcanoes Influence Climate-* [4] from UCAR, the Center for Science Education:

"Volcanic ash or dust released into the atmosphere during an eruption shades sunlight and causes temporary cooling. Larger particles of ash have little effect because they fall out of the air quickly. Small ash particles form a dark cloud in the troposphere that shades and cools the area directly below. Most of these particles fall out of the atmosphere within rain a few hours or days after an eruption. But the smallest particles of dust get into the stratosphere and are able to travel vast distances, often worldwide. These tiny particles are so light that they can stay in the stratosphere for months, blocking sunlight and causing cooling over large areas of the Earth.

Often, erupting volcanoes emit sulfur dioxide into the atmosphere. Sulfur dioxide is much more effective than ash particles at cooling the climate. The sulfur dioxide moves into the stratosphere and combines with water to form sulfuric acid aerosols. The sulfuric acid makes a haze of tiny droplets in the stratosphere that reflects incoming solar radiation, causing cooling of the Earth's surface. The aerosols can stay in the stratosphere for up to three years, moved around by winds and causing significant cooling worldwide. Eventually, the droplets grow large enough to fall to Earth."

Reading this brief from UCAR's scientific paper, we have to ask ourselves: is it that far-reaching to consider that people who are intent upon dimming the light from our central star, for purposes of "cooling" the planet, might be interested in zapping a few volcanoes? We know the military has the technology and the equipment to blast just about

---

4   https://scied.ucar.edu/learning-zone/how-climate-works/how-volcanoes-influence-climate

anything it wants, anytime, anywhere on the planet, and that the pro-liferation of weapons in space is unending. Is it that much of a stretch to consider how volcanic ash and dust, released into the atmosphere during eruptions, shade sunlight and cause temporary and long-term cooling of the planet? Wouldn't that be of great interest to the mad scientists—especially those who would prefer not to see us climb up Dr. Kaku's scale to become a Type One planet, where we would progress to such a point that we would be utilizing our central star for all our plan-etary energy needs?

For the moment, SCoPEx has been tabled, but you can bet it is not **off** the table. Supposedly, this latest scheme to come from Mr. Gates is altruistically intended to trigger global cooling of our purportedly overheating planet. I do not trust it. I understand that the wealthiest individuals on the planet have their sights set on owning the Earth and everything within and upon it, but I would like to point out here that experimenting with cosmic dynamics, such as our planet's interaction with the sun and other planets in our solar system, is pure insanity—just as it is a crime, perpetrated against Planet Earth's own divine sov-ereignty, to strip her of all her resources, while they genetically alter plants, insects, animals and human beings.

No excuse from the latest greenhouse agenda storyline can erase the fact that we are already being denied vital sunlight at every level of biology on this planet, and it is interfering directly with the galactic design of our small corner of the universe. It interferes with our health, our joy and well-being. And, similarly, do these obliterators of the sun's rays plan to block the etheric light from our very DNA? What of that?

What if there were indeed a far more sinister plan underway by transhumanist overlords, to somehow unplug or disrupt our connec-tion to the light of Source, our nourishment, in order to disrupt or re-move the God Code from our DNA and to replace it with something dark and sinister, something say, such as a "Luciferian" signature, code or I.D.?

If crazed geneticists, funded by such a nefarious power structure, whose Satanic/Luciferian tentacles are attempting rapaciously to choke the light out of our living planet, were to develop a delivery system that could unwrite the God code—what of that? And what if they were to find a way to erase it from our DNA, detaching us from that God-given divinity and light, and to implant, instead, a numerical or vibrational code so dark, so powerful when activated, that it had the capacity to serve as a destructive force within the Divine Blueprint—one that would work in opposition to the Divine?

What then?

What, in God's name, then?

Perhaps the greatest, most troubling question of our perilous times is this: are these insane world leaders, who are clearly set on a disastrous course to destroy 21st century civilization, driving what will remain of humanity from biological beings to transhumanist robots? Are they actually intent upon hacking the God Code, in order to detach every single human being from his/her spirit—from Source—just as they are intent upon detaching the planetary being from the light giver: our central star?

And more importantly, if all that exists is, in fact, an aspect or manifestation of God's master plan, can they actually succeed in turning the lights off on Planet Earth?

The answer is simple.

You either believe in God, or you do not.

If you do, you know the answer deep within you.

And that, my friends, is everything you need to know about the future of our world.

Chapter 8

Battle Station: Earth

These are the years that mark our passage from the Age of Pisces into the Age of Aquarius, whereby we are in the midst of an enormous transition away from ideological values based around global religion, faith and belief systems, to those that drive civilization towards expansion of human consciousness, innovation and science. First, it appears, we have to release ourselves from the old that is holding on with a vengeance, for immense change is never easy.

The post-war comfort zone that the more fortunate of the world's population have enjoyed is definitively behind us, and what will replace it is ours—the choices of the collective—to create. I feel that I speak for most humans on this planet, myself included, when I say that people around the globe are feeling the upheaval of this cultural, political and societal transformation in a very big way, as we experience ourselves and our world being blown, like rolling tumbleweed, down a perilously rough road, and wondering where we all will land, when we move beyond the wake of this Great Shift of Ages.

Ramping up the intensity of what that really means and what it is going to take to get through to the other side of it, is our progression, in tandem with the colossal transition of celestial ages, through the mind-boggling four-dimensional warp drive of our sun's ascension out of 3D, and the contemporaneous metamorphosis of all trailing planets that, in essence, form the chakras of our solar system. On a planet that corresponds to the communication center—the throat chakra—of our central star, the paradox of our being silenced, through censorship, and forced, for over two years, to wear suffocating masks over our mouths that disrupt and disable our speech and clear communication does not elude me.

From one dimension to another, and traversing the Great Cycles of cosmic no-time, the colossal cosmic force of such immense shifts can be so overwhelming to us that, sometimes, it feels we can barely stand up anymore. We are being pushed and pulled in every direction, thrown off balance deliberately, and struggling—day-to-day, hour-to-hour—to keep from going under.

Fighting to hold our ground against what appear to so many to be insurmountable negative energies is wearing people out; we see those around us becoming mentally and emotionally exhausted. And again, this is a global phenomenon. Tragically, the number of people taking their own lives, even young children, is climbing dramatically. More and more people are choosing suicide as a way out of what they perceive as a lonely, terrifying existence, with nothing more on the horizon than a hopeless, unbearable future. It breaks my heart that anyone could be in that much pain, and that the human condition at this time is so fraught with suffering and fear that escape through untimely death seems the only option for growing numbers of desperate souls.

We must find ways to help these people back from the abyss.

I have talked a few people down from the ledge in recent days, but there are so many, teetering at the edge of despair, who cannot be reached, and others still, who have no one there to extend a hand . . . and so, they leap.

The rest of us dig our heels into anything that will help us hold steady against the galactic winds of change and disruption that seem determined to uproot us all, constantly, furiously ripping us from our very foundations. If only we can catch our breath long enough to grasp the significance of this cosmic storm, we will get a glimpse of what comes after this wild ride. We will recognize that, in a very beautiful sense, rooting ourselves to Mother Earth is exactly where we need to be putting our energies, to prepare for what follows. If, indeed, we are to secure our own lives, while we help move the Goddess up the vibratory spiral on our evolutionary journey back to Source, we are going to need to send our roots deep into the heart of our beloved planetary deity, drop anchor and hold on tight.

Let us love and celebrate her beyond measure, and commit to being here now, to being part of whatever this is, and to staying the course.

Despite how we long to return to our respective stars, leaving this little pocket of celestial turmoil behind us, we, starseed, did not traverse the universe to reach this distant neck of the galactic woods merely to escape it "when the going got tough." We knew full well it would get plenty rough when we signed up to participate in what will eventually unfold as a glorious evolutionary milestone, currently scribing every detail of Earth's immense transition into the Akashic Record.

I know, in my heart, that we will look back, from somewhere up the road, reminded of our passing here at such an extraordinary time such as this. We will smile to ourselves then, and think: "I was there for that."

"I was there..."

In the meantime, in those moments when we feel fatigued and defeated, we are entitled to lay down our light sabers to wipe our brows, to breathe and gather strength. There must be time for that. What matters is that we come back even stronger, reminded that we came **because** the going would get tough, and we chose to be here for it, holding the light as embodied Homo sapiens—the New Aquarians.

Our ultimate empowerment comes from truly owning the fact that we knew exactly what we were getting ourselves into when we enlisted to serve with the light brigades, now . . . when the Great Armageddon would be playing out here on Earth. We stepped into this mortal flesh unflinchingly, with absolute determination, exercising our free will and honoring our mission. For many of us, it was a difficult choice, one that would tax our spirit, test our will and challenge our resolve to the limit, and yet, we made it willingly. Spirit warriors determined to take those giant leaps up the spiral of light that accelerate our eventual return to Source, we incarnated into a lifetime on Earth at this time to do just that: to be tested, to be challenged, to serve and be part of the ascension process of the remarkable celestial deity that is Gaia.

It is understandable that we will have moments when we are battle-weary, and feel we are losing ground. When we peer into the outer world, it can look frightening and foreboding, no matter how powerfully we know the Light is pushing forward, into those dark corners. Whatever we agreed to in spirit, we cannot deny that 21st century Earth might just be a little more than we bargained for, as we struggle to cope with so much upheaval and malevolence, and worse . . . coming face-to-face with the evil that fuels it.

But we do know how to deal with it, or we wouldn't be here, now, would we?

Just as light forces of countless star systems and parallel realities chose to take part in this drama, so did the forces of darkness, for, as we were attracted here, so was the opposition drawn to come and take antagonist roles in this theatrical appointment with destiny. Earth is the battlefield, and the great clashing of forces—good and evil—are playing out, as war games, through us all, to the bitter or sweeter end. I am reminded that somewhere very long ago we, sparks of light, plunged into the abyss to know the darkness; we, too, chose, as the Sirians say, "to drink of the dark wine, on our long journey back home."

Shakespeare expressed it beautifully in a soliloquy from his play, *As You Like It*:

"All the world's a stage,
And all the men and women merely players.
They have their exits and their entrances;
And one man in his time plays many parts…"

It is no coincidence that the cold-blooded overlords of Planet Earth chose this time, one of great cosmic turbulence and immense cyclical change, to wage their holocaust against humanity. Their brood have known for a very long time that these would be the coordinates on the time-space continuum to make their final move, to attempt to impede the Earth from realizing its true destiny and hold us back from ever progressing on our trajectory into higher dimensions—out of their clutches!

The individuals who lord over these secret societies are now out in the open, masks off, using corrupted political pawns and controlled media to twist public opinion into embracing their final destruction manifesto: Agenda 2030. Let us remember that its ultimate purpose it is to eliminate ninety-percent of the population, and to mutate what remains of biological human beings (and animals), after the culling, into transhumanist robots and chimeras: soulless creatures that would be bioengineered solely to feed the hive mind control grid, for biological body parts, or simply for the perverse entertainment of very sick creatures, near and far.

To win this final war, they must control the narrative, holding as many people as possible in a state of hypnotic obedience. They have been extremely successful at that for a very long time, but never so much as now, since Covid first made its entrance. A carefully constructed terror campaign that has stripped our freedoms and filled us with dread, the "plan-demonic" has seen billions of people adhere to it vehemently, as if their very existence depends on embracing every word, and following every rule. Tragically, many of them are already dead; others are maimed and suffering grave and chronic health conditions. More will die in the months and years ahead.

Those, instead, who are aware—those who cannot be mesmerized and mind-controlled—media puppets classify as dangerous conspiracy theorists, radicals and extremists. I know, for I am perceived that way by some, simply because I dare to question authority, follow my gut, and find my own answers.

Whether awake or asleep, we are kept at an ideological distance from one another, in a perennial state of hyped-up antagonism: fighting for space, for dominance, and for that proverbial piece of cheese—like frenetic rats, prisoners of their electromagnetic cages. They believe they must beat the compassion out of us until we are left with no reverence for life, whatsoever, in any form. That aspect of our humanity has to go, and with it all hope, joy and even the smallest thing that serves to raise our spirit. They must keep us distracted, so locked into the lower chakras, that never, not even for a moment, can we rise from feelings of powerlessness against them to realizing how few they actually are, and what they are intent upon imposing upon the many that constitute the entirety of humankind—and our growingly dystopian, divided world.

Seated on their gilded thrones at the golden capstone of their power pyramid, they are a mere two thousand puppet masters, dangling their marionettes on tightly-wound strings, and making them dance around before the green screen of illusion—where they lip synch empty platitudes and feign emotions they no longer possess, in order to mislead the masses.

If you can bear to look into their eyes, you see the long, empty corridors of their emptiness.

There is nobody home anymore.

Pity the wooden puppets, for they are bound to those who, in turn, bow to the dark lord. However fierce their threats and menacing mandates against us all, they are nothing more than vacuous figureheads, possessed, who sold their true human emotions, along with their souls, to the highest bidder . . . way long ago.

On the other hand, we, "cattle," as they affectionately regard us, are nearly eight billion and growing. To say that they are outnumbered is a statement of epic proportions. Truth be known, the power elite are actually quite terrified of the unstoppable rising tide of human beings across the globe, as we unite and stand in defiance. We are on to them, and they know it. That which they fear—a global uprising—is already happening, and they know they cannot stop it. They are using every tool, every trick at their disposal and weapons we cannot even fathom to exert their power over us and quell any and all resistance. Yet still we rise.

Still, we rise.

More people are shaking off the hypnotic programming coming through their televisions and cell-phone mind-control devices, and reclaiming their sovereignty. They are awakening at last: alert, and seeing clearly. Very soon now, others will step into the light and join this Great Awakening, where all the dirty secrets are being revealed, and where true justice will prevail.

What the upper echelons of the cabal and their minions are most concerned with, what frustrates them beyond measure, is that it is their very abuse of power that is provoking this awakening in the masses. They can see that the more they disrupt the social order on this planet, encroaching upon our liberties, the more they mess themselves up, thwarting their own agenda and sabotaging their "Great Reset" for all of humanity. Imagine the frustration and rage of these omnipotent "bosses," as they come to terms with their own incompetence?

They have already begun cannibalizing each other.

At the zenith hour of the Armageddon, they are beginning to realize that, despite the omnipotence they were so sure they possessed— despite all the money, the black magic, all the manipulations, the runaway corruption—somehow their agenda is not quite working out as they had planned. They've backed themselves into a corner, caught in their own trap.

What a monstrous blow to their huge collective ego! Nowhere in their grand design could they ever have foreseen themselves yielding to a civilization of beings they perceive as their "inferiors." That simply does not compute. Yet, as we join forces—standing up to them in town halls, city squares and thoroughfares worldwide, refusing to comply, saying "no" to their poison darts—they cannot help but be aware that it is because of their rapacious acts against us that we have been driven to reversing their mandates, exposing them and their controlled media for what they really are, and breaking their chokehold over our beloved planet.

Despite the unyielding narrative and endless lies, despite the threats and false flags playing out in strategic time and at pre-determined locations, we are, in fact, neutralizing their power. They simply cannot believe it. They have made that egregious mistake of underestimating the human spirit, and the forces of light—layer upon layer— that stand with and behind us, pushing us forward.

Big mistake.

Nothing short of an all-out thermonuclear war can stop what is coming and, although they threaten us with it daily, that will not be allowed. Our planet is under constant surveillance not only by menacing ET races, but also by galactic peacekeeping forces capable of neutralizing all nuclear arsenals on this good Earth. They have been doing so since WWII, and they will not allow the insanity of beast and misguided man to execute the kind of destruction that would blow a planet to smithereens, tearing a gargantuan hole in the fiber of the galactic field, and sending a devastating shockwave through the Cosmos of Soul . . . a force so immensely catastrophic that it would ripple through the multi-dimensional universe for all eternity.

What a dilemma for the Luciferian architects. The only thing they know to do now is to drive their flawed agenda forward, no matter what, come hell or high water. Hell, they can have: it is an end of their own making, and they are already living at the outskirts of what awaits them there. The "high water" is us, the awakening human race, and we are rising very quickly now, washing away the old corrupt control systems and breathing new life, new vital energy unto the sandscapes of forever.

We are winning.

We know enough of karma not to wish any suffering on any other being and we give thanks to Spirit, trusting in Divine Justice to exercise the appropriate measure, where justice need be served. But, oh, how the universe does love to add a good dose of irony when it serves up its karmic retribution. Who knows? Perhaps we will live to see these nasty critters ejected off our planet altogether, to a barren one they cannot destroy . . . in a universe far far away.

*

I wish to emphasize how important it is that we never give up on people who are still asleep and unwilling to shake off their opiate stupor, to see with their own eyes what the Order is throwing at them. Once we dedicate ourselves to taking the next step, locking arms as one race, undivided, we will overthrow the tyrants, and restore the balance. Those secret underground cities they are so counting on are being destroyed—bombed, and flooded out—so they will not be escaping to their million-dollar condos in the sub-surface world any time soon. Neither will they be allowed to walk freely amongst us, here on the surface, for they are dead men walking. And most likely, no civilized planet will welcome them, should they attempt to announce themselves, uninvited.

No amount of cunning, manipulation, high-tech control systems and weaponry will save them, now that they have unleashed Armageddon. They will be left with no way out, because, as we all know, you cannot escape karma—particularly now, in the fourth dimension, where karmic retribution is so instantaneous and bold. Their puppets, their covert activities, the corruption and abuse of power are being exposed for who and what they are. Not even the controlled media can restrain truth's fury. And no amount of trickery and deceit can distract this growing tide of light warriors any longer. It is futile in the long term, for, the tighter they squeeze us, the freer we become.

They have seen that their agenda, which they thought was fool-proof, is not fooling us at all, and that it is only making us stronger, and the light brighter, than ever before. No matter how much they exacerbate the evil of their acts, no matter what tricks they have left to pull out of the magician's hat, they see the victory of light over darkness, because they can access that luminous future—**our** future—through the Looking Glass: the *Orion Cube Stargate*. No matter how they skew data they feed into the time machine ... no matter how they play with probable outcomes and altered realities ... they always come up losers.

We, the people of this Good Earth, have no need for futuristic computers that can look into other timelines to predict the future, because we possess our own, inner looking glass, and that is the heart, and the eyepiece of the human soul.

We have the ultimate advantage of knowing what love can do. And, as we watch the loveless slowly self-destruct, consumed by demons they themselves evoke and call into their beings, we know what hate cannot.

Always remember that they do not resonate to love, just as they cannot bear the Light. They can't even get close to it, so far down the vibrational spectrum is their bandwidth, in the snake pit, where they stay locked into negative energies that thrive on their contempt for the other, and an insatiable hunger for power over everything and everybody. They have no idea how to operate within the vibrational energy field of the heart, and they know no other way to manage us than to destroy this pesky thing—LOVE—they so detest, to pull us down into their resonant fields through fear, sensory lust and all kinds of abuse: mental, emotional and physical. Along with all their demons, they exist in that low-frequency field: the vibratory signature of war and dissidence ... pain and perversion ... hate and greed.

The vibratory signature of peace is unconditional love.

They cannot bear that.

They cannot drink of our energy or dim our light, when we are seated in the sanctuary of the One Heart.

They can't have us loving each other, living prosperous, harmonious lives. Love and the light it emanates are what they fear the most. It is hard to believe that they could be far more afraid of our light than we of their darkness, but they are. They are terrified of what light can do.

If we are just able to stay in the heart, expelling fear, where they want to take us. They will never be able to place us under their absolute control. Hate, distrust, destruction, and the terror they create everywhere around us are where their power proliferates. They, and all their demons, exist in those low-frequency fields: the vibratory signature of war and dissidence . . . pain and perversion . . . and greed.

They are living in a metaphorical haunted forest, surrounded by their own demons. That is all they know. Their Armageddon is against everyone everywhere: pitting people against the other, dividing us and attempting to lure us off the path, to disconnect us from Source. Their false ideologies and lies target our limitless capacity for love, and armed, like missiles, they strike wherever they perceive our strength, our purity and light.

To this end, these creatures have made great strides over the last few years, wreaking havoc upon our societies, inciting upheaval, disruption and misery around the world—suffocating freedom.

Still, we rise.

What is more than clear to me, as it is to many of you, is that what is really rolling out on our war-weary planet is a systemic program, decades in the making, that has as its purpose a coup to steal the soul out of the very heart of humanity—one person at a time, disconnecting us from the God light.

Then, when most of our species, the "useless feeders," have cleared out, and when all that is left to make of a robotic, barren Earth is a shrouded mining station in cold, dark space, they believe they will be able to turn out the lights permanently on this jewel they so disdain . . . to disconnect the third rock from the sun from all that is divine and flourishing in Creator's perfection of life, love and beauty.

Wretched creatures are they, oozing their way through the mud and black goo. I cannot imagine the horrific destiny that awaits them when they try to crawl out to dry land, only to be sucked back into the fetid swamp.

Let us never forget, not for one moment, how blessed are we to have chosen the light, as we feather our wings in preparation to fly above the clouds.

Chapter 9

Biowarfare: Plain and Simple

On January 9th, 2020, the World Health Organization announced that a spate of extreme pneumonia-like cases (fifty-nine to be exact), had broken out in the human population of Wuhan, China, where there just happens to be located a high-security pathogen lab, the Wuhan Institute of Virology, extensive facilities whose laboratories cover roughly two football fields, surrounded by twelve times as much land.

Of noteworthy significance is the fact that the top-security, top-secret facility has enjoyed funding from the U.S. non-profit organization, EcoHealth Alliance, which claims to be in the business of "stopping pandemics before they start," from as early as 2017. Details of that co-operative alliance have been made available to the non-profit organization, Judicial Watch, by the National Institute of Allergy and Infectious Diseases (NIAID) in a document[5] released under the Freedom of Information Act.

We hope active investigations into these organizations' potential involvement in the origins of the Covid outbreak and its rapid spread across every continent will lead to indictments against those who allegedly committed crimes against humanity. Hearings and legal ac-

---

5   https://www.judicialwatch.org/wp-content/uploads/2022/01/JW-v-HHS-Wuhan-Prod-6-00696.pdf

tions are currently underway in the U.S. House of Representatives and through concerned citizens, such as Tom Fitton, the president of Judicial Watch, that bring into question:

1. The role of the NIAID, headed up by Anthony Fauci, who reportedly approved a $3.7 million dollar grant to EcoHealth Alliance in 2016, for Gain-of-Function research (ie: weaponizing viruses for biowarfare) to be developed at the Wuhan Institute of Virology.
2. The alleged involvement of Peter Daszak, president and lead researcher at EcoHealth Alliance.
3. The activities of Shi Zhengli, a virologist working at the Wuhan Institute for over fifteen years in the field of—you guessed it—Gain-of-Function research.

Acting as the lab's spokesperson, Shi Zhengli, also known as the "bat lady," for her particular fascination with the potential risk of human infection from bat-origin viruses, insists that there was no connection between the virus and the Wuhan Viral Institute.

Two weeks after that initial announcement from the WHO, seventeen people in China were reported dead and several hundred more were declared "infected" with the yet unidentified "virus." The Chinese government made the drastic move to seal off Wuhan completely, locking down its eleven million residents by force. They restricted access in and out of a nearby province, Huanggang, where another eighteen million people were immobilized—but not, they asserted, before some people "escaped" on flights out of the country. That, supposedly, is how it spread beyond China's borders, carried by infected people who were not **that** sick that they couldn't escape Chinese police, military and airport controls to fly, mind you, on a few commercial flights to Italy, the U.K., France and Washington State, in the U.S.

In Wuhan, horrific scenes of people be carried off by Chinese "medical" authorities—some against their will, others appearing to be too sick to care—were exacerbated by sensationalistic media, inflaming people's terror of what so soon after was declared a "global pandemic."

I say "appearing" because I have never believed the narrative and never bought the photo bombs produced by the manipulated media.

Lockdown of the entire planet, from Alaska to Zanzibar, soon followed: methodically, deliberately stripping away our freedoms and manipulating the fear meter to such a point, so quickly, that the majority of people got down on their knees and lapped up what was being fed to them. They obeyed. The healthy got tested, re-tested, and tested again . . . and again. Not only did they accept being masked and quarantined, they begged to be vaccinated, locked down, and sealed up in their houses, alone. The unrelenting global media, directed by the puppets of the New World Order and owned by a mere seven oligarchs, whipped humanity so quickly into such a froth of irrational fear and aberrant behavior, that their meticulously constructed worldwide panic set in overnight, precisely as they planned it.

And the world as we knew it ceased to exist.

An Orwellian nightmare has been playing out ever since, with those of us who are non-compliant being condemned as evil, dirty criminals to be cast out, denied basic human rights, bullied, imprisoned—even murdered! This, while absurd manipulative propaganda is being politicized to such a point that any and all rebellion and rhetoric against the agenda underway is instantly classified as "racist," making questioning the narrative, or speaking out against it, an act of "terrorism" against society at large.

How can anyone equate questioning an untested "vaccine" and its rushed use on the citizenry, "racist?" Do people even know what the word means? The globalist media played this bizarre racism card over and over again, to a feverish pitch, condemning everything that didn't fit the script—and they still do today, two years later, to the point that everywhere you hear said: "If you do not get your vaccinations, you're a racist."

The great division of peoples was set in motion, in 2020, on the grandest scale ever attempted on our planet. The globalist plan, which had laid the groundwork well in advance of what was thrust upon humanity in the months to come, was underway, full throttle, prepping us all for the more or less forced inoculations that soon followed. In the new global apartheid, never before seen on this planet, the "vaccinated," who asked no questions and blindly rolled up their sleeves for the unknown chemical/genetic modifier injection, were reeling against the "unvaccinated," who dared to question authority and to demand to know what dangers lurked in those vials.

We became a people divided, suspicious and paranoid. Many exhibited unbridled hysteria; plenty more engaged in violence against their brother, sister, the neighbor, a friend: anyone who wasn't adhering to the new Corona rules and regulations—masking, testing, sterilizing everything, and allowing themselves and their children to be injected with an unknown substance, against a mysterious "virus" that has a reported 99.7% recovery rate.

If only recovery from the injections were so remarkable!

Almost immediately, some of us realized that we were witnessing the beginning of World War III, and that it was going to be a war unlike anything we had ever seen: a war waged by the designers of the New World Order, against the entire global population.

Others bought it hook, line and sinker, and many of them still do, although, as the draconian infractions against their liberties roll out, and they see what is happening around them, a growing number have awakened all at once, with a force akin to a sonic boom going off in their consciousness.

*

Just who are the true perpetrators of this war and what is their end game? People are eager to place the blame on Pinocchio politicians, because they still do not know who the puppet masters are, even though some of them show their reptilian faces now and then. These hyper-elite designers of mass destruction still tend to operate from the shadows of their murky ambiguity, sending forward their minions to do their dirty work.

Adolph Hitler, Vladimir Lenin, Joseph Stalin, Idi Amin, Chairman Mao and other ruthless despots were mere amateurs: cunning, evil and insane neophytes. What we have at work today, set upon the destruction and elimination of all light and life on the Earth, is all of them rolled into one putrid ball of hideous evil, with a sprinkling of cold-blooded extraterrestrial design thrown into the mix, on steroids.

This war, the final war of Earth, is an orchestrated psycho-biological global takeover of the entire planet, led not by the body politic, or what we refer to as the "Deep State," but rather by hybrid offspring of reptilian earth-dwelling shape shifters and other ET species, interfering in our planetary affairs. It is their final thrust, driving their transhumanist agenda that has, as its ultimate objective, the eventual kill-off of the biological human being—for once and for all.

They wish to move Homo sapiens out of the way, to prepare the planet as their mining station in space, run and operated by AI machines, robots and semi-human cyborgs.

You may choose to believe that what I am telling you is science fiction or mere fantasy . . . my delusion. But it is the right now of our existence. Whether it is our future depends entirely upon how quickly the human race shakes off the drug and moves into action.

The war from the "unknown enemy" has been set in motion.

It is up to us, sovereign starseed, lightworkers, light warriors and God-loving human beings of the Earth ship, to overturn their evil agenda and release this breathtaking planet from their filthy talons at last.

I remember so many years ago, back at the outbreak of AIDS in the early 80's, watching a late-night public service television program entitled, as I recall, *AIDS: The New Epidemic*, in a round table discussion format that hosted a politician, a priest, a professor and a long-haired, bearded man, who worked in an underground laboratory. I mention his appearance only because at the time I thought that it seemed he was deliberately camouflaging his identity. Soon into the program, I understood why.

The debate, which set out to explore the explosion of AIDS, was centered around two primary questions: What was this virulent virus that was wiping out so many thousands of young men, particularly in the gay population—and where did it come from?

While the three officious representatives of church and state offered their theories and opinions about the why and how so many gay men were dying, so quickly, in hospitals from coast to coast, the man from the laboratory sat there, listening, looking like he was about to explode. The politician was concerned about the financial impact it would have on the local community; the priest pontificated about the immorality of homosexuality, and whether AIDS was God's revenge for their "sins."

When the visibly agitated man from the lab could no longer bear the inane conversation, filled with uneducated speculation and anti-gay judgement calls, he finally spoke out. "I work in an underground laboratory," he said, "One of many. We develop lethal viruses and bacteria for biowarfare—to kill people," he stated. "What do you think we do there? We have strains that are so virulent that a thimble-full, slipped into the water supply of any major city, would kill the entire population within twenty-four hours."

As I watched, intrigued, the show suddenly cut out. The station flashed a sign that said, "Please excuse our momentary interruption of our program. No adjustment of your set is necessary."

Seconds later, the program returned, but the man from the underground lab was gone.

His truth had been silenced, but not to me.

Soon after, we would learn that key cities, such as San Francisco, Los Angeles and New York, had delivered a targeted vaccine program that had encouraged thousands of gay men to take part in what they suggested was a government-sponsored, sexually-transmitted diseases study, focused on hepatitis B. They lined up, willingly, never imagining that their own government would use them as guinea pigs, or that Ronald Reagan's "moral majority" policy would actually target the lives of those they determined were the "immoral" minority.

What those men got, in those injections, was full blown AIDS. The gay communities of those key cities, particularly San Francisco, were ravaged. I was living there at the time, so I saw it all unfold first hand.

According to an article[6] in the Washington Post, dated February 1, 1987:

"By 1987, health authorities had learned at least 600 of the 6,700 participants and acquired immune deficiency syndrome. About 375 of them were dead from it. And a sample survey taken showed that about 70% of the participants tested positive for the AIDS antibody – indicating that they were likely carrying the disease."

Later, we would be told by government and health officials that this deadly virus had been contracted from a monkey from Africa, and that is how the story came to be inculcated in the minds of those who believed the narrative of those times.

---

6   https://www.washingtonpost.com/archive/politics/1987/02/01/map-of-aids-deadly-march-evolves-from-hepatitis-study/47cd206c-c8d9-4082-896f-a075e53bd221/

In an article published in the *American Journal of Public Health* [7] in June 2016, by Theodore M. Hammett and Roderick T. Bronson, it was from a monkey that an estimated seventy-eight million people had ended up infected, thirty-nine million of them died and countless millions had been left living with HIV. They stated:

"AIDS was recognized in humans in 1981 and a simian form was described in the years 1983 to 1985. However, beginning in the late 1960s, outbreaks of opportunistic infections of AIDS were seen in monkeys in the United States. This apparent syndrome went unrecognized at the time. We have assembled those early cases in monkeys and offer reasons why they did not result in earlier recognition of simian or human AIDS, including weaknesses in understanding disease mechanisms, absence of evidence of human retroviruses, and a climate of opinion that devalued investigation of infectious disease and immunologic origins of disease. The "epistemological obstacle" explains important elements of this history in that misconceptions blocked understanding of the dependent relationship among viral infection, immunodeficiency, and opportunistic diseases. Had clearer understanding of the evidence from monkeys allowed human AIDS to be recognized earlier, life-saving prevention and treatment interventions might have been implemented sooner.

A form of AIDS in monkeys (caused by simian immunodeficiency virus [SIV]) was described between 1983 and 1985. However, outbreaks of opportunistic infections of AIDS were seen in monkeys in primate centers and laboratories in the United States starting in the late 1960s, with some evidence for virologic and immunologic etiologies. This apparent syn-

---

7   https://ajph.aphapublications.org/doi/full/10.2105/
AJPH.2016.303085

drome went unrecognized at the time. We have assembled those early cases in monkeys and offer reasons why they were not connected. We also speculate on what earlier understanding of these outbreaks in monkeys might have meant for the recognition of and response to AIDS in humans."

Monkeys from Africa, bats from Wuhan wet markets . . . they all seem to have it out for the human race. But viruses just don't jump from animals to humans without a lot of help and interference, which is precisely what they're doing in those biowarfare labs—extracting viruses from animals and then genetically altering them with the intent of making them more transmissible and infectious to humans.

That is what "Gain-of-Function" is all about.

What we have learned from experts who are daring to speak out, and from the National Institute of Health itself, is that not only was there was "Gain-of-Function" technology applied to the "bat" virus in Wuhan labs, but that the NIH used U.S. taxpayer money to fund it.

Despite outright denials from U.S. health officials, not least of whom is Anthony Fauci, the NIH's principle deputy director, Lawrence A. Tabak, wrote a damning letter to Representative James Comer of the United States Congress, in which he blamed the EcoHealth Alliance (a New York non-profit which was caught sending US funds to the laboratory in Wuhan) for not coming clean about the goings on in that biolab. He disclosed that spike proteins from naturally occurring bat coronaviruses circulating in China were capable of binding to the human ACE2 receptor in a mouse model.

What do I think they do in those bio-warfare laboratories?

Gain-of-function research: that's what I think.

By February 11th, they had already named the new strain of SARS the "SARS/CoV-2," or "Covid-19" virus. That there already existed a patent for it years prior seemed irrelevant; no one seemed to want to pay attention to the pesky details. Fear and panic ruled. Lockdown, the stripping of constitutional and human rights, became the order of the day, and by mid-2021, an untested, unsafe "vaccine" protocol had been miraculously created with "warp speed" in the labs of Big Pharma: Moderna, Pfizer, AstroZenica and Johnson and Johnson: the four horses of the Apocalypse.

Two years hence, it is estimated that between fifty- to seventy-percent of the global population has bowed down to the omnipotent rulership that daily denies more and more liberties to those who dare question what it is that is being injected into their bodies. They have taken the jab, and the consequent "booster" shots that supposedly strengthen one's immunity to the not-so-deadly Covid-19 "virus."

It is not working.

Where are we now . . . booster number five? We are seeing so many die or be injured with paralysis, aneurisms, seizures, Bell's palsy, myocarditis and other heart diseases. Countless other side effects continually manifest in victims around the planet: young and aged, healthy or comprised.

Pushing aside, for the moment, so-called "conspiracy theories" regarding the covert depopulation agenda and the rapid encroachment of an AI/transhumanist override of our natural, biological human design, we cannot deny—no matter what side of the fence on which we sit— that the statistics are staggering. Despite relentless propaganda from the media, we have doctors and medical professionals telling us that it is the vaccinated who are flooding the hospitals with life-threatening symptoms, not the unvaccinated, as the authorities want us to believe.

If you've seen Pfizer's list of adverse reactions from the study, the list they did not want to published until 2089, you can see it all spelled out for you, in black and white.

Despite the fact that the presumed virus that has never been isolated in a laboratory has an estimated 99.7% recovery rate (higher in children), and despite the fact that effective treatments do exist, those treatments are banned everywhere. You are not allowed access to them.

Period. The New World Order has stripped you of your right to cure your own body, so that you will shut up, take the poison shots (and/or end up in a hospital with a respirator tube jammed down your throat) or be damned.

It doesn't take genius to recognize that something far more sinister than that to which we have ever been exposed, in all the years of unnecessary war and orchestrated famine, pestilence and suffering, is underway.

It appears that the bioweapon the long-haired man from the secret underground lab warned us about back in 1980, when he tried to tell us what was really going on in those secret laboratories, has been administered to the human race: not in thimbles, mind you, but in hypodermic needles. Investigations into the source of Covid-19 is still centered around the "virus" itself, and whether or not it is indeed "Gain-of-Function" research from a lab in Wuhan that created the monster.

The Satanic/Luciferian agenda is in full swing. That oh-so-dark opposition to the Light has its claws around every level of government, the judicial systems, media, medicine, education systems and the international corporate structure. The subversion of society is the goal—the dimming of the light and love and laughter—the splendor of our godliness; the wonder of our humanness. Innocence and beauty are being obliterated by the vulgar and profane: ugliness and fear.

The proverbial black cat is out of the bag.

Come on out. Show yourself.

We know how to tame the beast.

Chapter 10

The Messenger RNA Injection

Let's Stop Calling it a "Vaccine," Shall We?

It is time we define what a vaccine really is, since, apparently, we seem to have forgotten. Perhaps we never thought to question it in the first place, because, by and large, people simply follow their doctors' recommendations and trust the health authorities, even if they are being proven wrong. If they are told that they and their children must be vaccinated against certain obscure diseases, they comply, without question. Clearly, though, it is becoming more dramatically obvious to us all that it has never been more urgent and important to ask that question than now.

That is one positive aspect emerging from this so-called "pandemic" and the injection campaign.

Most people understand a vaccine to be a preparation of a tiny amount of a dead or "attenuated" virus or bacteria that corresponds to one of a host of infectious diseases. Usually administered by injection, it is supposed to provide the body's natural immune system the opportunity to create antibodies against the given disease, so that, should the body ever be exposed to it in a more virulent form down the line, it will be immune to it.

That, in a nutshell, is what a vaccine is supposed to be and do, and we cannot deny that it has been used, effectively, to fight certain deadly diseases for a very long time over the evolution of medical history. Whether we need to be loading up our babies and children with thirty or more such vaccinations by the time they reach puberty, as they are subject to today, however, is a very different matter that merits much closer examination and scrutiny.

Perhaps it is time to re-examine that faith and trust we have afforded the purveyors of the burgeoning pharmaceutical industry.

We weren't given hardly any vaccinations when I was a child, and we seemed to be so much healthier and stronger than the kids of today. There was no autism then either, that I can recall. Of course, the world was a safer place back then—far less toxic, and so many environmental factors contributed to our overall well-being.

But still. Are all these vaccinations really necessary?

While the debate rages on as to whether the Covid-19 "virus" was ever actually isolated and identified, we know that a lot more than a "dead or attenuated" version of what they claim to be the virus is being administered in these shots, which, alongside of other toxic substances, inject the body with synthetic nano-technology that overrides the DNA and commands it to perform a laboratory-designed function . . . supposedly, to produce spike protein to combat the dreaded virus.

This is fact.

So, let's stop calling it a vaccine now, because that is not what this is. May the war and condemnation against people who refuse to take the injection—marginalized, castigated as "anti-vaxxers" and denied basic civil rights afforded the "vaxxed"—be ceased, because **that is not what this is.**

We may yet be uncertain of what is really going into people's arms, but we do know it is not a vaccine, certainly not an effective one, because, for one thing, nobody appears to be immune after taking it! By definition, they should have had immunity after the first shot; that is what vaccines are designed to do. Is that not what people signed up for . . . or did I miss something? And yet, everywhere around us, and in countries around the world, jab after jab after jab we see that the "vaccinated" still are getting sick from Covid-19.

These same inoculated people are constantly filling hospitals with symptoms of the so-called virus, or from dire adverse reactions to the shots themselves. There are definitely more vaccinated people being hospitalized for Covid than there are those who never took the jab in the first place. That is also a fact.

We hear the horror stories every day now . . . we see the suffering. We see people dropping dead.

Something is not working, here.

It appears, from reports, that this "emergency experiment" includes different batches of the poison, with different potencies. There is a lot of speculation as to whether certain cities or demographic groups are targeted for the more virulent, or more benign; we are also told that in the early days of the "test study," a percentage of those inoculated received a placebo.

If that is true, they were the fortunate ones.

Some people are dropping dead immediately, or soon after the first inoculation. Healthy eight-year-old children are being diagnosed with myocarditis after being injected, and some die of heart attacks. Athletes, some of fittest people on the planet, are dying everywhere around the world; we watch in horror as they keel over on playing fields, race tracks and tennis courts. Reports of these heartbreaking events are leaking out of the mainstream media into public awareness.

Some experience only mild side effects from the first shot, so they go on to take the three or four doses more, recommended by health authorities and required in order to retain the coveted "vaccinated" status that allows them to work, travel, attend social functions, etc. They are still getting sick. Despite all the denial, reports from several hospital medical staff reveal that high percentages of people, recovered for Covid, are those who had the shots—which, I repeat, were supposed to give them immunity. The list of recorded reactions and health conditions that arise from them, from Pfizer's shocking report alone, would make their hair stand on end.

Vaccine enthusiasts do not want us to see the casualty statistics of the dead and maimed, but they are becoming available, as we enter year three of the extended "emergency experiment." They are controlled by the pharmaceutical companies, the government and the health organizations, but still, the numbers are so overwhelming and sources contributing to the data gathered so numerous that even skewed reports cannot prevent the truth from being exposed. One source is the U.S. government's own *Vaccine Adverse Event Reporting System* (VAERS), managed by the CDC and the FDA to monitor the safety of all vaccines licensed in the United States. There you will find a database that collects and reviews (at least some) reports of adverse events that occur after vaccination.

Knowing what we do about who is funding these organizations, we must read their reports with discernment, yet we still can glean some truth surrounding so many adverse reactions, and deaths, from injections undertaken.

The evidence is available. Many of us are risking our lives to bring it out to the public. What people do with the information is up to them.

How great is people's terror of what they have been told is a deadly virus that could kill them, if bearing witness to people actually dropping dead from the "vaccine" does not have them stepping out of their place in line and running for their lives? How possibly is it not registering in their minds that they could be the next person to hit the pavement?

It is very difficult for me, personally, to understand that fear, or how people can sacrifice themselves to it, because I have always questioned arbiters of authority, and always stepped away when being told to take my place in line. By now I've made it abundantly clear that I do not trust government and all the corporate/military systems that thrive on the business of war, for that is what this is really all about—war against the whole of humanity, the perpetuation of our enslavement, and genocide.

I do truly feel compassion for anyone who still believes government has his best interest at heart, while Big Pharma and the colluding power structures of the world render the sanctity of our health and welfare invalid. And yet, these colossal forces suffer no consequence for their actions, which are now being charged as crimes in several law suits against them. But will they be incriminated? They made sure they were legally protected before the experiment began. It shall be very interesting to see if we still have remnants of a judicial system that has not been corrupted, to uphold the laws and bring these criminals to justice.

How can people still trust these organizations, after they subjected the world to an experimental medical procedure, pushed on billions of healthy people—people who were too afraid to ask a few simple questions, like: "Why am I taking an untested, unknown substance into my body, when the virus has a 99.7% survival rate? Why am I not allowed alternative treatments, denied to hospital patients, and refused by pharmacists, even when prescribed by doctors? Why are the vaccinated still getting sick, after five consecutive injections?"

These people now have nano-technology implanted inside of them, and it is rewriting their DNA. This has been confirmed, in part, by the study from Lund University. They don't really know what it is and what it does, and they may not even care (just yet), but it is there. They either wake up, prepared to examine a growing amount of scientific data that exposes what is being imposed upon them, or, regrettably, they may very well be faced with the irreparable consequences we already see unfolding in the population.

How many more have to fall to the ground, before our eyes—in newsrooms broadcasting live on television, on football fields, tennis courts, in line for their next injection, or just stepping out the door of the vaccine center—before they say "Enough!"

The glaring truth is that an effective vaccine does not require multiple doses, strategically timed a few weeks and then months apart. Whatever they are claiming builds immunity clearly is not. It is an obvious lie. What exactly is in those vials and why is that information still unavailable to the public: the human guinea pigs? Why is there no list of ingredients, or side effects and other warnings in the box that comes with the vial? Why does the "vaccine" need to be stored in subzero temperatures, and what happens when it is warmed up to human body temperature?

Is some bizarre, alien parasite being activated in that substance, when the heat rises to human body heat of 98.6? We have microscopic images from marginalized researchers that attest to the fact that strange, unidentifiable organisms are appearing and **growing** in the blood and tissue of those who have received the poison.

People need to understand that they are actually accepting software—a synthetic gene-altering device—into their DNA. Is it permanent? They must be made aware that, besides the poisonous chemicals, strange biological material (to include aborted human fetal tissue, and animal DNA) and toxic adjuvants in the shots, it appears that graphene oxide nanoparticles are also being deposited in the cells.

If they know all of this, and still insist on being punctured, then that is a conscious decision. They consent to it. That is their free will and so, whatever consequence evolves from it is their destiny and, eventually, their responsibility.

But why? Why, in the name of God, would anyone agree to it?

*

Clearly, gene therapy is the next big thing for Big Pharma. The people running this horror show tell us that the way forward for all medicine of the future will be the employment of these laboratory-designed synthetic mRNA and DNA therapies, implanted in the body by means of injection, that supposedly will go into the nucleus of the cells to re-pair our "damaged DNA." Eventually, it will also be delivered orally, nasally and even via treated foods. Their public relations campaigns are centered around the idea that injecting people with synthetic mRNA, cooked up in their biolabs (so much smarter, apparently, than Creation itself) will be the way forward. We can look forward to miracle gene-al-tering therapeutics for all genetic diseases that we may not even have, once they have successfully re-set the modified DNA in our bodies, and we effectively become the genetically modified beings they so long for us to be: "Homo sapiens 2.0."

Bio-geneticists are talking about how they can turn genome se-quences off and on **remotely**, once we've got our implants, sensors and links to the Internet of Bodies. They have the technology; they just have to push past the resistance of a growingly aware public, so they can deliver it from the laboratories into our bodies. These transhumanists, who extoll the virtues of the Internet of Bodies, are telling us that a new computer ecosystem is going to be collecting our private health information, linking up pacemakers, reading body statistics (through sensors and implants) and basically eliminating the need for any per-sonal contact with doctors—unless it is over the internet. Or, I imagine, in the event you require surgery, the plan is to have robots (like Elon Musk's Neurolink skull-drilling mechanical surgeons) take the place of humans in the E.R. They want us to think this is an absolutely natural progression.

Sorry, but they cannot convince anyone who is awake and using his brain that being mechanically linked to a computer network is a natural process—a good thing—no matter how hard they try to persuade us to drink the Kool Aid. The natural way to understand more about the body is to be in tune with it, to avoid toxins of all kinds as much as is humanly possible, to expel what we can of them, and to nurture good mental, spiritual and physical health as best as we can. It is not about having a sensor in the chest or an implanted nano-robot reporting into a computer every move, every inner sound and brain wave activity of the sacred body electric.

If the Kahunas of the pharmaceutical industry were to have their way, our personal approach to health and well-being, a state of being in harmony of body/mind/spirit, would not be ours to safeguard any longer. We would be plugged into this "Internet of Bodies," whereby every single bodily function would be monitored through the almighty Internet, and where treatment would be determined by various mRNA injections that we are now being told is the medicine of the future. Period.

I do not believe they are going to have their way on this. The plan is falling apart as people realize what has been done to humanity. And our numbers are growing.

They will not be able to enforce this upon those of us who refuse.

*

For as long as globalized commerce has existed, we have been sold product that claims to resolve whatever it is about us that is deemed damaged and inadequate by the mega-corporations that rule over world economies. That has been the model society has been based on for what seems forever ... certainly from the Industrial Revolution on. It will be interesting to see how their forced consumerism breaks down, when the orchestrated crash of our global economy hits bottom, and people are struggling to buy a loaf of bread, over an eighty-dollar jar of designer youth serum.

Corporate psychological manipulation of the human mind has never been more rigorous than it is today, because convincing people they are not good enough sells just about everything, whether they need it or not, and often times, whether they really want it or not. Peace, unity and self-love do not move product. We are constantly being programmed, through industry and the owned media, to believe that we are inadequate, and that their branded products can fix us: cosmetics, the burgeoning plastic surgery industry, weight loss products, pharmaceutical drugs, fashion, luxury items, gaming—you name it. They all sell product based on the principle that human beings, in their natural and pure states of being, are physically flawed, and that only by aspiring to those pre-determined standards of beauty and fitness and (the appearance of) wealth, can we feel worthy and complete. This endless cycle of wanton consumerism, all of which purports to "fix us," by guaranteeing status in a competitive world, where we can never be beautiful, youthful and cool enough, keeps us racing around the caged rat's wheel: chasing something that isn't there . . . and never arriving.

We are used to corporations and industry bombarding us with how flawed we are, when compared to the unachievable standards of beauty and coolness, standards we are supposed to emulate by buying their beauty, fashion and status products. But now, they are telling us, we are damaged, right down to the DNA within us. Not to worry, though. They have a high-cost, low-quality solution for that too. What today they are declaring to be technologies to repair us, to fix what they deem broken, is tomorrow's made-to-order, GMO human. It is just a matter of massaging the population into acceptance, which is happening in the right now of our lives, as they race us towards their end goal: a new, bio-techno hybrid species: Robo sapiens.

I am not so naïve to proclaim that genetic diseases do not occur in humans, and in other species. We know that we inherit certain traits and pre-conditions from our parents and they, in turn, from earlier up the ancestry ladder, and that genetic mutations can be carried through generations. But that does not give the uncontrolled biotech/pharmaceutical industry free access to human beings across the globe, to be experimented upon with secret technologies which, in the case of these repeated Covid injections, are misleadingly and downright falsely labeled "vaccines."

Of course, in examining illness and disease in all populations and species, there are factors that damage the body system at the cellular level. But what these cold-blooded laboratory experimenters do not understand, nor have they any intention to do so, is that we are not merely physical creatures: neither are the animals, nor the fauna of this planet. Where there is disease there is a reason, one that the pharmaceutical industry completely ignores, unless there's a way to medicate the symptoms, which is so often the way medicine is practiced today. It is a vicious cycle, and once you're in it, your body, reacting to the "cure" instead of the cause, perpetuates the state of dis-ease that emerges from environmental, psychological and emotional issues—and the effect of constant chemical bombardment from pharmaceuticals in the body.

And yes, we do also have hereditary traits that can manifest as disease as well.

Most doctors today, obligated to follow the guidelines of the CDC, do very little more now than to test and medicate, test again—and medicate again. The ones who really care about their patients are either being forced out of practice, or are so belabored with government bureaucracy that they simply cannot give the time they want to their patients, to truly practice medicine, as they used to.

In an interview given to Bloomberg January 10, 2022 the CNN-awarded "Businessman of the Year," CEO of Pfizer[8], Albert Bourla, declared:

"Another area we announced today in partnership with Beam (Beam Therapeutics, Inc.) are the rare diseases. These are diseases, mainly, that have as a cause a mistake in your DNA, a genetic mistake. Something is wrong with your DNA and as a result you have a disease. What we try to do with the base enzyme editing technology, of which Beam is a master," he states, "is to target what will be delivered through mRNA that

8   https://www.bloomberg.com/news/articles/2022-01-10/pfizer-deepens-commitment-to-genetic-drug-future-with-deals

will be able to correct those mistakes. Last but not least is the codex. What is codex technology all about? They are **creating DNA** instead of biological manufacturing, it means that it is synthetic."

There you have it, on record. From the mouth of the Pfizer giant himself comes the admission that they are "creating synthetic DNA" to replace your biological codex, there where they believe "something is wrong with your DNA." And yet, still we are being misdirected about the function of the synthetic mRNA, and how it doesn't necessarily interfere with the DNA. Still, we are being denied access to in-depth information regarding the content in those vials. Still, people are being told that these multi-staged shots are "vaccines," which they are not. And still, they discredit anyone trying to share the truth—truth that Albert Burla himself has shared—that they are "creating DNA and that it is synthetic."

Teams of scientists, bioengineers and medical professionals, who work with people like Albert Bourla, are operating on the supposition (one they may or may not actually believe) that all human beings are damaged at the cellular level, but that they know how to fix us, by implanting synthetic mRNA into every human being on the planet. That is the goal of the pharmaceutical cartels that are moving gene therapy into pole position, as their new trillion-dollar business model. It is a burgeoning industry, designed to genetically modify the human race by invading our cellular design and reprogramming what they claim is our "broken" DNA to repair itself—not as it was divinely designed to do, but as **they** determine it is necessary to do.

Don't take my word for it. Just remember the alarming statement from Bourla himself: they are creating synthetic DNA in their labs and it will be injected into humans.

It doesn't get much clearer than that.

*

In his recent book[9], *Covid-19 And the Global Predators: We Are the Prey*, prolific author and psychiatrist, Dr. Peter Breggin, explains:

> "These injections bear no resemblance to anything else in human history that has ever been called a vaccine. They most nearly resemble a Trojan horse.
>
> DNA (deoxyribonucleic acid) contains our genetic code—the blueprint for our biological existence. It is found in the nucleus of every cell in our bodies. An enzyme enables the DNA to morph into RNA (ribonucleic acid), which can become mRNA, the messenger with instructions for the cell to make proteins. Both types of vaccines use genetic instructions copied from SARS-CoV-2 which enable the deadly virus to make the spike protein that gains entry into human cells.
>
> Instead of taking the genetic material directly from SARS-CoV-2—an expensive and painstaking task—scientists reproduce the genetic material artificially in the lab. In both DNA and mRNA vaccines, the genetic material induces our body to make the same spike protein that is on SARS-CoV-2. In effect, as the recipient of the vaccine, our own body receives an injection with a "message" to create an alien SARS-CoV spike protein known to be very toxic to mammals, including humans. Hence, our comparison to the infamous Trojan horse. The theoretical concept is that our immune system will then attack the spike protein that its own body has just produced, which, hopefully, will induce some degree of immunity to SARS-CoV-2 if it challenges us. But that is not what happened when the hidden Greeks crept out of the gift horse in

---

9   Covid-19 And the Global Predators: We Are the Prey, Peter R Breggin MD, Ginger Ross Breggin, Lake Edge Press 2021, pgs 175-177

the middle of the night, slaughtered the Trojan guards, and opened the gates to the Greek army.

We will find a number of problems associated with all the cells in the body being directed to produce the alien spike protein. The spike protein itself is part of the disease process of COVID-19. Among other harmful effects, it damages endothelial cells in many organs of the body and in the blood vessels this can cause bleeding and clotting, and even death. In addition, the spike protein can elicit severe immunological overreactions, leading to the kind of potentially deadly cytokine storm seen in COVID-19.

There are two important differences between mRNA and DNA vaccines, the last of which are called viral vector vaccines. The first difference is the method of delivering the piece of genetic code into the human body. The mRNA, which is sealed in a nanoparticle package, enters the blood stream and finds its way to the RNA. The DNA vaccines, as the term viral vector suggests, instead use a non-replicating animal adenovirus to carry the strand of DNA genetic code to the cells in the body.

The second difference is that the mRNA vaccines send their genetic strands into the blood stream directly to the RNA in the cells with no intermediate steps. e mRNA provides genetic code with the orders and the plan to make the SARS-CoV-2 spike protein. In contrast, the DNA vaccine involves two steps. First it finds its way to a messenger RNA in the body which then tells the RNA to produce the same SARS-CoV-2 spike protein.

It is untrue that the injected materials and their effects are limited to the injection site. e messenger coding goes throughout the body, potentially affecting all cells in the body.

So far there is no evidence that the mRNA or DNA vaccines directly impinge upon DNA in the cell nucleus, but thoughtful journalists and scientists do worry that the process could end up modifying human DNA and the genome. e process may be similar to the "reverse-transcription" by which COVID-19 may be changing the genome of some patients The cavalier dismissal of any such concerns is incompatible with ethical medicine, science, or public health policy."

Before people roll up their sleeves and welcome in any more of these overwriting laboratory-created synthetic messengers, they had truly better wake up from their opiate slumber to ask the question: are they really willing to hand over their human genome to the trillion-dollar biotech/pharmaceutical industry, that has declared their DNA "damaged" in the first place? What is that injectable, synthetic messenger telling their deoxyribonucleic acid molecules to repair? How is it altering people, permanently, and why should they allow anyone to override the innate knowledge and design of the divine blueprint, re-directing human evolution?

Have we learned nothing from their take-over of the food supply, which has now given us genetically modified, tasteless food that has, as its objective, longer shelf life—i.e., more profit?

It is truly time we educate ourselves to the workings of basic biology, and explore the actual role of RNA in the body. We understand that the coiled DNA is housed in the protective nucleus within every cell. In order to perform vital functions required in the healthy life of the organism, the information contained within that original blueprint has to be communicated from the nucleus, out to the rest of the cell—the cytoplasm—which is where the vital proteins that perform so many of the body's functions are assembled.

Messenger RNA (mRNA) is the term given to those specific sequences of DNA code that are carried from the nucleus out into the cell, to produce proteins that are deemed necessary through instructions from DNA Central, for whatever purpose it understands is required for the healthy function of the organism, to include repair and protection of cellular integrity.

In an article[10] entitled *What is mRNA?* published by Texas A&M University in The Conversation, by Associate Professor of Function Genomics, Penny Riggs, she explains, in relatively simple terminology, what the role of mRNA is in the communication of DNA instructions to the cell. She states:

"As the intermediary messenger, mRNA is an important safety mechanism in the cell. It prevents invaders from hijacking the cellular machinery to produce foreign proteins because any RNA outside of the cell is instantaneously targeted for destruction by enzymes called RNases. When these enzymes recognize the structure and the U in the RNA code, they erase the message, protecting the cell from false instructions.

The mRNA also gives the cell a way to control the rate of protein production – turning the blueprints "on" or "off" as needed. No cell wants to produce every protein described in your whole genome all at once.

Messenger RNA instructions are timed to self-destruct, like a disappearing text or snapchat message. Structural features of the mRNA – the U in the code, its single-stranded shape, ribose sugar and its specific sequence – ensure that the mRNA has a short half-life. These features combine to enable the message to be "read," translated into proteins, and then quickly destroyed – within minutes for certain proteins that need to be tightly controlled, or up to a few hours for others.

---

10   https://theconversation.com/what-is-mrna-the-messenger-molecule-thats-been-in-every-living-cell-for-billions-of-years-is-the-key-ingredient-in-some-covid-19-vaccines-158511

Once the instructions vanish, protein production stops until the protein factories receive a new message."

It sounds to me that the messenger RNA within us needs no outside orchestrator interfering with that intricate and miraculous process that determines just what is needed to combat invasion from outside of us. Why then, would we agree to having a synthetic messenger, a technology that overrides the natural information highway within, to trigger the body to start producing spike proteins, with no cut-off valve, in opposition to the body's own capabilities?

The Center for Disease Control wants you to know and understand, from their own website,[11] that what they call the mRNA COVID-19 vaccine does not act like other "vaccines."

Indeed not. Because, and I repeat: it is not a vaccine.

In its own words, the CDC explains the function of the mRNA injection being utilized as a "Covid vaccine" as follows:

"To trigger an immune response, many vaccines put a weakened or inactivated germ into our bodies. Not mRNA vaccines. Instead, mRNA vaccines use mRNA created in a laboratory to teach our cells how to make a protein—or even just a piece of a protein—that triggers an immune response inside our bodies. That immune response, which produces antibodies, is what protects us from getting infected if the real virus enters our bodies.

First, COVID-19 mRNA vaccines are given in the upper arm muscle. The mRNA will enter the muscle cells and instruct the cells' machinery to produce a harmless piece of what is called the spike protein. The spike protein is found on the surface of the virus that causes COVID-19. After the protein piece is made, our cells break down the mRNA and remove it.

---

11   https://www.cdc.gov/coronavirus/2019-ncov/vaccines/different-vaccines/mrna.html

Next, our cells display the spike protein piece on their surface. Our immune system recognizes that the protein doesn't belong there. This triggers the immune system to produce antibodies and activate other immune cells to fight off what it thinks is an infection."

The essential purpose of the biological tools provided to all life on this planet and, no doubt, across the universe, is to adhere to the divine imprint in its DNA genetic coding, to be birthed, to grow and thrive, and to survive against attacks on the organism for the cycle of life that is endemic to its given species. How to assure that occurs is written in meticulous detail in its genome, the infinite architectural genius of Creation. This is common between all God's creatures, which all house an immense highway of information—the story of their genus—coiled within every cell of its being. That is Creation, pure and simple, and it has Creator's love, wisdom and light laced all the way through it.

The real messenger RNA is already there, all laid out in the great design. It is that wisdom within each and every one of us, the Source, that sends the messenger RNA to the cell, the tissue, anywhere and everywhere the survival code is needed. The organism's immune system goes to work, just as it is designed to do, to surround any invasion and flush it out. It knows how to instruct the cell to reproduce, to repair itself, how to fend off an enemy, and even when to die.

The body does not need to be taught how to make a protein by a team of scientists in a bioengineering lab, who claim to have the best interest of humanity at heart. How can anyone believe they do, knowing what we know and seeing what we've seen? Your natural bioelectrical life form does not need to be taught how to "trigger your immune system to produce antibodies and activate other immune cells to fight off what it thinks is an infection."

That capability came hardwired in your Divine DNA and it knows exactly what to do.

Unless you allow men playing God with human life, concocting disruption of our natural God-given life support systems in their secret laboratories, to tamper with your own divinity, that divine wisdom will work for you throughout your lifetime. It will continue to birth the new, and to kill off what needs to be released, supporting, nurturing and protecting your body for the lifetime of your passing here.

When we allow the body to do what it knows how to do, spontaneous healing often occurs. But how many people give the organism time to burn out an infection by elevating the body temperature in a fever, or to fight off an infection without antibiotics and disinfectants, chemicals that hinder the natural process? Of course, allopathic medicine has a place in the fight against disease, but how far has it run away from the real target, when treating a health crisis?

And now they are injecting people with a synthetic technology that rewrites the DNA, telling it what proteins to produce. This can only be described as collusion between Big Pharma and Big Government to alter the biological nature of life on this planet.

What are we going to do about this?

One thing we know with certainty is that whatever is in these shots is telling the body that it does not know how to protect itself against infection. And it requires no great leap of consciousness to realize that neither does the invasive cocktail of substances communicate to the organism that it actually possesses the wherewithal to protect itself from the messenger itself.

What makes more sense for the overall well-being of living beings of this Earth is to close down the laboratories once and for all, so that the proliferation of weaponized viruses and super bacteria, which we know are being created there, can be stopped.

These are the great weapons of this Armageddon war: bioengineering, biowarfare and synthetic, AI intrusion into the natural biosphere of all living beings. Big Pharma has already disrupted the plant kingdom, hybridizing and genetically modifying the food supply, herbs and medicinal plants. They've mutated the animal kingdom as well, always with a particular focus on the food chain, so that they can get their genetic mutations into humans. And now the diabolical plan is to colonize all human beings—every last one of us—with synthetic prions, in order to slowly remove our divine essence from our genetic codex—stripping the God Code out and replacing that infinite brilliance with the false light of what they affectionately call "Luciferin."

It will be an ice age in hell before I allow a lab white coat in service to the dark side to determine what unnatural aberrations will be injected into me to mutate my cellular make-up, in such malevolent consequence that it deliberately overrides Creator's own perfected divine blueprint. I will never allow it. May my natural mRNA, the messenger from Source through my DNA light sequencing, keep me healthy and thriving, and may you, too, stand in that power and determination.

It is time for all people—no matter what size, shape, gender, race or creed—to recognize the ultimate grace of our being truly human.

Honor the divine wisdom within you. And stand for that light that shines from your heart and soul, against anyone or anything that wants to dim your brilliance.

This is a battle we have to win, spirit warriors. And win it, we will.

For the love of God, people.

For the love of God...

Chapter 11

Souls in Shut Down

"The time will come—and it may not be far off—when people will say: 'It is pathological for people to even think in terms of spirit and soul'. 'Sound' people will speak of nothing but the body. It will be considered a sign of illness for anyone to arrive at the idea of any such thing as a spirit or a soul.

The soul will be made non-existent with the aid of a drug.

People will invent a vaccine to influence the organism as early as possible, preferably as soon as it is born, so that this human body never even gets the idea that there is a soul and spirit. The heirs of modern materialism will look for the vaccine to make the body 'healthy,' that is, to make its constitution such that this body no longer talks of such rubbish as soul and spirit, but takes a 'sound' view of the forces which live in engines and in chemistry and let planets and suns arise from nebulae in the cosmos.

Materialistic physicians will be asked to drive the souls out of humanity.

The spirits of darkness are now among us. I have told you that the spirits of darkness are going to inspire their human hosts, in whom they will be dwelling, to find a vaccine that will drive all inclination toward spirituality out of people's souls when they are still very young, and this will happen in a roundabout way through the living body. Today, bodies are vaccinated against one thing and another; in future, children will be vaccinated with a substance which it will certainly be possible to produce, and this will make them immune, so that they do not develop foolish inclinations connected with spiritual life—'foolish', of course, in the eyes of materialists.

A way will finally be found to vaccinate bodies so that these bodies will not allow the inclination toward spiritual ideas to develop and all their lives, people will believe only in the physical world they perceive with the senses.

With such a vaccine, you can easily make the etheric body loose in the physical body. Once the etheric body is detached, the relationship between the universe and the etheric body would become extremely unstable, and man would become an automaton, for the physical body of man must be polished on this Earth by spiritual will.[12]

—Rudolf Steiner

One hundred years later, the visionary Rudolf Steiner's soul-snatching vaccine-that-is-not-a-vaccine appears to have arrived, delivered, on cue, by "materialistic" physicians. The time **has** come, Mr. Steiner.

However, the question of "choice" is in play here, manifesting with particular vehemence and absolute preeminence over world affairs, specifically with regard to the construed Covid threat and the disproportionate response to that threat.

After all, it was the first time in vaccine history, at least that we know of, that they would be implanting nano-technology directly into humans beings—their willing test subjects. Whether we were going

---

12   The Fall of the Spirits of Darkness, A Future Vaccine to Prevent Knowledge of Soul and Spirit, Rudolf Steiner, October 7, 1917, Rudolf Steiner Press, Bristol, 1993, GA 177, p. 85. (edited)

to allow the unrelenting propaganda machine of the media to drive us into compliance, so that we would simply line up to take whatever they wanted to put into us, in massive numbers, or whether we would refuse and resist, was the unknown.

To achieve their desired outcome, one that would see an estimated seventy to eighty-percent of the world populace injected many times over, they had to create such hysteria at the onset that an immense swathe of people would go into panic mode, freeze up emotionally and obey.

They were not disappointed. Much of humanity eagerly rolled up its sleeves and said: "Save me from whatever it is that you say can kill me." Not only did they welcome the mystery poison into their bodies—they demanded it. These same people turned their children over to those same health officials, for all the same reasons. No one was asking what was in the shots, the tests and the masks, and no information was available to those who would have tried.

It was an "emergency," after all. There was no time for pre-trials, questions, and research. And still people said "Yes!" lining up around city blocks for hours, fighting to get to the front of the line.

And that was that. Mission accomplished. Big Pharma and the machine behind and in front of it were successful. The media drove it hard, convincing people to obey the government, fervently, without hesitation, because this was an epic pandemic that would kill millions around the world. Those who took the shots either believed what they were told was a raging pandemic of such monstrous proportions that people would be dropping dead on the streets all around them . . . or were slightly skeptical, but knew that without taking the shots, without the proof of inoculation (and the ensuing Covid "passport") they would be denied access to just about everything society formerly had to offer them. They acquiesced, because they felt it was just easier to take the jab, so that they could get on a plane, go to a restaurant, and enter the building. What that had to do with actually trusting that what they were accepting into their bodies was good for them, or whether it could cause harmful adverse reactions (as we have seen now in hundreds of thousands of regretful individuals) seemed to be a matter of little or no consequence—one to override and ignore.

Out of desperate, irrational fear, the majority of people obeyed strict and unreasonably severe mandates: they stayed home in isolation, locked down by government edicts and media hysteria. They eagerly downloaded the tracking "app," allowing the government to locate them at all times, to identify with whom they had been in contact, and to command them to report for a PCR test, if and when local health officials deemed it necessary.

People only dared to step outside their cages, and were only allowed to do so, provided they were fully masked and sanitized, and only to buy "essential" items, like food and medicine. They lined up like good little soldiers to receive the poison dart—the so-called "vaccine" that was supposed to protect them—one, two, three, four and now a fifth time but which, they sadly came to realize over a year later, did not protect them at all.

The CDC's own director has made that very clear.

After the greatest global inoculation program ever undertaken (one that slid past years of required testing because of that "state of emergency" declared by the World Health Organization) the "vaccine" was finally recognized to be not only ineffective but, conversely, it has proven to be the cause of severe reactions and death in massive numbers of people.

Once the facts started slipping past the media's protective shield, and people started seeing the adverse reactions and deaths happening all around them, Rochelle Walensky, Director of the Center for Disease Control, declared, in an interview, that "Nobody ever said the vaccine was going to work."

Really, now? And so, people are taking it because...?

*

This perceived threat of the Covid-19 "virus," and the greater risk posed by injecting repeated doses of untested substances into perfectly healthy men, women and children, have taken our lives away—for some, permanently—mutated our social structures, and stripped us of our freedom. The way in which the Covid debacle has been managed by government and health officials has separated families, destroyed friendships, and divided us into opposing camps. It has basically broken the global economy. People gave away their civil liberties to it willingly, obediently, and allowed those who rule over governments to shut down life on this planet for over two years and counting. Sadly, as the crisis rolls on, and "deviant" strains are introduced (with their respective "booster" shots), it has become all too clear that life as it was before this agenda was rolled out and thrust upon the human race will never return.

And yet, despite all that we have learned and continue to observe, the on-going war between the vaccinated and unvaccinated rages on. The never-ending pandemic is being projected into the future, too. People like Dr. Anthony Fauci and Albert Bourla are preparing to launch yet another "booster," all the while telling us even more are going to be needed.

What kind of vaccine have you ever heard of that needs a booster shot every few months, because the one you took a month or so earlier had "worn off?" Whatever is one's understanding of "the science" of immunology, a vaccine cannot be considered effective, and is not creating immunity, if it has to be repeated, month after month, year after year, with the excuse that the always unidentified virus is "mutating." The officials who are responsible for the health mandates on our planet would know that, just as they already know that another "pandemic" is on the way. They are grooming people to prepare for it, because you can bet the vials are already filled, ready for roll out.

Anthony Fauci keeps telling us that something worse is coming. And he would know, right?

Ah yes, but then, when you think you may just, in fact, be a little paranoid, you dig just below the surface, on the CDC's own funding page[13] and find that this organization "manages approximately $2.1 billion in financial and resource investments for global health. In addition to Congressional Appropriations, the CDC receives approximately $12 million in global funding through foundations and other donors including the Bloomberg Family Foundation, the Bill and Melinda Gates Foundation, and the CDC Foundation."

In other words, the same people who are funding the CDC are also funding Big Pharma and pushing the "vaccine" program (you know, the same global vaccine program the CDC is supposed to be regulating?) around the world.

*

An unprecedented 55,000 pages of documentation out of Pfizer, revealed after U.S. District Judge Mark T. Pittman, of the Northern District of Texas, forced the FDA to release clinical date on the vaccines, a list of over thirteen hundred recorded adverse side effects, many of them extreme, life-changing health crises—many permanent. More damning evidence is forthcoming, since the judge ordered the FDA to produce at least that many pages per month. It is comforting to know we still have representatives in the judicial system who are truly concerned about the people, courageous truthers who are also established medical professionals, such as noted Dr. Peter McCullough, MD, Aaron Keriaty, MD and Harvey Risch, MD, PhD, from the non-profit organization, *Public Health and Medical Professionals for Transparency*, which sued the FDA in September, 2021, based on the illegality of the FDA denying the re-

---

13   https://www.cdc.gov/globalhealth/pdf/global-Health-Funding.pdf

lease of COVID-19 vaccine review documents, in accordance with the Freedom of Information Act.

According to MedPageToday:[14]

"After the FDA distributed the first batch of the documents last week, Public Health and Medical Professionals for Transparency posted the files on its own website. The content of the documents ranges widely, with no real explanation of what the files entail. One listed de-identified data on clinical trial patient demographics and medical history, while another detailed the FDA's response to Pfizer's request for fast track review. One included post-marketing safety data based on voluntarily reported adverse events.

Zach Zalewski, PhD, JD, a regulatory strategy consultant at Avalere Health, said that many of the documents that will be released were submitted to the FDA up through the vaccine's emergency use authorization and full approval, and may not be material to an overall analysis of the vaccine's safety and efficacy. The FDA already published a drug approval package for Pfizer-BioNTech's COVID-19 vaccine, which consists of summaries of the FDA-reviewed data. The documents that the agency is required to release will likely comprise the unabridged version of this report, Zalewski said.

'This will literally include every scrap of paper that was submitted to FDA for the entirety of the pandemic', Zalewski told *MedPage Today*. 'If transparency is what they want, transparency is what they'll get'."

Anti-vaccine advocates have already capitalized on the release of these documents to further call COVID-19 vaccines into question. Children's Health Defense, a nonprofit that has taken a stance against the use of COVID vaccines in kids, highlighted a list of adverse events

---

14   https://www.medpagetoday.com/special-reports/exclusives/97544

reported in the documents—a list that includes any adverse events that occurred in people who participated in the clinical trial, even those who received placebo.

But experts have said it is misleading.

"There's a risk of cherry picking and taking things out of context," Zalewski said. "Just because you will have all the data in front of you, that doesn't mean you'll reach any different conclusions."

It is no wonder that the Food and Drug Administration, which claimed it would take decades to process the data, tried to hold back the results of that trial as far into the future as 2096—seventy-five years after the first injections, when nobody would be left alive to worry about it. That is reprehensible and it is an outrageous betrayal of all those who succumbed to it.

Thank God they did not get away with it.

The shocking Pfizer report revealed that extremely high numbers of people, in the preliminary trials, died immediately or shortly after being injected. What's more, it provided a nine-page list of every adverse reaction conceivable. We are already seeing what they wanted to hide, and there is no need to "cherry pick" at the data!

Some of the more devastating include: lung embolism, brain hemorrhage, cardiac arrest, paralysis, acute kidney failure, and epilepsy; the complete list is published on Robert Kennedy Jr.'s website: www.childrenshealthdefense.org. You may not yet be aware of the Pfizer report, because at the same time this information was being revealed, the media was meticulously redirecting public attention away from Covid and the "vaccine" debate, to the crisis in the Ukraine.

But you do need to be aware of it now.

You need to be very, very aware.

While information in the report is of the ultimate importance, my focus here is not to delve into the adverse physical reactions being experienced by growing numbers of unfortunate victims. From the psycho-spiritual point of view, one that will most likely never make any official, documented list of adverse reactions, I believe that what we are witnessing in a significant segment of the "vaccinated" population is deliberate chemical and genetic tampering with the original blueprint, the human genome—resulting in the shutdown of the astral portal, detachment of the etheric sheath, and consequent disruption of the entire bioelectromagnetic human system.

Considering what we know about bioengineering and the experiments being performed to alter the human genome, and what we heard directly from Albert Bourla, I do not think it is a stretch to say that this synthetic messenger RNA is quite specifically designed to alter the DNA. And there are plenty of other researchers and medical professionals who agree that the synthetic mRNA can indeed enter and permanently alter pure, biological human DNA.

And again, I ask you: what if the God Code is being isolated and then removed from our God-given human genome, and replaced with a different signature code, or overriding vibrational sequence? How long would it take us to figure out what had been done to so many innocent people? What would that even look like in individuals, and then from the bigger perspective ... what would it mean to the very fiber and future of civilization?

The idea of zombified, vacant shells, as they are being constantly portrayed and served up to us as entertainment in films and horror stories, comes to mind. Is that what the Center for Disease Control was hinting at when they published their article, entitled: *Preparedness 101: Zombie Apocalypse?*" on their "science-based" Public Health Matters blog? Now retired, after the CDC received a ton of kickback in the media for what they defended as simply "educational entertainment," the blog claimed to have used "popular cultural reference to zombies to promote preparedness for different emergencies and disasters"[15] merely

---

15   https://www.cdc.gov/cpr/campaigns/index.htm

to draw more people to their site. Would you call that "clickbait," or manipulation, or both? I fail to see the entertainment value in scaring people any more than they already are, for the sake of "entertainment."

When the nation's primary health protection agency, which is supposed to be safeguarding human health, sanctions dangerous experimental medical procedures never before tested on humans as an "emergency response" to a potential threat, and when the agency's own director says they never said it would work, we—subjects of their genetic manipulation and poisons—need to demand absolute proof that the threat is so overwhelming that it warrants a "solution" that is not worse than the problem. If they brush off the failure of their evil experiment in that way, and people become devastatingly ill and disabled, or die, is there any reason at all why we should allow them to continue to hold those positions?

We need those chemical concoctions to be tested and approved by an unbiased government agency, if we can find one, and we must be allowed to read exactly what is contained in those vials . . . and what the potential side effects are: before, not after the fact. That used to be standard operating procedure when pharmaceuticals are launched in the market, but once again, these products and the organizers of the injection campaign are protected in the name of an emergency response to a global health risk.

Will they be held accountable?

No matter how the "pandemic" was portrayed in the media, in the first phase of induced global hysteria, we know that the science renders unwarranted the extreme measures taken, since the facts presented us from early on established that 99.7% cure rate in adults. It was so much higher children, close to one hundred percent, yet parents, the medical and educational professions and governments around the world saw fit to inject their babies, nonetheless. Age five and up are now subject to injection and they are coming for your newborns!

Why would a parent would risk a child's health, whose natural immune system is still developing, by allowing that they be injected with this dangerous substance, knowing that survival in youth is almost one hundred percent? It is pure insanity.

Still, the injections continue. So do the endless PCR tests, invasive probes that go so far past the upper sinus cavity that they can actually penetrate the blood brain barrier, dangerously close to the Pineal Gland. What are they really after, twirling around their ethyl oxide swabs deep inside people's delicate nasopharyngeal membranes . . . and, more frighteningly, what are they **delivering.**

If this is such a virulent virus, why won't a drop of saliva suffice?

Never mind the dunning reports and overwhelming scientific data from expert doctors, geneticists and pharmacists who have had the courage to speak out. The extremely profitable business of probing people with those nasal swabs and injecting people with gene therapy is alive, and thriving.

Have we forgotten what happened back in the days of Thalidomide, which resulted in the maiming of over ten thousand newborns, and the death of thousands of those same babies? Most people today have no knowledge of how or why Thalidomide was administered to pregnant woman when it came out after WWII, and they are completely unaware that it was developed by Heinrich Mückter, a high-ranking medical doctor, pharmacologist and chemist, a Nazi who repeatedly experimented on concentration camp prisoners in Buchenwald, near Weimer, Germany. He avoided prosecution for those crimes and managed to enter the German pharmaceutical industry as Head of Development for a relatively new pharmaceutical company, Cherie Grünenthal, established by a man named Hermann Wirtz, Sr., also a dedicated member of the Nazi party.

Adding to the collection of gruesome Nazis in key positions in this company were Martin Staemmier, a medical doctor and proponent of Nazi eugenics programs, Heinz Baumkotter, chief medical officer at the

Sachsenhausen concentration camp, located twenty-two miles north of Berlin, and last, but definitely not least, Otto Ambros, Hitler's very own adviser on chemical warfare. This nefarious individual just happened to serve as chairman and member of the board of Grünenthal's advisory committee when the horrific chemical, Thalidomide, went into development, and soon after, when it was sold to the public—first in West Germany, in 1956, and later worldwide.

Thalidamide was sold under the name "Contergan," as an over-the-counter medication, promoted as an aide for people with anxiety and trouble sleeping. It was given to pregnant mothers as a treatment for morning sickness, even though there had been no trials run with pregnant women. I wonder how many people have any idea at all that the number of extreme birth defects in babies born to mothers, who used the drug during pregnancy at that time, was over ten thousand, of which a reported forty percent or more died at birth.

Did the end "justify the means" then?

As an aside, Muckter and others at Grünenthal were put on trial in Aachen, Germany in 1967-8. The company was indicted with intent to commit bodily harm and involuntary manslaughter, but, despite the overwhelming evidence against them, criminal charges were mysteriously dropped. Grünenthal agreed to pay German Thalidomide victims thirty-one million dollars in retributions and, surprise, surprise . . . the Nazi monsters were acquitted of their crimes against humanity.

This same drug, pulled off the market in 1961 because of those birth defects and deaths, was approved in the United States in 1998, for use as a treatment for cancer. Hard to believe, isn't it? It has been reintroduced and is available today as a generic medicine—Contorgen, or Thalomid—and it actually appears on the World Health Organization's List of Essential Medicines. Poison, developed by Nazi eugenicists who experimented on innocent prisoners in the camps from hell—poison proven to destroy, maim and kill—has been back on the market for decades and not only is it back in commerce . . . it is actually sanctioned and marketed by the World Health Organization!

The Food and Drug Administration and other regulatory agencies have also approved marketing of the drug; the only caveat is that people need to be made "aware" of the risks and avoid pregnancy.

Clearly, we cannot trust these governmental organizations to be watching out for our health and life expectancy, especially when something as poisonous as Thalidomide, developed by Nazi eugenicists, is on their lists of recommended medications.

And when the CDC, that same government body that is supposed to serve as our point of reference for safety and scrutiny of the medical profession, claims posting instructions for humans to prepare for a zombie apocalypse was merely "tongue-in-cheek educational entertainment," questions must be asked, such as: "Define 'entertainment'."

As precarious as the world is today, I want valid information, not entertainment, from a government agency charged with the responsibility implied in its name: disease control. I find nothing entertaining about their zombie apocalypse instruction manual. They are mocking, not protecting us. We should, at the very least, be infuriated.

But heh, there's nothing to see here, folks . . . move along.

It's just a little "educational entertainment" for the masses.

Chapter 12

The Great Disconnect

I wish to elaborate my personal experience of the psycho-spiritual impact of what I believe is really going on, as foreseen by the great Rudolf Steiner.

Over the course of my spiritual lifetime, throughout which I have conducted thousands of clairvoyant, healing readings either in person, or over the zoom screen of the Internet, I have never before observed such a profound divide amongst people. So many are surfing the "ascension" waves, awakening to their true divinity, whilst others, still the majority for the moment, seem to be living through a terrifying spiritual disconnect, in varying degrees. Sadly, some are facing a very grave existential crisis . . . one of monstrous proportions.

Since the onset of the worldwide inoculation campaign, I have witnessed this phenomenon first-hand, in people who feel shut down from spirit. I am not merely referring to warring religions, a rise in atheistic, communist doctrines, or to the mass hypnosis syndrome that has billions of people bowing down to the pharmaceutical empire, believing its fear-driving propaganda and obeying whatever they are told, or remotely "mind-controlled" to do. Nor am I addressing the issue of how a vast swathe of humanity has abandoned the pursuit of spirituality, community and relationships to the almighty control screens of the techno god.

I have been the uncomfortable observer of a form of "soul disconnect," in people for whom I conduct psychic readings and remote healing sessions, since this roll-out began. I never believed such a phenomenon could possibly manifest in a living, conscious being. But it does, and apparently, other psychics and sensitives are having similar experiences and observations in their healing practices. Rudolf Steiner's vision, which I only just read about for the first time, when gathering information for this book, appears to be unfolding exactly as he prophesized it would, right before our very eyes.

What I am seeing, or rather what I am **not** seeing in the energy fields of people who have been several times jabbed, is the luminous *sahasrara*, the crown chakra, the portal of connection to source: soul's direct byway to Source.

It simply is not there ... or at least it does not appear to my mind's eye.

This is the energy vortex spiritualists world-over understand serves as our bridge to Source and all the higher realms, expressed in what we understand to mean a broad-reaching perception of existence. It is the portal of divine light that bathes the energy body, the spirit and soul, and it is from that brilliance that we are always reminded of our true essence: spirit temporarily residing in a human body, or physical form, in order to experience matter and the sensate world.

It is at this point in the etheric system of our electromagnetic, biological energy bodies where our awareness of "self" connects directly to the higher, universal consciousness. It can be considered the byway of our transcendence, from the limited awareness defined by the state of separateness and the material, to our emergence into Oneness and the multidimensional expanse that permeates realities we have yet to fully experience. From that state of consciousness that soars beyond the matrix of our current constraints in the three-to-four-dimensional perception of a material world and all existence, we are rapidly shifting our perception to this next phase of our ascension, where the illusion of time and space eventually disappears altogether.

From the crown chakra, we enter and exit the physical body in the dream state, in astral journeys. At the hour of our passing from life, it is through the crown that spirit moves on, into the eternal light, in a "permanent" astral journey, when one's lifetime as a physical being ends—or rather, when the life that we know as human beings, earth walkers, is transmuted to its next phase of soul transition.

What it would mean to the soul's journey if that cosmic byway were absolutely disconnected from its body temple presents the metaphysical philosopher with a staggering conundrum. It brings to mind an image of someone coming home from a journey to find his house boarded up and the lights out, with no possible way to enter. Where would the wandering soul/spirit essence go, if the entryway to its physical house were sealed up, and the highway of lights that guided it home were completely blacked out? Would the soul believe that the body had died, even though it had not? Would it thus float away, beyond the astral field, and precipitously snap the astral cord, as it does in the death process?

We understand that the soul is attached to its physical manifestation by the *sutratma* or silver cord, which in Sanskrit describes the linkage that connects the *atma* (higher self) to the physical form. Many describe seeing this cord clearly during out-of-body journeys, claiming to be fully aware that it serves as a lifeline that pulls the astral body back to its physical being.

Once the astral form is in close proximity to the auric field that emanates from the physical body, it is guided back in, re-entering through the crown—also fully aware that it is the crown chakra that serves as the gateway, or point of re-entry. I have had several of these experiences myself, and can personally attest to seeing the silver cord, when I am coming back from those extraordinary astral journeys that I have been blessed to recall with clarity. It has always given me a sense of safety, knowing that I, the soul that defines my "I am" awareness, am tethered to my physical body. And I do always experience the uncomfortable sensation of having to condense the unconstrained, formless astral body down to a size small enough to pass through the crown.

How such a vital and prominent aspect of the human energy field simply could not appear to be there, in a living human being, does not align with a metaphysical understanding of the attachment of body and soul—at least, not in my experience. We believe that when the time of death comes, the soul leaves the body temple behind, exiting through the crown chakra, and this cord becomes severed, freeing the soul to journey on to its next phase of experience. But in the time of **life**, if people are not feeling that connection to spirit—or rather, if they feel the soul has already left the building—what then?

In now fourteen people whom I have scanned psychically, I was, in every case, unaware at the onset that the individual had taken one or more of the injections. I had not solicited that information before beginning the reading. I gather no knowledge of anyone before a session, as I never want to influence the pure psychic perception with information and impressions gleaned from the client. I believe it is not an ethical approach to the service I provide. Rather, I rely strictly on what is shown to me through my psychic screen, which is what people come to me to receive.

For the crown chakra not to appear to me at all, when I open my third eye to perform that psychic scan of an individual's energy body, is extremely alarming and disconcerting. In each of those fourteen instances, I was perplexed that I could see nothing at all at that critical point in the individual's electromagnetic field: no spinning vortex, no sparkling light . . . nothing that I could define as "energy" at the crown.

To then have all of these people declare that they could no longer feel God, or meditate, or connect to guides or Spirit, was a confirmation that something truly dehumanizing is happening to them, and it is something we have never experienced before.

More and more people are describing that post-injection trauma as feeling like "their soul has left them." They describe feeling desperate and depressed, with an unshakeable sense of being separate from everything and everyone. They tell me they cannot feel God. They describe how they cannot seem to shake feelings of apathy and indifference to others around them, and they admit, in varying degrees of sadness and depression, that they have an overall lack of compassion or connection to anything outside of them. Materialism—their new god—seems to be the only thing that matters, whilst spirit appears to have deserted them entirely.

Imagine how many are afraid to speak out, and how many are unable to fathom what has been perpetrated against them at the spiritual level. In my limited experience, fourteen out of fourteen vaccinated people—one hundred percent of those who had been injected—appeared to me with no visible crown chakra, and a weakened, diminishing etheric body. Every single one of them described feeling a disconnect from Source ... from God ... from the light.

Rudolf Steiner described just that one hundred years ago.

It cannot be a coincidence.

As truth about what is really in those needles begins to seep through the cracks, and more and more of those who accepted the poison see people around them become chronically ill or dying from the injections, they are filled with regret, realizing they have made a terrible mistake. Caught in the vehement polarity of society's pro- and anti-vax stances, these people are struggling, afraid to ask the questions that need to be asked, with nowhere to turn for answers.

Try telling an allopathic pro-vax doctor that "you can't feel God within you anymore," or that you're afraid you have somehow been "disconnected" from Source after taking the injection. Those who dare are being diagnosed as "psychotic" or "depressed," and it goes without saying that they are being referred to psychiatrists, and/or prescribed mood-altering, numbing medications to deal with their duress, because it appears too few medical professionals are prepared or allowed to confront an issue so deep and unprecedented as a conspiracy to disconnect or scramble the God Code within our DNA.

Suffice to say that they are not teaching "soul disconnect" in med school.

It was most telling and alarming to learn that all fourteen of the people in question had received a double or triple dose. How many hundreds of thousands more, who have allowed themselves to be repeatedly jabbed, are silently grappling with the ultimate existential crisis, cut off from Spirit, with no one to turn to? What dark, parasitic mechanism has been injected into these people, and what has caused their light to be diminished? Is anyone prepared to listen?

What explanation could there possibly be for this aberrant disruption of people's energy systems that appeared to be shutting off the crown chakra? And why, in all fourteen instances, were these same people describing the same eerie sensation that, somehow, they had been cut off from the God source? Their terrified comments ranged from feelings of diminished spirituality, inner light and joy to those of hopeless despair that, somehow, God had "left them."

I asked myself: had the injections somehow cloaked or shadowed the vital energy wheel at the crown? Had it shut down the connection completely? Had the Divine Blueprint been disrupted? And perhaps the most important question of all: would it revitalize in time, and how?

When it comes to the etheric and astral realms, all manner of apparitions and phenomena can occur. As an objective observer and psychic healer, I often find them very difficult to interpret and then deal with. I have seen it all: from ghoulish demonic entities and vampiric leeches that suck the life force out of the host, depleting the energy field, to far less harmful attachments of non-malevolent spirits, who get lost somewhere in the ethers, and hook onto the individual energetical-ly, like parasites, feeding off the physical being's vital energy to survive.

There have been countless manifestations of what I have been gift-ed, all my life, to be able to see through the psychic eye: some fright-ening and threatening, others mysterious and curious—aspects of the multidimensional universe that manifest in the etheric field. All of it fills me with wonder and immense curiosity, and I have been moved, with great compassion, by those innocuous, harmless energies that are lost in the in-between. As a healer, I was often able to assist a lost en-ergy/spirit to detach and move on, to its rightful place in the etheric realms. It is far more difficult to feel that same compassion for the more demonic entities who have moved into people's energy bodies, and in many cases, taken possession of them.

Even if I were able to release that kind of malevolent spirit, how would I know where it was meant to go, and would I be capable of assuring that it didn't simply move on to invade another? In those rare cases, my protective shield keeps them at bay and distant, by necessity.

So many times, people make karmic choices that call these ener-gies to them. Is it the healer's role to interfere? These same questions arise when I encounter this disturbing new phenomenon: an empty void above the crown, where usually there are sparkling lights, beams, even spirals emanating from that sacred space, traversing the auric field and shooting off into the ethers. And in every case, these individuals described the same, exact sense of feeling disconnected from Source, feeling like the God force has left them ... feeling lost.

Around and around in my head whirls the thought: how can I help them get it back? And then, there is a consideration that other healers and psychics do need to ask themselves as well: will my intervention, on any level, interfere with the karma the individual has created, by willful-ly allowing a foreign substance he knows nothing about to be injected into the body temple? Would it cord my own karma to theirs, in the process?

Those who roll up their sleeve to the omnipotent administrators, unquestioningly accepting their poisons over and over again are, in essence, making a covenant with something or someone of which they have no conscious awareness. If only they would stop to think that by accepting this synthetic operating system to override their God given one—allowing the system to inject whatever it wishes to impose upon their biological being—they are essentially saying "Yes, do what you will with me," yielding their sovereignty of mind, body and spirit.

That is some pretty wild abandon, considering that the virus from which people are supposedly protecting themselves, with the vaccine that is not a vaccine, has such a high cure rate. They are unwittingly saying yes, absolutely, inject me with a chemical cocktail filled with unknown substances that also contains nano-technology—synthetic mRNA—delivered into the molecular body, altering the cellular composition of all human beings who take it. It overrides the sacred, the God Code, and sets a whole new template into the Divine Blueprint, with a new set of commands that now appears to be injurious to the body, and apparently the soul—but yes, give it to me.

Shoot me up, lock me up ... take my breath away.

That synthetic transcription in our mutated DNA and the genetically spliced, false neon light of DNA from non-human species, which they have begun inserting into our naturally luminous beings, contains what they call "Luciferin," and that is exactly what it is: Lucifer "in."

Does that fear-based compliance that causes people to rush to the local vaccine center mean that on some level of unconsciousness they are actually saying "Yes, I accept Lucifer in?" For the most part, I highly doubt that. So, what does such acquiescence mean, not only to one's body and present lifetime, but to the journey of the soul? What kind of karmic bond is being created? What kind of pact? Does that choice remain to be healed through countless lifetimes, subverting the ascension of the soul? If that is the case, which I suspect it is, how far down the spiral of the soul's journey will they fall? Do those who accept the poison realize the karmic noose they are placing around their necks for many lifetimes that follow?

Most people have no idea what's being administered to them. They ask no questions, waving their sovereignty to whomever or whatever frightened them into becoming test mice for the pharmaceutical, medical and bioengineering cabal, which, in turn, is working with DARPA, the Defense Advanced Research Projects Agency of the United States military. This highly-secretive entity has brought us things like GPS tracking systems, stealth planes, speech recognition, self-driving cars, and plenty of other technologies designed to control human beings—or at the very least, to alter our behaviors.

If you still have trouble believing that your own government is colluding with Big Pharma, I share with you DARPA's own declaration, taken from their website:[16]

"DARPA's Pandemic Prevention Platform (P3) program, launched in 2017, focuses on rapid discovery, characterization, production, testing, and delivery of efficacious DNA- and RNA-encoded medical countermeasures against infectious disease. This foundational technology pioneered by DARPA under the *Autonomous Diagnostics to Enable Prevention and Therapeutics (ADEPT)* program provides the body with instructions on how to immediately begin producing protective antibodies against a given threat. Just two years into a four-year program, P3 has performers at AbCellera Biologics, AstraZeneca, Duke University, and Vanderbilt University, all of whom have been able to quickly pivot to rapidly identify antibodies for COVID-19 in less than ninety days. This process traditionally takes several years to complete."

Let us never forget that the body already knows how to "immediately begin producing protective antibodies against a given threat." It is

---

16   https://www.darpa.mil/news-events/2020-11-10

called the natural immune system. So, what exactly did the Big Pharma/DARPA coalition have in mind for us, when they came up with the plan to globally inject every walking human being with a so-called "vaccine" that is actually a delivery mechanism to invade our DNA? And why is a highly secretive branch of the military so heavily involved?

*

Of my encounters with this strange and disturbing phenomenon of disconnected souls, the first was with a woman who had been injected two weeks prior to her session, which I conducted over the internet. I will call her "Lily."

I had worked with Lily a year or so prior to that session, before she received the "double jab" injections. She was a vibrant, very connected and dedicated spiritualist, whose metaphysical practice was centered around her established yoga center, where she taught courses, and from where she also organized yoga retreats. She was truly a centered, luminous, high-energy individual.

One year later, I saw a very different person looking back at me through the screen. She was lifeless, and grey. Her energy field was opaque and dull. The sparkle and the warmth in her eyes were gone.

When I told her that I was "having trouble" seeing the crown chakra, she told me that she had "lost contact with Spirit," and could no longer meditate. She described how she had struggled to keep her center open, but had had no other choice but to close, when the really tough mandates were rolled out. Like those who would follow in subsequent sessions, Lily's terrifying experience was one of feeling shut down, completely turned off to her higher self, and disconnected from everyone and everything around her. She had hoped that a reading with me would help her get to the root of it, and clear any blockages I might be able to pinpoint in her energy body.

Lily had not associated her state of alienation with the "vaccines," until I asked if she had been injected. She replied that she'd had the first shot when they were first being administered, because at the time she believed she had no other choice, if she wanted to keep her center open, and that she'd just had the second one two weeks prior to our session. She reported having no particular adverse reactions, other than a sore arm and muscle aches throughout her body after the first dose, and then a fever, a crushing headache that lasted for days and a general state of malaise, with the second, that lasted even longer.

I dare say those were definitely adverse physical reactions to the injection! And now here she was, two weeks after the second shot, shut down, lights off, feeling spiritually vacant and, understandably, depressed and afraid.

Needless-to-say, the spiritual side-effect of being injected with whatever is being imposed upon all these innocent people is not a conversation taking place in the mainstream debate. If you dare to discuss anything at all that can be construed as an "anti-vaccination" position— and that includes highly-qualified researchers, doctors, health care professionals and even whistleblowers from the pharmaceutical companies—you are attacked relentlessly and persecuted, with every attempt made to silence and destroy you. You lose friends, and family too. Merely electing to refuse the injection for one's own body is being decried as a form of terrorism against society.

At the time of this writing, several government heads and citizens themselves are even calling for the "unvaccinated" to be jailed in concentration camps, or "re-education centers," as they're being called, which are popping up in countries all over the world.

*

I refer back to the Nuremburg Code of 1947. Wasn't it written so that the world would never again see medical experimentation performed on unwilling victims of a rogue state? Do we need to be reminded that one of the basic tenets of that post-war code of medical ethics stated that "the degree of risk to be taken should never exceed that determined by the humanitarian importance of the problem to be solved by the experiment?" It should be clear to anyone with a mind to see clearly that a 99.7% cure rate does not warrant the degree of risk engendered in an experimental, never-before-utilized genetic modification "vaccine," that uses unsuspecting human beings, who trust their doctors and their political leaders, as mere test subjects.

In this environment, where most people dismiss adverse physical reactions to the experiment as being "psychological" in nature, to attempt to open a discussion on the subject of the Covid-19 "vaccine's" effect on the spirit and soul of a human being will surely be met with resistance, hostility and ridicule. This aspect of the problem simply doesn't enter into most people's equations, for most are not in touch with that facet of their being to begin with. After all, if one is witness to someone dropping dead at the head of the line and still submits, then he is not seeing, not thinking, and not understanding at the most basic of levels.

Whether it is a state of mass hypnosis, misguided trust or outright denial that blinds people, especially to another's suffering, it is unconscionable that anyone would proceed, taking the needle, in such a circumstance. Would the question of being interfered with at the spiritual level, whereby it is just possible that whatever is going in is capable of severing people from Source, hacking the God Code within their DNA, even cross their minds?

The possibility of delivering pure evil to the innocent by means of an experimental injection or drug, something so all-pervasive that it could transmute the chakric/aura energy network and quite literally turn the lights off in one's spirit body, is beyond most people's comprehension and scope. It is very difficult for heart-centered people to imagine anything that seethingly wicked, even though the proof is absolutely available to anyone willing to open his eyes and truly see what is unfolding. And then, of course, there is the mind-numbing mainstream media, owned by those same forces, pushing from the illusion of objectivity . . . to persuasion . . . to subjugation of all opinion and thought, that dares oppose the official narrative and governments world over.

When we consider that it is a spiritual war raging across our planet, with armies of dark and light warriors already in full battle position, it is not so far a stretch to recognize that the ultimate conquest in question is not about countries, riches or power.

The emperors of darkness already possess those.

No, the goal now—the final conquest—is the subversion of the soul of humanity that gives itself over willingly, submitting to the Satanic force, bowing down to it in absolute obedience and surrender. That requires a means to disconnect the masses from the God light.

It is total subjugation they feed upon, the loss of faith in one's own godliness . . . the relinquishing of self to the master: fear.

The conquest these evil despots seek is the soul of any and all human beings they can bring to the dark side. To dim the light everywhere, within and around us, is their intent. Once that disconnect has been effectively achieved, what remains of our vacated beings they plan to assimilate into the artificial intelligence hive, via technologies we still cannot imagine. But they have them. And with every day that unfolds, even as I write these words, diligent researchers are exposing how their AI nano-robotics are being delivered through those hypodermic needles. And yet, still people go for the next shot, and the next one after that, still allowing probes to penetrate almost across the blood-brain barrier, still breathing their own carbon dioxide behind their "protective" face masks, and still taking the knee to the lords of their enslavement.

This may sound completely far-fetched, frightening or insane to you. But I can tell you this: from my personal experience through encounters I am having with people who are well along on their spiritual path, but who now are feeling that they can no longer "connect with God," the disappearance of the crown chakra, to which I am witness, is a very real phenomenon. Those who are experiencing it first-hand, growingly aware that they have made a terrible mistake, are terrified.

And yet, no matter how far we distance ourselves from Source— whether through fear or ignorance—there is always a way, and there are always varying degrees of solutions to any problem. They are not always what we hope they will be, but in the end, we manage to move ahead.

In my experience, which I dedicate this book to sharing, that is all about being absolutely focused upon setting the intention to reclaim one's sovereign DNA, and then restoring whatever has been altered, by way of powerful vibrational frequencies that reweave what has been tattered, restore the music, the light and the broken pieces . . . and if possible, remove whatever has been implanted in one's holy temple through the desecrating needles and swabs that have been unlawfully utilized against them.

As one of the pioneers who first brought the idea of activation and repair of DNA into communal awareness almost three decades ago, I have been concerned with the question for a very long time, along my journey as healer and guide.

It is just that the stakes are higher now . . . much much higher.

With that in mind, I invite you to join me, as I stare the demon straight in the eyes, to get to the absolute core of the problem facing us all and then, resolute in that knowing, and understanding how it operates, we will be empowered to transmute it: for ourselves, for those fourteen souls who feel disconnected, and for hundreds of thousands more who will be desperate for our help.

The survival of our species and many others is at stake here.

We are Homo sapiens, whether walking in our brilliance, or bent in fear, shadowed from the God light. We are human beings.

If you wonder why you have to go through this, struggling and weary from what feels like an endless battle, just remember that the war is on not only for your own soul, but for the soul collective of the entire human race.

So, shields up, everyone.

Do not be afraid. It only enchains and disempowers you.

We can talk about all of this—all the evil—and take it apart, piece by piece, in order to examine every bit of the cog and stop the devastating wheels of opposition to love from turning.

Feel the immense power of knowing you can look right down into the belly of the beast and never give way to its force, for it has no power over you, unless you are prepared to yield your power to fear. Always remember that it needs the adrenaline you pump into the ethos for fuel; it needs your fear to survive, to cloud your thinking and disrupt your emotions, and to spread across the oceans of human consciousness, staining the mind of the collective, like indigo ink in crystalline waters.

Call upon the God light that is within and around you, and let nothing enter you that is not of the highest intention. Your mind can either function as the ultimate shield against anything that wishes to invade you or, if you allow it, as a programmable magnet that forces outside of you can utilize to manipulate and deter you.

Remember that you are a child of Creation and that you bear the God Code in every cell of your being. Wherever needed and required, your natural mRNA delivers all necessary information, constantly, to every tissue, organ, and bodily system, designed to build, preserve and potentiate not only the physical body, but also the spirit, the soul and the brilliance of your capacitated mind.

Beyond the biological DNA, powerful energies and influences in the quantum field serve and assist you, in a constant interplay of information sourced of light, with your sacred, biological being. Understand that. And know that no force of evil—no matter how dark, no matter how powerful—can ever take what you are not willing to give away.

You have to be willing. That is how they steal it from you, whether you sign away your soul for fame and fortune, in a contract sealed in your own blood, or whether you roll up your sleeve to take Lucifer In, in order to quell your fear.

Without your compliance, their game is off, because they need you to give yourself away. That's where their ultimate power lies. That is what they are after.

So, check your obedience meter and then repeat after me: "I am a sovereign being, a child of the Earth and stars."

And sovereign we shall forever remain.

Chapter 13

Honor the God Code Within

Bioengineering is the tip of the poisonous spear of the medical/pharmaceutical empire, on a collision course with destiny, imposing invasive chemical, synthetic and genetic tampering upon the sanctity of our godly beings: plants, animals, and humans alike. And let us never forget how miraculous it is that we exist at all, and how godly we are at the very core of our being, beyond personality and physicality, as we are all created in the omniscient vision of what or whomever we consider that incredible architect of all life to be.

Some souls—"new souls" as they are often referred to—choose to manifest form and be birthed into this realm at a very early stage on the path to eventual enlightenment and, mesmerized by the sensate world and the lure of pornographic sexuality and meaningless materialism, they choose to wallow in those illusions, where shadow veils the light. Others, well-traveled souls of the no-time, come in with a higher vision, a mission and gifts that unfold throughout the lifetime—gifts to be lived and shared with the community, enhancing and lifting the lives of the many.

To each his time, rhythm and pace.

Dark or light, new or old, we are all cut from the same fundamental cloth from which all biology is constructed, and that is a coalescence sourced from the subatomic, infinite microcosmic universe, from which the actual molecular material—the DNA—is derived, exhibiting extraordinary consciousness and supreme intelligence through its incredible form, vibrational essence, and function.

From the non-invasive point of view, healers, spiritualists and mystics, such as I, have learned so very much about the etheric nature of DNA: how the actual molecule responds to negative or positive thought, sounds and vibrations, interacting with the unified field. We recognize how the body's cellular memory, reflecting the waters and crystalline essence of the biological being, serves as a resonance chamber for every thought we have ever thought, every word we have ever spoken, and every sound we have ever taken to heart and allowed to enter our sacred halls of "be-ing." And we are more than clear that the ninety-percent DNA within us, that has been labeled "junk" by the scientific and medical research communities, is anything but that, for there is nothing in all of Creation and its boundless expression throughout the Cosmos that is superfluous.

The explanation put forth in the Sirian Revelations that fragments of ten of our original twelve strands (which the geneticists refer to as "non-coded" or "junk") have been scattered and lie dormant within the cells is by far more credible, in my humble opinion, than the official narrative: that nine-tenths of our DNA is purposeless waste, with nothing to do and nowhere to go ... and that it is comprised of vacuous bits and pieces of debris that, apparently, Creation forgot to clean up.

Let us be very clear about what I can only call an "undeniable truth." Of all the living indigenous animal species that share our space here on Earth, only man creates "junk"—and a lot of it—tons upon tons, hour by hour, laying waste to every ecosystem on the planet. It does not exist anywhere in nature where, in a perpetual dance of individual and collective purpose that expresses itself in breathtaking beauty, all living beings co-create an interdependent environment that thrives, where man does not interfere.

Creation saw fit to design all manner of life forms which, in perfect synchronicity, know how to perpetually birth the new, but also to remove decay and death from every ecosystem, holding nature in perfect balance. Maggots, vultures, hyenas and many other animals feed on dead carcasses and clear away death. Even the tiniest creatures, such as the ant, serve as scavengers that remove and consume waste; others feed on dead plant material as their food, which vitalizes new growth.

That is not to deny that humans who live in respect of nature do wonderful things when they cultivate gardens, protect the animals, and live in harmony with their environment, mindful of the flow of life and the beauty of Creation. So many of us are seeking out that connection, leaving the toxicity of cities, building sustainable homes and taking care to create as little waste as possible, aware of our "footprint." And when we take that extra step to carry away the plastic and garbage others have left behind in parks and beaches, as custodians of the environment, we perform a very conscious role in the dance of life. We become conscious contributors to the interdependent system of nature.

We bow to the beauty, in great humility and respect . . . and the goddess, Gaia, bows back.

Isn't it amazing, when you really stop and think about how everything fits so harmoniously together in our mutually dependent natural world? We have only to examine the perfect balance of the pure earth, sea and sky, and all Earth's blessed creatures, to recognize how life co-creates, in such an exquisitely choreographed dance of life, and how nothing in the great scheme of our world, and beyond, is without its reason to exist.

Nothing in the divine design is superfluous. Everything that exists has purpose: in nature, in the macrocosm of the multidimensional universe, and in the microcosmic patterns that define the cellular make-up of all living beings. When we look at life through that lens, recognizing how things fit together, so seamlessly, throughout the bountiful landscapes of our Great Earth, we can only assume that, if scientists of the biological fields that study the etymology of our particular species have never been able to identify ninety-percent of our divine blueprint, it is because there exists a ninety-percent problem in their approach to the field.

We metaphysicians have come to understand that the ninety-percent has everything to do with our inner eye, the Pineal Gland, and how we were designed to access and consciously connect to the quantum universe. Those disassembled light strands and dormant signals are currently scrambled in a quagmire of broken segments, awaiting the impulse and conscious direction that will magnetize them back into their original form, structure and purpose and plug them back into the master switchboard.

Also required for full twelve-stranded activation of this scattered DNA material is the de-activation of the electromagnetic grid placed around the planet, which has us locked into a lower energy field that is antithetical to the luminous Christ-like energy that is our original birthright.

I read with great interest recently that forty out of forty-nine of Elon Musk's Starlink satellites, vital to his invasive SpaceX "communications" system in space, crashed to Earth in February, 2020. SpaceX was quick to put out a press release that claimed, contrarily, that the "deorbiting" satellites were not at risk of collision with the plethora of satellites encircling our planet and that by burning up in space there would be no debris, and nothing careening through our atmosphere and crashing to the ground.

So, apparently, there was no crash.

All manner of speculative claims, dependent upon whether someone sees Musk as a heroic figure, or a villainous one, immediately surfaced on social media, as to whether it was White or Black Hats that shot them down. The debate rages on. A statement from SpaceX itself reported that the satellites were significantly impacted by a geomagnetic storm. May there be many more of these storms, if that is indeed the case. And may so many more high-tech, potentially weaponized surveillance satellites be blown up outside of Earth's atmosphere, clearing our space . . . in space.

Although we understand that we must serve as determiners of our own destinies, to be the saviors some believe we are waiting for, it is my personal impression that forces still beyond our perception are assisting humankind at this treacherous time on Earth. Whether, just as our own personal spirit guides assist us on our individual paths, there are peace-loving, off-planet civilizations helping to steer the future of our ascent out of the quagmire in which we find ourselves today will remain a mystery, until we have undeniable, irrefutable contact. What we must not overlook, in the meantime, is the extraordinary conscious interplay between the planets and our sun, the source of heat and electromagnetic energy that operates our solar system. Such powerful energies from our ascending star are, in fact, more than capable of disintegrating the electromagnetic cage that surrounds our planet, which permeates our atmosphere with extreme radiation, and has an extremely negative effect on all life here.

The horrific grid that encases our planet needs to come down and it is going to—one way or another. Whether that will involve peace-loving ETs, willing to give us a hand down here on Terra Firma, or whether the sun itself will fry the entire array in a monumental solar flare and knock the debris out of Earth orbit, it is time that this techno/mechanical girdle around our planet be removed—not tightened, with tons more technological equipment raining down even more powerful electromagnetic frequencies on our world.

We have had enough of it. Let this weaponized radiation cage be incinerated in space and carried away, like dead animal flesh on the savannah, by well-intended galactic scavengers—the clean-up committees—in space.

The take-down of the electromagnetic grid encasing our Earth is vital to our progress: from the microcosmic universe—the atoms, protons, neutrons of subatomic consciousness—to the macrocosmic energy exchange between our sun and all celestial bodies involved in its sphere of influence, and with all species that live and thrive on those planets, moons and asteroids within our solar system. And I reiterate: it is necessary for full reactivation of those additional strands of DNA that currently lie scrambled in our DNA matrix, like tiny bits and pieces floating around in a pot of microwaved minestrone.

I cannot ignore the question of how this grid affects the DNA of animals and plants, as well as humans. Researchers claim that junk DNA also exists across many species and, since we know that we share amazingly similar genetic building blocks, it stands to reason that the interference that involved scrambling ten strands of our Christed DNA would have affected fauna and flora across the board. That over 100,000 years ago, ancient aliens would have deliberately utilized some futuristic form of electromagnetic radiation to scatter our DNA, an act capable of diminishing the brilliance of a society of Christed beings and sabotaging our evolution, is an utterly fascinating proposition ... as much as it is perplexing. And that the animal kingdom would have experienced chromosomal disruption and mutational genomic interference as well cannot help but fill our minds with more questions. To what insane weaponry did those divisive alien creatures have access? And what, exactly, are the modern-day exterminators planning to do with what they have now: in space, overhead, on land and deep within the sea?

*

Notwithstanding the small problem of this pesky ninety-percent mystery DNA, which prominent Darwinist theorists dismiss as left-over waste—a by-product of evolution—21st century geneticists believe they have successfully sequenced the entire human genome, which they have not. Far from it. They do now possess highly sophisticated technology, no doubt. It was acquired decades ago, from sources light years ahead of humankind's technological capacity at that time. From what we understand was President Dwight D. Eisenhower's trade agreement with off-planet beings, he allegedly gave permission to extraterrestrial visitors to experiment on us "Type Zero" human beings, in exchange for advanced technology, and related scientific knowledge that has clearly altered our evolutionary progression.

Whether the president even had a choice to accept the terms of that "deal" or not, and if he did, in fact, make that trade, it was a bad one—a very bad one indeed, across the board. For the thousands of abductees whose lives were dramatically traumatized, and for civilization, conditioned by and subjected to information and systems way too advanced for our unprepared societies, the benefits from President Eisenhower's handshake with aliens appear to have served the military-industrial complex he warned of, but not the healthy advancement of life on Earth.

Whatever its source, alien or human, it has been well established that the military and government-recruited scientists have available to them technologies that are believed to be at least forty years ahead of what is publicly known today. Seeing how the cabal, its foot slammed on the accelerator from the onset of the 21st century, has been utilizing those tools since Eisenhower's encounter, I shudder to think what they are capable of imposing, not only on this planet, but on others they intend to invade and conquer.

From as far back as the hour of the despot, Adolf Hitler, all life here has been the subject of a relentless experiment that involves every imaginable and unimaginable invasion of the divine against all biological species. In 2008, an organization called The Global Crop Diversity Trust, a non-governmental organization with headquarters in Rome, engaged with the Norwegian government to build the Global Seed Vault (a structure not unlike the mythical Noah's Ark) in the side of a

Norwegian mountain at Svalbard. Would you be surprised to hear that Bill Gates Foundation/UN Foundation is the second biggest donor of the project?

Once the organization and the money behind it collected and stored seed of every living plant species of Earth, which they embedded in permafrost conditions in that freezing Global Seed Vault, the breathtaking flora of our Earth—particularly cultivated crops and medicinal herbs—came under attack of being poisoned, burned to the ground, genetically altered and driven to extinction. The remaining plant and tree kingdoms of the Garden of Eden are being genetically modified to increase production, to resist infection and pests, and most definitely to introduce unnatural DNA material into the food chain, along with synthetic mRNA, pharmaceuticals, insects, and gene therapies.

How did Mother Earth manage, so beautifully, before?

All I can say is, "Be extremely careful about what you eat." Seek out organic foods wherever possible. Be aware and make the best choices you can; grow your own, or join up with community farmers and neighborhood garden projects.

Plant trees to cool down the Earth, plant flowers for the bees, and grow food.

Animals, of course, have been experimented on forever. Animal DNA has been spliced, hybridized, mutated and conjoined with that of other species to create new bizarre mutations—chimeras—for reasons that are far from altruistic, and which have paved the way to the current experimentation of mixing human DNA with theirs, altering the natural biological body of Earth's biome altogether, and most likely forever.

With a diabolical world government intent upon fusing human DNA with the technology of Artificial Intelligence, all stops are out. Like irresponsible neophytes, recklessly playing God not only with the very now moment of our existence but with the future of our lives, government-funded university and laboratory researchers are having a field day, bioengineering their dystopian fantasies in test tubes worldwide. Since the onset of this 21st century, they have been given much broader license and free access to some of that futuristic alien technology Ike signed on to, to forge ahead with no constraints, free to mutate the divine molecular software inherent in a simple leaf, the bird, a mighty whale ... the human being.

It appears there is a very one-sided race underway to alter, splice and rewrite that God-given code across all life forms, probably, deliberately. Beyond interfering with and altering your divine blueprint ... beyond any altruism attributed to the work of the bioengineers, "applied genetics" is big business—big, huge business—and that equates to big money for big industry. Areas that are being explored for their profitability to Big Pharma and potentially for undisclosed governmental and military use include:

- Mining data that regards the human genome, categorizing genetic information growth areas in the sector for Big Pharma, government and other private interests
- Determining genetic predispositions for disease of the fetus or newborn – and interfering with the genetic code if deemed "necessary."
- The development of new gene therapies
- Profiling: targeting certain pharmaceuticals and gene therapies for people with certain genetic and traits
- Testing human-animal genetic mutations
- Creation of bio-warfare, as in the case of the mRNA inoculations
- Creation of "designer" babies
- Modifying the human genome to re-direct the evolution of the species

Reading this list of just some of the "growth areas" of the burgeoning genetics industry, one can only surmise that, no matter how they spin it, invasive practices that interfere with the sanctity of human life, through testing, probing, injecting, modifying and drugging, are the order of the day in the Big Pharma/Biotech professions.

Practice in those sterile, cold laboratories, where they experiment on the DNA of those fetuses, newborns, children and adults mentioned above, is too painful to elucidate here. It is too dark for any heart-centered, conscious human being to bear. Many will never be able to fathom or believe what actually goes on in those facilities, for it is very difficult for loving souls to contemplate the horrors that are concocted there: whether at the cellular level, in their test tubes and petri dishes, or whether experimenting on unwilling, captive living beings.

We do not want to think about it; we do not want to talk about it. But horrors there are and they are proliferating at lightning speed. We have turned the other cheek for far too long.

Many years ago, I encountered a woman who worked in one such a laboratory, specifically one that experimented on animals for the cosmetics industry. I will spare you the horrific details. I remember thinking how utterly shut down she was as a human being, and how strange it was to me that a mother of four children could do what she did to those tortured animals. When I asked her how she could bear to bring such terror and pain to those innocent, endlessly suffering creatures, she replied, matter-of-factly, that they were "only animals."

I reminded her that we too are animals, to which she replied, coldly, "You had better toughen up for what's coming or you're not going to survive it."

Decades later, those ominous words haunt me more and more each day, as I see what has come, and what more is on the way. I never have "toughened up" to suffering and never will.

Suffice to say that, from as far back as World War II, mad geneticists have been replicating, replacing and mutating animal and plant DNA for reasons that have nothing, or, at best, very little to do with the advancement of any sentient species. In those unfathomably cruel and torturous laboratories, and in the boardrooms of corporate lords who finance them, their attention, in the last few decades, has turned from mutating and mutilating the plant and animal kingdoms to the modification and sabotage of human DNA.

Funded by governments, Big Pharma and the military-industrial complex that Eisenhower warned of, back in January 1961, in his *Farewell Address to the Nation*, appear to have no restraints, no ethical or moral limitations, and no limits whatsoever. In the anonymity of their relatively secret world, anything goes when it comes to the field of bioengineering, and that includes experimentation on every life form indigenous to Earth, and probably from beyond. Some will argue that they are also creating hybrid species merging human DNA and that of select extraterrestrial races. Tens of thousands of abductees claim to have some experience of that alien agenda—far too many to be ignored.

Suffice to say that bioengineers have been given carte blanche in those laboratories. God help the poor animals and humans, and even eventual extraterrestrials who end up in their cages, as it appears is the case in Area 51 and other top-secret military bases.

God help them all.

Whatever claims the geneticists do publicly admit to—claims like those that promise how the developing field of biogenetics medicine, or gene therapy, will vastly improve the way disease is treated, extending our lifespans—the truth is far more sinister. The reality is that the world's most profitable industry thrives on our being dependent on pharmaceuticals, the legal drug trade . . . not upon wellness. Applied genetics are no different. It's money—huge money—for Big Pharma and the downline of "corruptibles" who make the right policy decisions for them.

A well-respected, well cared for body knows how to maintain health, although the toxicity of our environments has taxed our immune systems to the limit, as has our dependency on the pharmaceutical fix. There are, of course, exceptions. I am not so reckless to suggest that there have not been great achievements in the field of medicine, or that there are no well-intended professionals in these fields, and I am not qualified legally to make any medical calls at all. Scores of ethical health workers are risking everything, in order to speak their truth of what is really going on in hospitals and clinics around the world. But it is clear that, today, the assault of an unbridled pharmaceutical industry, in bed with the medical profession, holds sway over a lot of innocent people, who still do not realize how deleterious are their prescribed chemical poisons and gene therapies to their health and well-being.

A healthy society is not a profitable society for a machine that poisons for profit and corrupts the political class to do same. It is the way of war as well, because peace is not profitable. That is the very sad state of affairs that defines bellicose policies worldwide, and our paid politicians' mockery of the health and welfare of their citizens.

Are you aware that the healthcare industry is reported to be the second largest lobby in the United States? According to a Reuter's report[17] from October 25, 2021:

"The industry, which traditionally gives more to Republicans, channeled around 60% of donated campaign funds to Democrats this year. It has spent over $177 million on lobbying and campaign donations in 2021. Nonprofit political action committees (PACs) run by Pfizer Inc (PFE.N) and Amgen Inc (AMGN.O) and the Pharmaceutical Research and Manufacturers of America (PhRMA) were among the biggest donors, according to political spending data from OpenSecrets, formerly the Center for Responsive Politics."

---

17   https://www.reuters.com/business/healthcare-pharmaceuticals/capitol-hill-drug-pricing-reform-opponents-among-biggest-beneficiaries-pharma-2021-10-25/

Republicans will have gotten a significant piece of that pie as well – let us not believe for a minute that only one side of the political body is corrupt! The article goes on to say that:

"Nonprofit political action committees (PACs) run by Pfizer Inc (PFE.N) and Amgen Inc (AMGN.O) and the Pharmaceutical Research and Manufacturers of America (PhRMA) were among the biggest donors, according to political spending data from OpenSecrets, formerly the Center for Responsive Politics."

Once people truly understand how corrupt government officials collude with corrupt pharmaceutical giants for money and the power they acquire from it, things may change. When more of us realize that a huge percentage of the pills and shots and vaccines and treatments and remedies and surgeries prescribed to the well and unwell are the honeypot of a ruthless industry, one with the capacity and express intent to interfere with the natural state of health of almost eight billion "customers" on this planet, more people may finally start taking better care of their bodies, and shun the system altogether. They may think twice before turning their babies over to the medical industry, which starts pumping their tiny bodies with chemicals, hormones, and injections from birth, setting up a state of drug-dependent dis-ease within these individuals for life, if they even survive at all.

And, if Rudolf Steiner has it right, as I believe he does, they are disconnecting the newborns from Spirit, so they never even contemplate the soul and its journey, just exactly as the transhumanist team visualizes the GMO, Human 2.0.

What will become of them?

So many in those white coats we thought we could trust have long abandoned the Hippocratic oath for profit and ease, within a controlled system of profit-making and neglect of the true human condition. When the global society recognizes how dependent human populations have become on Big Pharma's chemicals and drugs—for themselves, and even for their beloved pets—more people will come to terms with the reality that something has gone very wrong in medicine. They will understand, at last, that the caring, sensitive family doctor is being usurped almost everywhere in the world, and in his place is a system whose purpose, by and large, it is to administer legalized drugs and other invasive, highly toxic substances to mask or reduce the symptoms of disharmony in the psycho/biological body . . . or, in the case of genetic technologies, to mutate it altogether.

One has only to read the insert in any prescription to become immediately aware that the substance to be ingested, at the behest of the prescription-writing "doctor" is, at the very least, questionable and most often highly dangerous. You are not encouraged to read the side effects (if and when they are even provided) and when you do, the doctor, who will firmly remind you that **he** is the doctor, most often will tell you to ignore the paper, ignore the warnings, and take your meds, as you're told. All too often, that enormous list of potential side effects warns of conditions, symptoms and reactions to the medication that are far worse than the problem you went to get help for in the first place!

I remember time ago when I was hospitalized for pneumonia. I dared question the doctor about what meds he was prescribing in the massive cocktail of pharmaceuticals being pumped into my dangerously weak body. He answered sharply, "I'm the doctor here," to which I replied, "Yes, but it is **my** body, Doc. Let's not forget that."

If you are really paying attention, it is not difficult to recognize how, while some of their concoctions may extend the average lifespan of 21st century man, they are certainly reducing the quality of life for a vast swathe of drug-dependent human beings. If you do not believe that, ask yourself how many people you know, yourself included, who do not possess a medicine chest full of the stuff. How many of your family and friends are on prescribed meds, and how many others self-medicate with over-the-counter symptom chasers, whose chemical and toxic contents they have no understanding of at all. When you take the time to investigate what poisons are in those pills and vaccines you unquestioningly allow to be put into your body, and the potential side effects they can provoke, you can't help but revisit your approach to your own health care, or at the very least, to start asking questions of your doctor . . . and demanding answers.

We do still have committed physicians who are speaking out for the human race and choosing the ethical, moral high ground in service to us all. We do still have dedicated health workers who are doing what they can to serve and assist us all, honoring the commitment of their profession. I am so very grateful to those who are standing up to the omnipotent system, questioning the authority, and putting their practice and sometimes their very lives at risk. Seek them out.

We have strength, in numbers.

More are coming forward, now that so much is being revealed.

*

Pharmaceutical/biotech industry giants are gearing up for the next generation of pharmaceutical interventionism: gene therapy, synthetic technology that penetrates the DNA with the supposed purpose of correcting, or "fixing" a gene that may be defective. Where is the list of side effects for that? Do we truly intend to allow an invasive, multi-trillion dollar industry free passage into the human genome, to rewrite what it believes must be altered or "fixed," without truth or consequences? If so . . . if people willingly accept the rewriting of our human genome by a synthetic messenger (mRNA) that has the capacity to go into our DNA and cut, splice and paste it, to the whims and fancy of whomever is doing the editing, then they had better prepare themselves for the rewrite—the edited version of their former selves: Homo sapiens 2.0.

How will this anti-human bioengineering industry, the medical profession and the chemists of Big Pharma, sheathed in white coats and Hazmat suits, cause us to mutate us as a species? What is the end goal? We had best be asking those questions now, because they are racing forward down a dangerous one-way track, like a runaway train, and if we do not stop them, and stop them **now**, there may be no pure biological human being left on this planet, in a future very much closer than we think.

Spiritualists, such as I, are concerned more than ever about the sovereignty of our sacrosanct DNA: its absolute self-awareness and consciousness, how it functions, and how it responds to stimuli that emanate from the higher frequencies of love, light and sacred sound. In essence, knowing what we now know about cellular memory and the impact of thought upon every single cell of every living being's mental/ emotional/physical bodies, we are many who seek to share the wisdom and knowledge that can protect, restore and heal our increasingly damaged DNA.

In today's world, it is under constant attack from all manner of toxicity in the air, water, soil. We are bombarded by hypnotic programming designed to perpetuate fear and disempowerment. It permeates a huge swathe of human beings who resonate to those manipulations, affecting the collective consciousness and the etheric substance that surrounds us all. And now, human DNA is the target of unrelenting chemical, synthetic and bioengineered alteration, for reasons that are all too clear to those who are paying attention and holding their ground: sovereign souls passing through this earthly existence at this dangerous time in Type Zero earth consciousness.

What we are up against is a politicized, runaway corporatocracy in Big Pharma, in collaboration with tech giants, that appear (despite claims to the contrary) to be doing everything to shorten our lives or to be veering the biological human into a bio/synthetic life form of robotic creatures, where our human nature and innate biology will be supplanted by artificial intelligence, and whereby what is left of our minds will be utilized to serve as units of the hive.

This same system, guised in ecological rhetoric, openly declares that we are too many beings on the planet, and must be culled. In a presentation Bill Gates made during a Ted Talk lecture back in 2010,[18] he spoke these chilling words:

> "First, we've got population.
> The world today has 6.8 billion people. That's headed up to about nine billion. Now, if we do a really great job on new vaccines, health care, reproductive health services, we could lower that by, perhaps, ten or fifteen percent."

Wait. Doing "a really great job" means culling the population?

No amount of damage control from Gates's public relations teams can erase this stunning pronouncement, although the mainstream media he funds have tried, for it is public record.

One decade later, we are an estimated 7.8 billion people on this planet and the globalists have every intention to fulfill the Bill Gates protocols, by reducing the population in any way they can. His vision, from back in 2010, is playing out as planned, attacking the health and welfare of the population, through "new vaccines, health care and reproductive services." It is integral to the Deep State's "Green Agenda," thrust upon an overtaxed global society at this time, and leading to the New World Order's looming Agenda 2030, whereby the political elite, and unelected, unqualified super wealthy like him have been catapulted into global policy-setting positions of power. There's just one minor adjustment: his quest to reduce the population is not at all about ten to fifteen percent of us; it is actually much more in line with the sweeping goal set forth in the four mysterious nineteen-foot-tall Georgia Guidestones.

The story goes that in June, 1979, a man who gave the name "R.C. Christian" commissioned the Elberton Granite Finishing Company to

---

18   Bill Gates, "Innovating to Zero," TED2010, https://www.ted.com/talks/bill_gates_innovating_to_zero/transcript?language=en

produce a mysterious stone structure, in granite, that would be erected on a five-acre plot of land there, in Elbert County, Georgia, which he subsequently purchased in October that same year. He explained that he and the group he represented, "a group of loyal Americans," preferred to remain anonymous.

The New World Order monument was erected precisely March 22, 1980, on that land, to which he later transferred title to the county, including ownership of the stones. Soon after, R.C. Christian disappeared into the shadows of his desired anonymity, but the ominous stones remain. Engraved upon them is a set of "guidelines" for the people of Earth, in eight different languages, that lists, as its first directive, the chilling words:

"Maintain humanity under 500,000,000 in perpetual balance with nature."

As we struggle through this stage of what is clearly a well-planned war against the human race, we recognize more and more that what is happening now was no accident, but rather, that it is rooted in an orchestrated stratagem that is several decades in the unfolding.

Killing us off is not the final solution. What they are after is the destruction of our eternal light, the dimming of all light, on all planes. It is our very soul essence, that spark of divinity within us all, that can only be extinguished when we surrender our God force to the darkness.

That is their primary target. It is their ultimate goal.

They believe that if they can achieve the perversion of soul consciousness, they can then assimilate what remains of our rapidly mutating species into the aforementioned hive mind units of their insectoid-like artificial intelligence technological matrix, already built, and waiting to assimilate the soulless beings of what will once have been the human race.

Anyone who understands and is aware of the transhumanist agenda, our run-away technological future, knows that what I am sharing here is not disinformation, as some would prefer to dismiss it. This is not mere fuel for "tin hats." Unfortunately, it is the very real, unfolding agenda of our globalist controllers, the depopulation plan for the entire planet. While all too many distracted souls are standing around at the station, transfixed by their cell phones, the train they never even noticed pull out of Grand Central is racing into a dystopian future.

Regrettably, as I observe the polarization of our societies and their rapid destruction, in the hands of a maniacal deep state, I do realize that the wake-up window of opportunity is closing rapidly, for so many individuals who have chosen obedience over freedom, and fear over love. Fortunately, however, we are entering into the time of Revelation, where all is being exposed. The undeniable truths we all will soon face are going to jolt the world out of its trance, in time to reach those who are not yet awake, so that they can override the orchestrations at work around them and reclaim their freedom, before it is too late.

This is already underway.

The time of the deep sleep, humanity's hypnosis, is ending.

*

If you intend to honor your sovereignty as a co-creating soul, passing into and through this lifetime, you will need to defend the very foundation of your physical presence on Earth, in the 21st Century. Today's world, deliberately driven by misdirected medical interference and bio-engineering tampering in the natural order of things, is faced with the deterioration of all life forms, on a planet in the midst of a global extinction event, from which we still can decide to recover.

Human DNA is now the battlefront between extinction and ascension. Alarming as that sounds, it is where we are now. Our DNA is under attack from every direction. In these recent years, there has been an extensive, far-reaching campaign, via collection projects that claim they want to help you "discover your ancestry" while, instead, they have been secretly compiling a massive DNA data base, from which to store and manipulate the human genome. Now, we learn that these DNA samples are also being sold to China for reasons that speak, at the very least, of racial profiling. I tend to think that their use in laboratories around the world is widespread, and not limited to the abuse of any one nation.

Most people simply do not think about these things. They do not want to confront anything that upsets the paradigm. They let people who are not even medically trained rub those DNA test swabs over the soft tissue in the cheek, never questioning what might be in those swabs, or what they are actually giving away, and to whom, and then off go their DNA samples to the unknown "collector." In their naiveté, they even pay to give that very private information away, with the promise of learning where their ancestors came from. What is done with the sample in a laboratory, and how these individuals are profiled for life, eludes them, for if it did not, they would never volunteer their essence to an unknown, random scientific experiment disguised as an "ancestry information" service.

People surely do need to be thinking about what is being done with those DNA kits. Will their sample be used to create test clones? Will it end up being joined with pig DNA, by mad scientists who are developing human-animal chimeras, in real time? Or, will it end up in a vial somewhere, in some obscure underground biowarfare laboratory, where it can be utilized in Gain-of-Function research down the road?

Remember that before genetically modified foods were disseminated around the globe, the mysterious Crop Trust Fund, backed by countries, corporations and private interests from around the world, collected natural seeds from every genus of every plant on the planet and secretly stored them all away, deep within the ice in Norway. Clearly, they knew well enough that, wherever they were taking genetic modification of the flora of the entire planet, it was not going to be good for the ecology of our world, and that it would be even worse for the living beings nourished and healed by Gaia's abundant plant diversity.

And now they are collecting human DNA, from every race and ethnicity, under the guise of those "ancestry projects," with the promise of having one's ethnicity revealed, but which we know is being purposed by the bioengineering industry. Some of that vital information will most likely be stored in some colossal techno-ark, to be utilized, if they have their way, like those heirloom seeds buried in the ice of Svalbard, to plant us somewhere else, perhaps ... once they have re-engineered us, or eliminated us completely from the planet they hold hostage: the formerly pristine Garden of Eden.

If you consider that the entirety of the digital computer technology is based on a binary number system code, it should not come as a surprise that the technology world would be scrutinizing the DNA code very carefully, to see how it can be similarly programmed to perform functions that are not written into the original code, or how it can be rewritten, like software, to follow a different design, function and purpose, or to be most effectively merged with the mega brains of computers, written with just two digits—ones and zeroes—and what might that mean to the potential capacity of DNA, with its four base codes.

Will computer programs revert from the binary codes currently in use, to be expanded into the language of DNA? In this world of outrageous science-fiction scenarios, whereby the merging of man and machine is fast becoming reality in our contemporary lives, it is not beyond the realm of possibility that this race for human DNA and its integration into computer technology might have everything to do with upgrading the entire computing system to the four-letter base codes of our DNA. Could it just be that the existing binary code structure is simply not going to be able to handle the computing requirements of the new digital frontier?

*

Then there's that nagging question of the "junk" DNA within us that just refuses to go away. Determined researchers are redefining the field's understanding of what function this "junk"—the "non-coding" bits and pieces of DNA—actually performs. They just cannot seem to figure it out!

Does it correspond to a different system, and does it provide a whole other composite of codes that respond to the ten additional light strands of DNA in the original blueprint of Homo sapiens? We believe it does, but they have yet to decipher what the stuff of our Christed consciousness is there for, nor how to reassemble the scattered pieces. I doubt any scientific mind will ever be open to what amazing information still awaits discovery in those deactivated information packets of our starseed heritage.

I am convinced that is a good thing.

Perhaps the scrambling of ten of our twelve-stranded DNA imprint was not simply the dismantling of our Christ Consciousness by intervening ETs after all, but rather, part of a far greater plan—a Divine Plan—to save us from that very end, at the moment when the darkness is using every means possible to dissect and destroy our "humanness" in the battle of darkness and light.

Perhaps . . . just perhaps, Creation determined that it was far too soon, in Earth's evolution, to allow unresolved darkness access to that intensity of light, walking, in Homo sapiens. Religious history certainly showed that to be true. We only need to remember what the story of the Christ showed us: that the world was not ready for such immense love and beauty to flourish here. If the immense impact of Christ also served as a test to see how civilization would respond to a twelve-stranded being, it failed, on the one hand, at the time of his walking here. On the other, it served as an eternal symbol for the Godliness within us all, if only we can "re-member" who we truly are.

It is just so very possible that the forces of the universe understood that there were no short cuts to achieving full illumination, and that playing God with Creator's signature, whatever the intention, was simply not going to be allowed, for reasons that had to do with interventionism then, as now. Even though we hold the bits and pieces of ten additional strands of DNA within us, scrambled and still undecipherable, we, as a global society, are not resonant, at this time, with the vibrational field of that level of consciousness . . . although we hold that potential within us.

Despite proclamations of a few gurus, cult leaders and self-aggrandizing spiritualists, who claim to be ascended masters, no Christed being could hold twelve-stranded frequency on the Earth at this time. But we are sparks of Divine Light, capable of reweaving some of those lost pieces into three- and six-stranded DNA formations, and I intend to elaborate that for you again in Part Two of this book, responding to the issues at hand: namely, how to deal with the imposition of synthetic mRNA through injection, and an overall approach to maintaining the integrity of our cellular memory: the DNA blueprint.

Using Dr. Masaru Emoto's work with water molecules as our model, which investigated how human consciousness could affect the structure and sacred geometric forms in those molecules, we know we must be capable of restoring broken fragments and healing the DNA, by creating sacred geometric forms within the nucleus of every cell, and calling those fragments back into the light of their original design.

Let us use our exquisite minds as the ultimate messengers, sending love light and healing into the coiled genome, to accelerate healing and to reflect our eventual ascending mastery that comes with knowing how to raise ourselves to higher heights, which will be potentiated when we leave the density of the earth plane.

We must never let anyone clutch that most divine of all rights away from us, our God light, no more than we can allow them to screen our skies with chemicals and aluminum particles to block the sun, to dim the light of Gaia herself.

Honor the God Code within and know that, right now, that is the most important thing you can do to retain your sovereign mission on this planet. Every crucial decision and every choice we make from here on out determines how quickly we overturn this agenda, and how we then can return to our collective appointment with the higher dimensions.

Chapter 14

YHWH
Deciphering the God Code

Some scientists suggest that
the three billion letter DNA code is so long and so complex
that it would take a computer software writer,
working eight hours a day, non-stop,
fifty years
to type the complete human genome:
the DNA Code.
Yet still we question
whether God
—Prime Creator—
exists?

Mystery has forever shrouded the name "Yahweh," the Hebrew word meaning "never to be spoken," or so it has been interpreted over millennia. The word has been feared, mistrusted, misinterpreted, blasphemed—even decried as the name of Satan himself, by those who wish to overturn that most sacred and powerful of pronouncements.

Examining ancient Scriptures, not from a religious perspective, but from a search for clues to secret codes and messages, I sought out the Holy Torah (a compilation of the five books of the Hebrew Bible), whose laws and teachings from oral traditions of God's revelations to

Moses are written in *Exodus 20:07,* the third of the Holy Commandments given to Moses. It reads:

"Thou shall not misuse the name of the Lord thy God, for the Lord will not hold anyone guiltless who misuses His name."

This revealing statement has been diluted over time, in the Old and New Testaments of the Bible and various interpretations of both, to mean: "Thou shall not take the Lord's name in vain." I often wonder what effect our modern-day avoidance of the word, "God," and how we have been conditioned to deny its utterance in even the most innocent expressions, has upon the greater ethos—and how much more powerful would be our prayers and sacred chants if we were to include the utterance of the name, Yahweh. With what we are up against now, we need, more than ever, to impregnate the subtle energy fields with the vibration and love that emanate from the invocation of that word and, more importantly, from our perception of and connection to Divine Creator.

Was the true purpose of the Third Commandment meant to assure that no one would ever disrespect or in any way dishonor God by pronouncing His name? Or does it contain, imbedded within it, a secret so all-encompassing that to correctly pronounce the word—or the sacred vibrational code embedded within it—might just serve to reveal, to those who have not evolved to a level of consciousness information, that which they are not meant to access?

Was protecting the secret God Code within our DNA the real purpose of the Third Commandment?

The millennia-old mystery surrounding God's name, in ancient Hebrew texts, and the deliberate substitution of the name, Yahweh, to prevent its "misuse," are most curious. If we read the Third Commandment from the Torah, drawing our attention to the word "misuse," a whole new message and meaning jump off the page. How could one "misuse" the word YHWH: Yahweh? Perhaps the original text provided a subliminal clue that, until now, historians and worshippers have missed entirely. Was the Bible actually saying: "You shall not **misuse** the God Code (embedded in the Divine Blueprint), and was that text warning humanity of the consequences of doing so?

The four letters, YHWH, are also referred to as the "Tetragrammaton," and refer, respectively to the Hebrew fire letters: Yod, He, Vav, He, read from right to left.

יהוה

Many are the phonetic interpretations of those ancient letters and their sequence, the *word that must not be spoken*. Why the name, pronounced "Yahweh" (one of several phonetic interpretations of the four-letter code), is never to be uttered should give theologians and seekers from all sides pause to reflect on what underlying purpose there might be in such a pronouncement.

Some choose to interpret the vowel-less word as "Jehovah." But it is indeed "Yahweh," that speaks or, rather, "sings" the vibrational codes of the Tetragrammaton.

According to ancient Hebrew Scripture, God said to Moses: "This is what you are to say to the Israelites: `I AM has sent me to you. I AM WHO I AM. Say to the Israelites, YHWH, the mighty one of our fathers . . . this is my name forever, the name by which I am to be remembered from generation to generation'."[19]

There has been such poor translation and deliberate obfuscation in the evolution of the Old Testament and ancient Hebrew texts, and the name has been removed in the New Testament. Hasn't that message about "misusing" the name also been mutated, along with the religious rule that we not utter the name of Creator?

YHWH, the "unspeakable" name of God from Biblical times to today, is the God Code, secretly woven into the DNA of all life. It is so

---

19   Old Testament, Exodus 3:14:15

simple, and so complex at the same time, which is the quintessence of all Creator's divine works.

In a treatise that he published as *The Hidden Name of Creator in Your DNA*[20], Rabbi Dani'el Rendelman explains the God Code as follows:

"A direct link can easily be found between the building blocks of life and the Creator of the universe. Mankind is fearfully and wonderfully made, with a hidden code within the cell of every life. This code is the alphabet of DNA that spells out the Creator's name and man's purpose.

Scientist discovered a "map" of four DNA bases that carry the ability to sustain life. These bases, known as chromosomes, are paired differently for each person. Human DNA contains 23 pairs of chromosomes, made up of hydrogen, nitrogen, oxygen, carbon, and their acidic counterparts. Encoded within these elements is an amazing blueprint of life that proves the Creator has put His own unique stamp upon every person. This stamp is actually His name as revealed to Moses thousands of years ago.

Now, compare this four-lettered name to the four elements that make up human DNA and discover an ancient secret of creation. "The key to translating the code of DNA into a meaningful language is to apply the discovery that converts elements to letters. Based upon their matching values of atomic mass, hydrogen becomes the Hebrew letter Yod (Y), nitrogen becomes the letter Hey (H), oxygen becomes the letter Wav (V or W), and carbon becomes Gimel (G). These substitutions now reveal that the ancient form of YHWH's name, YHWH, exists as the literal chemistry of our genetic

---

20   The Hidden Name of Creator in Your DNA, Rabbi Dani'el Rendelman, February 2012, http://www.greatgenius.com/hidden-name-of-creator-in-your-dna

code. Through this bridge between YHWH's name and the elements of modern science, it now becomes possible to reveal the full mystery and find even greater meaning in the ancient code that lives as each cell of our bodies.

When we substitute modern elements for all four letters of YHWH's ancient name, we see a result that, at first blush, may be unexpected. Replacing the final H in YHWH with its chemical equivalent of nitrogen, YHWH's name becomes the elements hydrogen, nitrogen, oxygen, and nitrogen (HNON)—all colorless, odorless, and invisible gases! In other words, replacing 100 percent of YHWH's personal name with the elements of this world creates a substance that is an intangible, yet very real form of creation! This is not to suggest that YHWH is simply a wispy gas made of invisible elements. Rather, it's through the very name that YHWH divulged to Moses over three millennia ago that our world and the foundation of life itself became possible. YHWH tells us that in the form of hydrogen, the single most abundant element of the universe, He is a part of all that has ever been, is, and will be."

The *Sepher Yitzirah* (also known as "the Book of Formation") is understood to be the earliest known text devoted to Jewish mysticism and Kabalistic philosophy, described by scholars and theologians as a treatise on mathematical and linguistic theory, through which ancient wisdom keepers were attempting to convey how the universe came into existence. It is the field of Creation theory. Interesting how so many texts and traditions from the Jewish faith hold, as the fundamental study of their search to know God, the geometry, mathematics and spatial relationships between number and form, and how these aspects are expressed in a divine alphabet known as the "fire letters."

The Hebrew language is esoteric, mystical wisdom of its own. Every letter is associated with a number and the vibrational essence of the numbers and how they are joined together, as words, hold hidden, sacred meanings that the novice cannot grasp. Not even the most devoted and scholarly Rabbis and academicians are able to break the codes buried within their alphabetical and numerological essence.

It is divine language—language many understand to be that of Prime Creator.

Rabbi Judah Ha Lévi (1075-1141), a Jewish poet and religious philosopher, wrote of the Sepher Yetzirah that "It taught us the existence of a Single Divine Power by showing us that, in the bosom of variety and multiplicity, there is a Unity and Harmony, and that such universal concord could only arise from the rule of a Supreme Unity." In Chapter Two of the Sephirah Yetzirah, which elaborates complex mathematical attributions to the numerical vibratory signatures of the Hebrew alphabet, it states:

"He hath formed, weighed, transmuted, composed, and created with these twenty-two letters every living being, and every soul yet uncreated."

So, let us examine the alphabet of DNA, in order to have a fundamental understanding of what the geneticists are working with, insofar as the coding of our biology is concerned, at this pivotal time in our evolution: plants, animals and humans alike.

Essentially, the DNA molecule is composed of a string of four specific "bases" or sub-units that are chemically linked to each other. For the sake of simplifying the field to where we are not struggling with the technicalities of "science speak," let us refer to them as the "building blocks" of DNA: the "nucleotides."

These four chemical bases have been defined as T C A G, corresponding, respectively, as: Thymine, Cytosine, Adenine and Guanine. How these bases are strung together—as strings of these subunits—

and how they then pair with other strings, so that the cellular mechanism can interpret them in order to create a protein, is what we refer to as the "genetic code." Miraculously, these bases pair with their equals in a second string, which we see represented within the double helix, as that twisting, coiled ladder of T to T, C to C etcetera, throughout the millions of molecules that contain this sacred formula. What results from that intricate structure geneticists have managed to translate into a highly complex, coded language.

Just as any given language is built upon a system of letters which, combined in countless clusters, form words that represent and convey thought, so does DNA language convey the thought of a supreme intelligence, or Prime Creator, whose divine design provides instructions (a sort of cosmic "owner's manual"), to be read by the cellular body. The sequence of these letters determines the structure of amino acids, which in turn greatly affects the form and function of proteins—essential elements of the cell—which perform close to every essential function of cellular life, determining the cell's shape, various structural aspects, and many aspects of cellular management.

In a paper from the Plant and Soil eLibrary[21], regarding DNA Structure, we find a beautiful explanation of how these nucleotides are "like letters in the genetic language."

"Just as we use letters to make words with meaning," the paper states, "the order of the nucleotides on a DNA strand codes information. They make 'words' that tell the cell how to make each protein. Furthermore, the genetic language is a universal language. Every living organism uses the same nucleotide combinations to code for its genetic information. This characteristic is important in genetic engineering. It allows the transfer of genetic information from one species to another while maintaining its meaning."

---

21   https://passel2.unl.edu/view/lesson/526205690468/4

This same theme is explored by biologist, Raymond Bohlin, PhD, whose approach to the mysterious wonder of life mirrors my own. In his brilliant article, the Language of DNA,[22] Dr. Bohlin writes:

"We use letters to form words, like DNA uses nucleotide subunits to form codons. Each codon codes for a specific amino acid. We use words to compose sentences. The sequence of codons forms a gene, and the sequence of amino acids forms proteins. We use sentences to form paragraphs, which are then grouped into articles or chapters of a book. Groups of genes and other DNA elements form chromosomes. When books and magazines are brought together, we call this a library. When chromosomes are assembled into the nucleus of a call, we call this a genome.

You could represent the parallels in the following table:

Letters	=	Nucleotides
Words	=	Codons (amino acids)
Sentences	=	Genes (proteins)
Books	=	Chromosomes
Library	=	Genome

What I'm trying to demonstrate here," states Dr. Bohnin, "is that the genetic code is a language. We use linguistic words to describe what happens to DNA. DNA is transcribed into mRNA, which is like a different dialect of DNA. The mRNA is then translated into protein, a totally different language. These linguistic terms accurately describe what is actually happening. The genetic code is an informational code or a language—it's even in digital form."

---

22   https://www.exploregod.com/articles/the-language-of-dna

This system of coded language, which communicates between the components of the cell, between cells and throughout the structures described above, has to have been written by someone, some force of intelligence ... something or someone so far beyond human perception that it has never been proven or unproven, across the annals of written history and more ancient myths, from which much of our human story is derived. Just as the most sophisticated computer software has to be written into the system by its inventor, so must the language of DNA be written by a Divine, Supreme Creator.

Nothing else makes sense.

Now that geneticists are deciphering the complex language it utilizes to operate the biocomputer of living beings, we can agree that it is a pretty undeniable fact that there is extraordinary intelligence and artistry in the biology of life. Who that grand designer is and what His purpose was for creating such magnificence as we are privileged to see and be part of on Planet Earth, remains the greatest existential question of our experience.

However, one thing we do now know with certainty from the scientific communities of genetics is that within every cell of our being is an extraordinary coded language designed to trigger, maintain and assure that life can thrive within the Earth environment—however harsh and unforgiving, however gentle and nourishing—until such time as it has lived its pre-ordained life span, and is ready to release from the body and move on.

What we will not hear confirmed from the engineers toying with human biology is that written into this language of infinite and loving biological expression and artistry, is the God Code: His language, His word, His signature. It is there and there it must remain: unaltered, untainted and pure.

Throughout known history, and no doubt beyond what we have gleaned from what has been written, many memorable people, through their intellect, power and vision, have in some way or another affected the course of human evolution. Some of their contributions have catapulted us forward in wondrous ways. Others have taken us backward, to ignorance, fear and self-destruction. One only has to contemplate a luminary, such as Alexander Fleming, whose discovery of penicillin in 1929 undoubtedly added to extending the life span of human beings. And then, we look back at maniacal despots such as Hitler, whose horrors and brutality almost succeeded in bringing the world to its knees. His presence on this planet left a stain, across the board, in human consciousness; the horrific memory of his inhumane insanity reminds us forever that evil does indeed exist. There are plenty more Hitlers walking the Earth today and they, too, are cold-blooded creatures whose intent it is to destroy love, life and beauty on this planet, for reasons no conscious soul can truly fathom.

True evil has a power with which we are forever contending, as we move through time and space, seeking to understand the human experience on this planet. But we must never forget that, in the cyclical nature of physical reality, all things have their time to be birthed, to reach their apex, and to slowly die.

These individuals and their participation in the unfolding evolution of our world come and go, and with time their existence here, while adding to the course of human events, fades, yielding to the forever-changing societal needs and desires of civilization. Over the course of centuries, their wars against humanity and all their evil deeds are often supplanted by the next generation of ideas, developments and inventions that move civilization further, in a given direction, which we want to believe is a forward moving, evolutionary pace . . . rather than a race backwards.

However, one man's discovery has so completely altered the future of humankind that, whatever his intention at the time, his work has bequeathed unto our civilization something quite different, something far more dangerous than even the most dreaded arsenals of thermonuclear weapons that proliferate around the globe. We are talking about Type Zero man's interference with the very essence of all biological life forms on this planet, whether indigenous to Earth or imported from other star systems and worlds.

This man was Swiss-born Biochemist, Fredrich Miescher.

Miescher discovered the DNA molecule in 1869, opening a Pandora's box for which, I propose, humanity is still unprepared—if we consider how the information has been abused until now. As a species, we do not appear to have evolved enough to tamper with what has been protected for so many ages in this Divine Blueprint, for it contains the secrets of Creator's ultimate design of life itself. It defines how every living being, and every single cell within that being, is designed to develop, replicate, reproduce and die off, as is optimal to the living organism, and that is a sacred library to which our current day purveyors of evil should never be allowed entry.

And if, as I stated earlier, evil or the "devil" is the opposition to Creator, then I shudder to think what twisted desires really underlie their invasion of our microscopic highways and byways, that form the roadmap of life—each with its unique and still universal construction.

To destroy and subvert the God Code? What greater desire could possibly exist for the darkness, whose intent it is to extend and replicate itself infinitely and inescapably, than to extinguish any and all light forever. Its program is to drown Creation in some unimaginably cold and inerasable smear of inky blackness, where no light passes, where no love can penetrate, where one can no longer feel God within . . . and where only the tyrant's mutations can survive.

They do now have the tools and the knowledge to initiate that process and they have, indeed, begun.

In an Armageddon war of dark against light, where the goal is to extinguish the light and kill the soul, it is not that difficult to figure out that what they wish to construct within our DNA and that of all sentient beings, after subverting the God Code that defines who and what we really are, is the light-snuffer, embedded within that acrostic "Lucif-erian" signature: the 666—Mark of the Beast.

Chapter 15

CRISPR
The Cut and Paste Gene Disrupter

We have become almost anaesthetized to the true meaning of the term: "genetically modified organism." We know geneticists are creating hybrids in plants, and in animals, and have done, for decades. We know they are cloning animals, first announced back in 1996, when they broke the news of Dolly, a female Finnish Dorset Sheep, reported by associates of the Roslin Institute to be the first known mammal to be cloned from the cell of an adult ewe's mammary gland. But, according to the non-profit organization, Understanding Animal Research, which claims to concern itself with the humane use of animals in medical, veterinary, scientific and environmental research in the UK, Dolly was not the first animal to be cloned.

They tell us that that Dolly was far from being the first cloned species in their labs and that before her came mice, frogs and cows—all cloned from embryos. What made Dolly exceptional, apparently, was that she was cloned from an adult cell and so, from Dolly we learned that they now had the ability to clone an entire biological organism from the DNA of a single adult cell.

They stop short of confessing that humans have been cloned as well. Are we really so gullible to believe that they went as far as Dolly, and then stopped? Although we have never had official confirmation of it from the bioengineering world, it would certainly seem they have cloned human beings too, judging from the bizarre replications we see of public figures in politics, and the sports and entertainment industries!

We know they are altering genetic information to create designer babies, genetically engineered, in vitro, to foster specific physical traits: super humans with exceptional intelligence, exceptional strength, beauty, etc. We know they are experimenting with human-to-animal chimeras. We know all of this and more. But what we still have not managed to get our heads around is how they are intent upon deleting Creator's imprint, the God Code, from the DNA, and replacing it with genetic information of their choosing—a re-coding of our light strings—while still managing to keep enough of our original genome to keep the physical organism alive and functioning: not healthy, and not happy, but functioning, until such time as the body no longer serves any purpose to the Borg.

As distracted as so many people are, watching our social structures fall into a state of extreme global degradation, and struggling to keep their heads above water to simply survive the barrage of geophysical, social, medical, and political attacks being hurled at us by the hour, the human race has, until now, been relatively unaware of what is going on in those secret laboratories, in countries around the world. I keep coming back to the orchestrations of the heavily funded, bioengineering companies that are conducting the most dangerous genetic experiments imaginable—methodologies that, unchecked, cannot help but alter our and other species' evolution forever.

What they needed to catapult the industry forward, to meet with their projections of the GMO human, was a new, reasonably inexpensive and easy-to-use technology that would enable bioengineers to remove a specific segment of the human genome, and replace it with genetic information from other humans, species, or synthetics.

Along came Jennifer Doudna, University of California Berkeley and Emmanuele Charpentier, now at the Max Planck Unit for the Science of Pathogens in Berlin, to win the 2020 Nobel Prize in Chemistry for their brainchild breakthrough technology, CRISPR (Clustered Regularly Interspaced Short Palindromic Repeats). It provides geneticists with the ease of a sort of cut-and-paste software that allows them to edit a specific segment of DNA: first identifying it, then altering it and/or replacing it with who-knows-what the experimenters decide to splice into it. Apparently, this new tool is cheaper, faster and easier to use than previous gene-splicing tools, opening the world of genetic modification to laboratories everywhere! Thanks to CRISPR, it's a veritable gene editing fest now, offering a wide variety of applications for basic biological research, the development of bio-technological products, and everything that has to do with the evolution of gene therapy.

It's programmable, too. Some in the biogenetics fields refer to its laboratory capabilities as being "as easy to use as clicking a button." Imagine?

This rapidly evolving science can use CRISPR technology to turn genes on or off, without altering their sequence. It has made it possible for bioengineering cowboys and gals to invade the microcosmic world of DNA, whereby they can click that button and edit parts of the genome, or cut a segment of the sequence they want to remove, and then paste something they want to add—something "foreign"—into the original blueprint, for reasons they and their teams alone know.

CRISPR has plenty of other applications: from "fingerprinting" cells and recording their inner workings, to creating gene drives (technology that modifies the inheritance of genetic traits in any given species), capable of directing evolution where they specifically want it to go.

Consider this: will the laboratory-created, patented synthetic mRNA technology, and CRISPR gene snippets, being injected into humans, mean that the holder of the patent, can claim ownership of your altered DNA—and subsequently—ownership over **you?**

An article entitled, Can Genes Be Patented?[23] from the National Library of Medicine, attempts to clarify the grey areas surrounding this pressing issue. It states:

"A gene patent is the exclusive rights to a specific sequence of DNA (a gene) given by a government to the individual, organization, or corporation who claims to have first identified the gene. Once granted a gene patent, the holder of the patent dictates how the gene can be used, in both commercial settings, such as clinical genetic testing, and in noncommercial settings, including research, for 20 years from the date of the patent. Gene patents have often resulted in companies having sole ownership of genetic testing for patented genes.

On June 13, 2013, in the case of the Association for Molecular Pathology v. Myriad Genetics, Inc., the Supreme Court of the United States ruled that human genes cannot be patented in the U.S., because DNA is a "product of nature." The Court decided that, because nothing new is created when discovering a gene, there is no intellectual property to protect, so patents cannot be granted. Prior to this ruling, more than 4,300 human genes were patented. The Supreme Court's decision invalidated those gene patents, making the genes accessible for research and for commercial genetic testing.

The Supreme Court's ruling did allow, however, that **DNA manipulated in a lab is eligible to be patented** because DNA sequences altered by humans are not found in nature. The Court specifically mentioned the ability to patent a type of DNA known as complementary DNA (cDNA). This syn-

---

23   https://medlineplus.gov/genetics/understanding/testing/genepatents/

thetic DNA is produced from the molecule that serves as the instructions for making proteins (called messenger RNA)."

In other words, if a genome extracted from Patricia Cori is utilized in the lab to make a modified version of that same genome, they then actually own the fundamental genetic information from my DNA. Correct? To unwrap the medical and legal terminology in that statement, we need to concentrate on the glaring question that remains unanswered after the Supreme Court's ruling.

The Court ruled that DNA altered in a laboratory is eligible to be patented.

This DNA, or cDNA, produced by synthetic messenger RNA which they have produced in laboratories, and now have injected into billions of people, can be patented. The glaring question that has yet to find a definitive legal judgement is this: would that "complimentary" DNA they CRISPR-modify in the lab and then inject into your body, via mRNA inoculation, render your mutated DNA their property, since it is their patented gene modification technology that is altering it? Because, if the answer to that question is yes, as the Supreme Court ruling implies, then Big Pharma will own your DNA, just like they own strains of GMO foods and plants—lock, stock and barrel.

To be "owned" at the cellular level? That takes our understanding of slavery to a whole other level, now, doesn't it?

CRISPR has been used in plants and tested on animals before, with particular emphasis on the development of biotechnological products that aspire to "improve" the natural biology of any given organism. We are already eating these GMO products in plant and livestock food supplies. But only now (that we know of) are human beings being genetically re-engineered by injection—the Covid-19 mRNA synthetic injection that, for all intents and purposes, is turning the population into a whole new species of genetically modified humans. I shudder to think what actual plans are in place, and what horrifying experiments are already being performed on animals, by bioengineering scientists who want to "tinker" with genes, to see what they do and how they react.

Where does this end?

Despite the ethics debate surrounding gene modification in humans, it has already been applied in China. A researcher at the Shezhen Southern University of Science and Technology, Dr. He Jiankui, recently gloated publicly over how he had successfully created designer twin babies, using gene-editing CRISPR-CAS9 technology. The procedure was performed on embryos before they were implanted into the mother's uterus, with the excuse that experimental gene modification was utilized as a means to make the babies more resistant to various diseases, including the autoimmune condition, HIV. Apparently, according to China's State Media, his work was performed on yet a third infant, before he was sentenced to three years in prison.

Recently, I read in the media that he had been released. So much for ethics.

We can be confident that Dr. Jiankui is not the only one who has been engineering embryos in those secret labs. He just went public with it, which prompted the government to take action to silence any global dialogue, at least temporarily, that may have emerged as to the ethics and morality of designer genome sequencing in vitro.

Hitler's dream has truly come to fruition, hasn't it? Imagine what he could have done with this terrifying technology, if it had been available at the time of his quest for the perfected Aryan race? I do believe that he reincarnated into the late 20th century, and is walking today, in the leathery skin of one of those who are intent upon mutating the human race into a transhumanist nightmare.

And then there are customized "Cas9 proteins," that do not actually go in and cut the DNA. They are designed to simply turn genes on and off, like a light switch. CRISPRa and CRISPRi, referred to as "base editors," can change one letter of the DNA code to another, altering the language of the DNA, and hacking the God Code.

Is that how they can splice in the Luciferian construct—the "language" of 666?

Essentially, this discovery, the CRISPER-Cas9 system (which they like to refer to as "DNA repair machinery") involves the utilization of two essential molecules that are capable of mutating the DNA. These are:

- Cas9: an enzyme that performs in such a way that it can cut into the double helix in a select location, allowing the researcher to then remove snippets of the genome, and potentially add other genetic material
- Guide RNA (gRNA): it binds to DNA and guides the Cas9 to the exact point of the intervention in the DNA sequence. The Cas9 follows the guide RNA to the location required, and then cuts into the genome. From there, they are enabled to alter the entire DNA genome: locate, snip, cut and paste and the change in the divine blueprint is done.

Why would anyone be willing to accept that? How much of what goes on in these university and secret underground laboratories ever even makes it into the mainstream arena? Are we really supposed to embrace the idea that all these technological impositions on our natural biological systems are for "the good of humanity?" When one thinks about the plan to convert Homo sapiens to a "new, improved" version, it is clear that the tools are found in the bioengineers' laboratories, and that what they suggest is the "future" is the now.

This war is not territorial—remember that. The real war against humanity is playing out in the laboratories of the world.

An article published March 30, 2022[24] on the National Library of Medicine's website, reported that genetically modified pig kidneys had been transplanted into a brain-dead person, and that the experiment was paving the way for clinical trials. According to a statement from the surgeon in question, Jayme Locke of the University of Alabama in Birmingham, they "transplanted kidneys from a pig donor with 10 gene edits (10 GE). Four genes were knocked out: three related to carbohydrate antigens known to cause hyperacute rejection (α 1-3 Gal, β 1-4 Gal, CMAH) and one involved the deletion of the pig growth hormone receptor (GHR). There were also six human transgene insertions. These edits were designed to further modulate the human immune system to help decrease inflammation (hCD47, hHO-1), and regulate complement (hCD46, hDAF) and coagulation (human thrombomodulin, human endothelial protein C receptor)."

She stated that they "launched the University of Alabama Xenotransplant Program in 2016 and invested heavily in building out the necessary infrastructure in order to make xenotransplantation a reality for the many patients in need. This included the development and implementation of a pathogen-free facility in which the donor source animal (pig) can be bred and raised in an environment that decreases/ eliminates the risk of viral or other disease transmission to human recipients from these pig organs."

What possibly could go wrong with that?

Ethics appear to be off the table completely now, but there is almost no outcry from humanity. Pig hearts and kidneys as spare parts for humans (failed experiments, I might add), human embryos merged with mice genomes, splicing, dicing, cutting and pasting . . . all of it is against the natural order of Creation.

I do not understand how human beings with even a drop of awareness of spirit, soul and evolution can perform such genetic aberrations on animals and human beings. They are basically driving the evolution

---

24   https://www.ncbi.nlm.nih.gov/pmc/articles/PMC9005640/

of man and animal mutations, fiendishly playing God with souls, cutting and pasting the genome of one into the other, to achieve freakish chimeras that will walk the Earth of the future. They are raising animals, probably humans too, for experimentation—for body parts—and then experimenting on the genome of each and the other, to achieve the mad scientist's dream: designer biological organisms: half-man/half-bird, pig, bat … woolly mammoth?

Who knows where their insanity leads?

*

It was a mere ten years ago that Doudna's team of researchers first unveiled its discovery of CRISPR gene editing, one of the most life-altering discoveries in the history of humankind's experimentation and discovery in the field of biology. It is hard to imagine how dramatically it catapulted forward research into editing the DNA of living cells, and with so little difficulty, endowing just about every bioengineering researcher in a lab coat with the life-altering tools to actually guide evolution in the direction they want to take it.

That is truly stunning, when you think about it.

I do not deny that these scientific inventions to alter DNA can and do have some benign applications, treating rare genetic diseases by "editing" out the culprit segment of DNA and altering it to remove the error, if that is even possible. However, seeing where the field of genetics has taken science in these last few decades, one has to admit that the potential for more sinister applications seem to far outweigh the beneficial ones.

We know that genetic modification was taking place years before CRISPR was first unveiled in 2012, but the technology was costly and progress was slow. However, this relatively new discovery has made the invasive manipulation of plant, animal and human genomes far easier, and far less expensive.

We have learned to live with genetically modified foods, no matter how much we try to avoid them. So-called "organically grown" foods are still cross-pollinating with fields of those that are treated. It is so difficult to isolate one from the other, because nature knows how to carry seed from one field to another.

We know about GMO mosquitos, bees and other insect species that are supposedly being modified for purposes that we still do not trust, nor should we, and although we try not to think about it, we do also understand that those secret laboratories are filled with mutated animals, as well as "cell lines" from supposedly "aborted" human fetuses—a practice that spans decades.

How can we ignore this? How can we allow this absolutely inhumane practice to be carried out in laboratories? How can anyone accept aborted fetal cells, reportedly kept alive in laboratories from fifty years ago but much more likely taken from countless aborted babies every day—into their bodies?

The explanation available from medical/biogenetics professionals is that viruses need cells to grow and that they grow better in cells from humans than animals. **They are using humans to grow viruses.** If this is acceptable to everyone receiving vaccines for varicella (chickenpox), rubella, hepatitis A, rabies, and Covid-19, then it would appear that we have abandoned ethics completely.

And that is not such a stretch, considering what horrors are emerging from the laboratories. It is not a stretch at all.

Let us grasp what that really means, and use what we glean from it to inform as many as we can what we are learning from their sacrifice.

Chapter 16

Lucifer In

If ever you have had the increasingly rare opportunity to observe glowing fireflies on a warm summer evening, you know you've witnessed something rare and magical . . . something that you know, in your heart and soul, should be protected, revered and held sacred. For some years, in my forested backyard in my country home outside Rome, I would watch them flittering among the trees, sparkling testimony to a mystical and wondrous display of nature's wisdom and perfection—with just a touch of whimsy. I was always awed and amazed at the spectacle, and never missed the opportunity to sit quietly beneath the trees those warm summer nights, when they would appear.

I always felt that just by reading my body electric they knew how much it meant to me to be in their presence.

Surely the firefly has added a rich texture to faerie lore and mysticism over the ages, all but gone now, as those pristine glens and forests become trampled, destroyed or simply razed to the ground by the encroachment of ruthless developers and the blind eye of industry.

Researchers' studies indicate that the firefly's light is something of a mating call, but that it can also be a warning to predators that they possess a chemical defense mechanism that can fend off any potential enemy. In the deep waters of our oceans, where light barely penetrates, several species illuminate their navigational fields with the most brilliant, colorful bioluminescent arrays, and there too, they warn predators to move on, and leave them alone, lest they get zapped with enough voltage to fry them, mid-stream.

How fascinating that nature can communicate offense, defense and other interspecies signals so efficiently, especially by way of electrical "no entry" flashing lights!

If only man would do just that: leave nature alone.

Just ... leave ... it ... alone.

Alas, the illusive firefly is disappearing—not only due to pollution, the razing of the forests and other factors, but because it has become another casualty in the mad scientists' laboratories.

According to researchers, the source of bioluminescence within the firefly, and an estimated ten thousand or more other species, is derived from a tiny molecule bio-engineering researchers have chosen to name "Luciferin," which Wikipedia defines as:

"A class of small-molecule substrates that react with oxygen in the presence of a Luciferase (an enzyme) to release energy in the form of light."

Needless-to-say, once the geneticists, molecular biologists and medical researchers discovered and isolated these bioluminescent molecules, they wasted no time determining how they could apply them in vitro and in vivo (bioluminescent sequencing). Their experiments, involving splicing Luciferin into the genome of laboratory rats and other animals, have reportedly been highly successful. We have neon pink glowing cats now, and laboratory rats that glow in the dark.

This, we are told, is "progress."

According to an article in in the National Institute of Health's National Library of Medicine:[25]

"Non-invasive *in vivo* fluorescence imaging of small animals as a method in preclinical research has developed considerably in recent years, and is used widely across a variety of disciplines such as oncology and infectious disease research. It provides a means of detecting a fluorescent signal within a living animal reflecting specific, mostly disease-related, processes, such as parts of the host immune response, inflammation, cancer growth or presence of pathogens. As well as offering many advantages as a stand-alone technique, it can also be highly complementary to other imaging modalities. This review discusses aspects of light distribution in animal tissue and the implications on in vivo imaging; the most widely used imaging techniques including planar and tomographic imaging; advantages and challenges of the techniques; fluorescent contrast agents and some examples of applications."

Let us consider, for a moment, that these experiments have now evolved to the point where they can inject the "Lucifer-in" compound into human tissue. Molecular biologists and the group of researchers interested in this application, insist that, too, would be "non-invasive." How this form of experimentation, which turns a helpless laboratory animal into a neon sign, can be called "non-invasive" eludes me but, clearly, we human beings do not all hold to the same standards and morality when it comes to the sovereignty of life forms on this planet.

---

25   Zelmer A, Ward TH. Noninvasive fluorescence imaging of small animals. J Microsc. 2013 Oct; 252(1):8-15. doi: 10.1111/jmi.12063. Epub 2013 Jul 11. PMID: 23841905.s

Can Luciferase be scanned? According to the FDA[26], the unsettling answer is a resounding "Yes."

"The luciferase-tagged G proteins (RSV-GA and RSV-GB) acted as "bait" to antibodies against the G proteins in samples of human serum (the clear fluid of blood without red or white cells), causing them to bind to the tagged proteins. The scientists added special protein beads that bind the antibodies with the luciferase-tagged G proteins to the bottom of a plastic test well. Then they added luciferin and measured the amount of light released when it interacted with luciferase, which enabled them to calculate how strong the antibody response was to the G proteins."

If you investigate any one of many proliferating biotech companies, such as *Creative Biogene*, you will find, readily available, information that should make your skin crawl. They are spelling out it, in plain sight (where they love to hide the truth), veiled in scientific jargon and confusing rhetoric. This one of many companies offers a smorgasbord of "pre-made virus particles," cloning kits and other treacherous biotech tools that (of course) are not meant to cross the ethics barrier.

Pre-made test viruses, a dual Luciferase assay kit (to observe cells using what they call "luminometers"), adjuvants, gene-editing kits, mRNA synthesis kits—all of this is right out in the open, for sale and readily available. They even openly describe their "cloning kits," for interested laboratories to clone DNA fragments, but, of course we know that cloning DNA "fragments" leads to cloning of entire organisms.

Step right up, ladies and gentlemen! Creative Biogene offers FreeClone™ Seamless Cloning Kit to streamline the interested laboratory in its research and development.

*

---

26   https://www.fda.gov/vaccines-blood-biologics/science-research-biologics/luciferase-immunoprecipitation-system-lips-assay-rapid-simple-and-sensitive-test-detect-antibody

Geneticists report that Luciferase is easily diffused in the blood brain barrier, the blood placenta barrier and the blood testis barrier. Make note of that little piece of information, especially since the PCR tests used in the on-going Covid testing protocols has administrators twirling an oversized swab around in the back of the nasopharyngeal cavity, as close to the blood brain barrier as it can get. There are several reported cases now where that barrier has been punctured because of that invasive procedure, with devastating consequences.

According to an article published in the National Library of Medicine:[27]

"Luciferase is likely to be a useful marker for monitoring virus dissemination and gene expression in experimental animals because assays for enzymatic activity are extremely sensitive and backgrounds are low in all tissues. In mice inoculated intraperitoneally (i.p.) with Ad5-Luc 3, luciferase activity was detected in the liver, spleen, kidney, and lung. A single i.p. inoculation of mice with Ad5-Luc 3 was sufficient to raise anti-luciferase antibody and Ad5 neutralizing antibody which persisted for at least 8 weeks. Even in the presence of circulating anti-luciferase and Ad5 neutralizing antibodies, luciferase activity could be detected in the livers, spleens, and kidneys of mice inoculated i.p. a second time with Ad5-Luc 3."

Strip away the scientific, medical terminology and what we read here is that they are using Lucifer-in/ase, among other things, to monitor how viruses spread with the organism, and to record what genetic

---

27   Pub med, 1993, Monitoring Foreign Gene Expression by a Human Adenovirus-Based Vector Using the Firefly Luciferase Gene as a Reporter: Mittal, McDermott, Johnson, Prevec, Graham https://pubmed.ncbi.nlm.nih.gov/8388142/

anomalies occur as a response to their experiments on laboratory animals.

If that is the case, then it is not a stretch to assume that the Luciferin/Luciferase system is being introduced into people's bodies as part of the inoculation program to track and record whether or not they have accepted the mRNA injection.

Clearly, there is much more going on here than a global pandemic.

Enter, Bill Gates.

Chapter 17

Microsoft Patent WO2020060606A1

"And he causeth all, both small and great,
rich and poor, free and bond,
to receive a mark in their right hand, or in their foreheads:
And that no man might buy or sell,
save he that had the mark, or the name of the beast,
or the number of his name.
Here is wisdom.
Let him that hath understanding
count the number of the beast:
for it is the number of a man;
and his number is six hundred threescore and six."
—*Revelation 13, King James Bible*

Bill Gates would have us believe that the wide-reaching scope of the Gates Foundation's "philanthropic" investments in the exorbitantly profitable pharmaceutical and bioengineering industries holds only altruistic visions for the advancement of civilization . . . if one can call "altruistic" using wealth and influence to lobby politicians and global influencers to push your agendas, while funding pharmaceutical and bioengineering labs to create whatever you see fit to inject into the population.

That is the case with Covid-19, which saw billions of people taking their "vaccine," for a yet-to-be-identified virus that, remember, had a 99.7% cure rate across the board—even higher, for people who managed to get certain medications that, mysteriously, were made illegal shortly after the injection programs began in countries around the world.

Now, that is what you call having a "corner on the market."

Despite attempts to distract truth seekers and the disinterested masses alike from what we can define as "factual information" provided by the patent office itself, in March 2021 (under the presidency of Bill Gates), the corporate behemoth, Microsoft Technology Licensing LLC, procured United States Patent Number WO 2020 060606A1, which bears the title: "*Cryptocurrency System Using Body Activity Data.*"

It does not escape me, or many others, that the filing number allocated to this particular patent just happens to have, embedded within it, the Luciferian vibrational signature code: 666. We are supposed to believe that this is mere coincidence, and nothing more. But, bearing in mind that the dictionary defines the term, coincidence, as "a striking occurrence of two or more events happening at one time," it feels less like a haphazard concurrence of events and more like a very deliberate choice that this transhumanist patent would bear the 666.

Personally, I doubt that the well-laid plans of the Cabal, with its agendas, programs and social impositions, leave anything to chance, but I guess it is possible—highly unlikely, but possible.

I suppose these, too, are coincidences:

H.R. 666: Anti-Racism in Public Health Act of 2021[28]

This bill establishes within the Centers for Disease Control and Prevention (CDC) a National Center on Antiracism and Health and a law enforcement violence prevention program. Among other activities, the new center must declare racism a public health crisis, collect and

---

28   https://www.congress.gov/bill/117th-congress/house-bill/666

analyze data, and administer research and grant programs to address racism and its impact on health and well-being.

Additionally, the bill specifically directs the CDC's National Center for Injury Prevention and Control, in coordination with the Department of Justice and other relevant stakeholders, to carry out the law enforcement violence prevention program by conducting research and supporting other activities pertaining to law enforcement violence and public health.

*"Racism" is a "public health crisis," under the jurisdiction of the CDC: the Center for Disease Control? Really?

H.R. 666: Department of Homeland Security Insider Threat and Mitigation Act of 2017[29]

H.R. 666 requires the Secretary of the Department of Homeland Security (DHS) to establish an insider threat program within the Department, mandates employee education and training programs, and establishes an internal DHS Steering Committee to manage and coordinate the Department's activities related to insider threats.

The bill requires that the Insider Threat Program provide training and education for Department personnel to identify, prevent, mitigate, and respond to insider threat risks to the Department's critical assets; provide investigative support regarding potential insider threats that may pose a risk to the Department's critical assets; and conduct risk mitigation activities for insider threats.

The bill requires the Steering Committee, chaired by the Under Secretary for Intelligence and Analysis, to meet regularly and discuss cases and issues related to insider threats to the Department's critical assets. The bill also requires the Under Secretary, not later than one year after enactment, to develop a strategy to identify, prevent, mitigate, and respond to insider threats to the Department's critical assets and develop a plan to implement insider threat measures.

29   https://www.govtrack.us/congress/bills/115/hr666/summary

H.R. 6666 116th Congress: COVID–19 Testing, Reaching, And Contacting Everyone (TRACE) Act[30]
To authorize the Secretary of Health and Human Services to award grants to eligible entities to conduct diagnostic testing for COVID–19, and related activities such as contact tracing, through mobile health units and, as necessary, at individuals' residences, and for other purposes.

Senate Bill 666 (2021-2022): Update Reqs./Advance Health Care Directives[31]
An act updating requirements for health care powers of attorney and advance health care directives, and authorizing the secretary of state to receive electronic filings of advance health care directives.

If we adhere to the dictionary definition, then yes, there **is** a definite co-incidence surrounding this 666 code, playing out the Bible's warnings with eerie precision. There are two distinct possibilities here. Either the Good Book provided a remarkably accurate and absolutely prophetic window on the 21st century, describing how we would be faced with this mark being implanted within our bodies, or the force pushing the Luciferian Agenda is following the Bible to the letter, fueling their agendas with fear of Biblical prophecy. Either way, the prediction in Scripture that has mankind being imprinted with the Mark of the Beast, and the transhumanist agenda that has us being electronically monitored from within, or from worn sensors, is all too terribly co-incidental to be ignored.

From reading the abstract on the white paper, we know that this latest "contribution" to civilization involves interfacing human biological activity with artificial intelligence, and that it is designed to function as an AI social credit monitoring system—controlling mind, emotion and body of the human being.

---

30   https://www.congress.gov/bill/116th-congress/house-bill/6666/text
31   https://lrs.sog.unc.edu/billsum/s-666-2021-2022

Before attempting to unwrap just what this AI patent is all about, I would like to draw your attention to the actual patent code itself and what appears to me to be an obvious, in-your-face numerical reference to what it really stands for, and what function it is intent upon performing, with regard to the technological interface of man and machine, via the transhumanist agenda.

In this government-issued patent are found the underpinnings of numerology and underwritten codes that convey satanic imprinting and subliminal mind control. It is comprised of:

- WO: (World Order)
- 2020: (the year the Covid 19 "virus" mysteriously appeared on the world stage)
- 060606 (666: the biblical "Mark of the Beast")
- A1 (also transcribed in many fonts as AI – Artificial Intelligence)

It could not be clearer to me that there is nothing random about the patent number assigned to this futuristic technology, which, of course, exists not in the future, but in the right now of their technological capabilities. It is a coded classification that communicates its essential purpose: that from the year 2020, the One World Order will introduce the Mark of the Beast through or as Artificial Intelligence.

We are seeing how everything links together in the transhumanist agenda: the invented pandemic, the injection program, and futuristic technology to merge implanted software within human beings to manipulate and control them, while rewriting the human genome. Let us examine just what elements are found in this patent, designed to allow remote access to us all, under the guise of giving us automaton access to cryptocurrency awards, apparently earned for "good behavior," all the while hooking us into a freedom-gutting, Big Brother social credit system.

The patent's documentation provides this opening statement of intent, or "abstract":

"Human body activity associated with a task provided to a user may be used in a mining process of a cryptocurrency system. A server may provide a task to a device of a user which is communicatively coupled to the server. A sensor communicatively coupled to or comprised in the device of the user may sense body activity of the user. Body activity data may be generated based on the sensed body activity of the user. The crypto currency system communicatively coupled to the device of the user may verify if the body activity data satisfies one or more conditions set by the cryptocurrency system and award cryptocurrency to the user whose body activity data is verified."[32]

In this proposed initiative, which mirrors China's already operative social credit score system, the philanthrope, Bill Gates, and his team are looking to merge our minds and bodies with artificial intelligence, in ways they would want us to believe are non-invasive whatsoever. But anyone with half a mind knows that AI invades every aspect our lives and that it is stealing more from us with every day that passes, with every new application in medicine, industry, technology and augmented, artificial reality.

Despite public outcry from the awakened, the Microsoft team aims to reassure us all that nowhere in the patent do they talk about implanting a microchip, but that, rather, the patent has to do with using harmless "sensors" near the body to monitor everything about us.

It is meant to be helpful in every way. Surely we simple folk, the Plebeians, can see that, can't we? Klaus Schwab, head of the World Economic Forum, seems to think so. He speaks openly about the merging of technology with humans as an inevitability of our evolution, touting

---

32   https://patents.google.com/patent/WO2020060606A1/en

how our future health will be determined by all manner of technological intervention: wearables, implants, all linking up with the Internet of
Things and Bodies. Schwab wants us all to embrace our transition from
Human 1.0 to Human 2.0 as a progression from inferior to superior
beings, one that involves giving more control of our mental and physical health, our consumption, and our place in civilization to technology
. . . whereby we let go of any foolish notions, apparently, that we know
best what is good for our own lives and our very souls.

Will "wearable technology" and sensors be monitoring the synthetic mRNA mechanism already inserted in billions of people through the
injection? The timing of these two systems—implantation of DNA-altering software through injection and "sensors" designed to read body
systems—is too perfect to ignore, even if those behind both would have
us believe it is all a big coincidence, including the unmissable 666 embedded in the government patent's code.

According to the abstract available in the patent material, the technology's objective is to create a monitoring system that will allow the
body's movements, the heat it generates, hormonal changes, heart rate
and even mind waves to be read by a computer, cell phone, or any other
"device" whose chip, supposedly outside the body in a nearby upgraded
device, will be programmed to interface with all bodily functions. The
data picked up by said sensors will then be fed into computer central
by the device that reads you, and registers the data gleaned from your
body functions and activity, including the electromagnetic charges from
your neural networks, which monitor your response to stimuli. From
these, with artificial intelligence mapping your behavioral progress and
your thoughts in every second of every day, you earn digital money:
crypto currency "rewards" that you will eventually be allowed to spend
on whatever Big Brother allows you to purchase. You earn cryptocurrency, that is, if your thoughts are in line with the company line: if you
eat what the government wants you to eat—most definitely "bugs" and

215

gene altering, poisonous foodstuff—say what the government wants you to say and, above all, succumb to any and all of their vaccines and synthetic injectables whenever they deem necessary.

That, my friends, is what patent WO2020060606A1 really holds in store for a consenting populace. One can only wonder what you earn if your thoughts are **not** in line, and if you dare attempt rebellion against a Microsoft technology you were told was designed to serve your best interests.

Details regarding the scope of this patent can be found in the white paper[33] itself. It reads:

"Some exemplary embodiments of the present disclosure may use human body activity associated with a task provided to a user as a solution to "mining" challenges in cryptocurrency systems. For example, a brain wave or body heat emitted from the user when the user performs the task provided by an information or service provider, such as viewing advertisement or using certain internet services, can be used in the mining process. Instead of massive computation work required by some conventional cryptocurrency systems, data generated based on the body activity of the user can be a proof-of-work, and therefore, a user can solve the computationally difficult problem unconsciously. Accordingly, certain exemplary embodiments of the present disclosure may reduce computational energy for the mining process as well as make the mining process faster.

Systems, methods, and hardware aspects of computer readable storage media are provided herein for a cryptocurrency system using human body activity data. According to various embodiments of the present disclosure, a server may provide a task to a device of a user which is communicatively coupled to the server. A sensor communicatively coupled to

33   https://patents.google.com/patent/WO2020060606A1/en

or comprised in the device of the user may sense body activity of the user. Body activity data may be generated based on the sensed body activity of the user. A cryptocurrency system communicatively coupled to the device of the user may verify whether or not the body activity data satisfies one or more conditions set by the cryptocurrency system, and award cryptocurrency to the user whose body activity data is verified.

Examples are implemented as a computer process, a computing system, or as an article of manufacture such as a device, computer program product, or computer readable medium. According to one aspect, the computer program product is a computer storage medium readable by a computer system and encoding a computer program comprising instructions for executing a computer process.

Communication network may include any wired or wireless connection, the internet, or any other form of communication. Communication network may enable communication between various computing resources or devices, servers, and systems. Various implementations of communication network may employ different types of networks, for example, but not limited to, computer networks, telecommunications networks (e.g., cellular), mobile wireless data networks, and any combination of these and/or other networks.

User device may include any device capable of processing and storing data/information and communicating over communication network. For example, user device may include personal computers, servers, cell phones, tablets, laptops, smart devices (e.g. smart watches or smart televisions.)

Sensors may be configured to sense the body activity of user. Sensor may be a separate component from user device and be operably and/or communicatively connected to user device. Alternatively, sensor may be included and integrated

217

in user device. For example, user device may be a wearable device having sensor therein. The sensor may transmit information/data to user device. Sensor may include, for example, but not limited to, functional magnetic resonance imaging (fMRI) scanners or sensors, electroencephalography (EEG) sensors, near infrared spectroscopy (NIRS) sensors, heart rate monitors, thermal sensors, optical sensors, radio frequency (RF) sensors, ultrasonic sensors, cameras, or any other sensor or scanner that can measure or sense body activity or scan human body. For instance, the fMRI may measure body activity by detecting changes associated with blood flow. The fMRI may use a magnetic field and radio waves to create detailed images of the body (e.g. blood flow in the brain to detect areas of activity)."

Since it is safe to assume that none of us will be walking around attached to an fMRI or an EEG machine, it isn't a stretch to realize that what they are really talking about here is **inserting** a sensor, in the form of a microchip, that will perform all these functions. Although Microsoft denies it, calling the idea that Gates has patented an insertable microchip a "conspiracy theory," we need to read between a few lines to draw the real intention from the broad-ranging terminology of the patent.

The claim here is that this would involve an external sensor specifically made for detecting and keeping track of human biometrics, such as implantable chips already developed by several tech companies in Europe, already in use by the Swedish company, Epicenter. But that is a ruse. After all, a microchip implant is the best sensor for biometrics, as it is literally inside the body. Clever of Microsoft, though, to sidestep that tiny detail for the sake of patent approval, and distracting the public.

True, patent WO2020060606A1 does not reference injectable microchips, but it does imply as much with regard to "sensors and scanners" that can measure body activity. Lo and behold, we have *ID 2020 Alliance*, operating under the flag of GAVI, the organization funded by the Gates and Rockefeller Foundations for "the well-being of humanity around the world." The digital identity program, cooked up by none other than Microsoft and Big Pharma, aims to monitor every single human being's immunization record by inserting chips into the physical body, with particular emphasis on the children.

Ah, but if insertable chips are not enough, we have a group of researchers from the Massachusetts Institute of Technology, who have found a novel way of addressing the problem of keeping track of vaccinations. Their engineers claim to have developed a way to store medical information under the skin, by delivering tiny dots of dye, along with a vaccine, by microneedle patches. Needless-to-say, the dye, which is invisible to the naked eye, can be read later using a specially adapted smartphone.

"Tiny dots," I ask, of Luciferin?

I remember when microchipping was introduced as "identifying integrated circuits," which they injected under the skin of our beloved pets and those poor laboratory animals. Developed by the VeriChip corporation and brought to the market in 1990, these were the first RFID (radio frequency identification) chips I'd ever heard of, and I was deeply disturbed that they were being forced on pet owners. The tracking system was sold to us as a "pet recovery" system, even though we were assured that it was not a GPS device per se, and that it could not actually track little Bowser if he strayed. We were assured that it would only serve to identify him once he was found. That is a pretty convoluted declaration of intent, if you ask me.

The chip also had the capability of recording the animal's vaccine history. Does that ring a bell for anyone?

It was pretty obvious to me at the time, I believe it was in the mid-nineties, that they were testing those implantable chips on animals first, as a trial run for what they had planned for humans, down the line. I was incensed, but no one else seemed too bothered at all. It was such an unnecessary invasion of our freedom, being forced to accept this untested and invasive technology into the bodies of our beloved animals, and we had no idea, despite assurance to the contrary, of what long term health issues it could provoke. In fact, there were countless occasions of adverse reactions around the insertion point, when that rice-sized foreign object migrated to other parts of the body, which it reportedly did all the time. There were cancers, infections and God knows what other side effects, but we had no choice. The veterinarians were all conscripted and the mandates were put in place.

In Italy, we were required to register our animals with local authorities; the chip was, of course, required for that too. No chip, no travel, was another constraint put upon the non-compliant human who did not want to subject his beloved pet to the unnecessary device. At first it was voluntary, so I naturally refused, but soon after they made it mandatory, which I had no choice but to accept, since my beloved Shitzu had to fly with me on a few occasions. That required a **"vaccine passport,"** which could only be obtained—you guessed it—with the chip in place. It broke my heart, watching the Vet inject her tiny body with the transponder, knowing it was anything but innocuous and realizing how my fur baby was an unwilling volunteer in a preliminary trial, for a tracking device whose target audience was not animals, really, but humans. I knew immediately that it was a test system for what would be coming down the proverbial pike for human tracking, and wondered why no one else seemed to care.

They called me paranoid.

Eleven years after the introduction and widespread application of the animal RFID chip, Dr. Richard Seeling, a research for Verichip's parent company, Applied Digital, supposedly just woke up one morning with a revelation: that their RFID chip could help humans! Imagine that? Unbeknownst to anyone in the company, he supposedly secretly implanted one into his own arm. Once he knew he was fine, the story goes, he told his colleagues what he had done and bingo! The human microchip was born.

Needless-to-say, Microsoft-of-the-external-sensors has partnered with Verichip manufacturer, the Digital Angel Corporation, since 2008.

The "Digital Angel?" What an odd name for a corporation. Are they referring to the "fallen angel," I wonder?

A Stockholm-based company, Epicenter, has now launched an RFID chip that stores your Covid-19 vaccine passport, which we are seeing increasingly mandated by countries around the world, particularly in Europe. It is so clear that they want to make it impossible for us to travel without a chip, just like our animals, which will verify from within whether we have taken the "vaccine." It utilizes NFC, ("near field communication" technology), which makes you compatible with any nearby NFC-compatible smartphone. How convenient is that, you ask, to wearing your Covid-19 vaccination passport in your arm, or in a chip inserted below the skin between the thumb and forefinger?

Epicenter has now begun successfully microchipping its employees. It is not mandatory as of yet, but it appears over 150 employees just could not wait to get theirs. They even held "chipping parties" at the office! Surely I am not the only one to see a pattern here: ice cream cones for kids getting the Covid "vaccine"; power shakes for people taking the chip, lottery tickets . . . you name it.

Advocates cite the benefits of accepting the chip into your body as:

- *Identification:* Passport, driver's license and all your identification rolled into one handy place.
- *Access:* Why carry around those pesky keys and plastic access codes when you can just wave your hand over a sensor and open the door?
- *Memberships:* Clubs, libraries, resorts

- *Health records:* Insurance companies will love that!
- *Theft protection:* No more fretting that a thug is going to poach your wallet or rip your purse off your shoulder.
- *Tracking:* If you get lost, someone will know where you are.

It is all about control—plain and simple.

Epicenter's website indicates Microsoft as one of its partners in a program entitled "Epicenter Accelerate." When it comes to vaccines, microchipping and bioengineering, it seems the illustrious Bill Gates is always there, accelerating the transhumanist agenda.

Dr. Carl Sanders, who was part of the General Electric engineering team that first invented the microchip, became the leader of the project way back in 1968. He claimed that, originally, the project was designed around the creation of a microcircuit that could reconnect the nerve endings in a severed human spine. They were unsuccessful. Soon after, they were approached by the government. In his own words, Dr. Sanders reported how that came down, as follows:

"Some men came to us that we were to find out were from the government, they were from the CIA and FBI. They asked us to design a microchip for identification. This was to be used not in human beings, not in animals but to be put in drug shipments to catch drug dealers. They came with a lot of money. And we were willing to do whatever we could. I want to tell you that at this point in time, I was not a Christian and did not want anything to do with Christians. We had developed the first identification device, and it was completed in the early 70's. They came back to us and said we want something better than that.

We said 'if you give us enough money we can develop something better'. I was not alone; we had over a hundred people involved in it. Some from General Electric, some from

Motorola, some were from the Bell laboratories, some were from Boston Medical Center, and some were from Stanford University. My responsibility was as project leader or senior project engineer. We began to work on the design of the microchip. When it was completed it was .75 mm in diameter 7mm long. It was the size of one-fourth of a grain of rice. Note again, I was not a Christian, and there were no Christians there. They said they wanted it to have a power source and wanted it to emit a signal. And they wanted us to use Lithium as a battery source.

Lithium is used in wristwatches and a lot of places. I designed into the microchip a little charging socket that would charge the battery. This sounds like a lot of technical things coming together but bear with me while I explain. You will see what God laid out about this microchip.

I needed a temperature change to be able to charge the battery. A change in temperature will cause current to flow to the charging socket that will charge the battery. We began to investigate to find out where in the body does the temperature changes most rapidly. We spent over a million dollars in tax payer's money. And when the result came back, there was a lot of information. We divided it up among three teams. We came back with that information. It was determined that there are two places in the body that are ideal for the microchip. One is just below the hairline on **the forehead**; every mother checks their children's temperature right there. I never saw a mother check the temperature on the ankle. The other place was the hand, preferably **the right hand**, because most people are right-handed. This did not bother me, and it didn't bother anyone else on the team. The hand seemed like a good place—nobody wanted it on the forehead. And so, the design worked, and everything was completed, the microchip was done. You are seeing it right now—some on discovery channel presentation. There are people that have received it as of now; it is real, not something that is coming way down the road.

I want to tell you is that this is real. The microchip implants are real. Credit cards are failing; they can be counterfeited, the new smart card can be counterfeited, they can be stolen, lost, all kinds of things can happen to a card. But you cannot lose your hand. Very quickly, they are going to move to the hand. No matter what anyone says to you, you cannot take it. God's words say you cannot take it.

Today there have been over 15,000 babies that have been given the microchip. Many companies are using the microchip as identification in their top-level employees. The Immigration and Naturalization Service has a better passport, the human hand. So many of these things are around us. We talked about the signs of the new world order; God has spelt out just exactly how as it is going today in the new world order. Satan desires to have a one-world government. From the time he fell, he said he wanted a one-world government. He wants to replace God. So we see a government put together by men, we see a one-world government.

The signs of the time are all around us..."[34]

*

They have been testing the implanted RFID chip on domesticated animals for at least twenty years now. We have asked no questions, and allowed them free access, so that veterinarians could store their vaccine data and, supposedly, to identify our beloved pets when they get lost. They are now in Phase Two of the experiment. They now have willing

---

34   https://voiceoutworld.wordpress.com/2020/05/12/dr-carl-sanders-the-man-who-invented-rfid-microchip-666-speaks-out/

human guinea pigs yielding sovereignty over their own being, allowing compliant doctors and, for some, the very company for whom they work, to insert the chip into their hand, or arm, so that they are enabled to unlock doors and perform magic tricks just waving an appendage over a sensor. Obviously, they are not at all concerned that their important data, medical history and vaccine record will all be recorded in their new hi-tech implant toy, or that everything they thought was private will now be accessible to anyone with a simple scanning device.

Who gets access to the data? Law enforcement? Employers? Controlled media? Dark forces in the government? And what do they plan to do with it? What happens when a hacker gets hold of you? Imagine how important it will be then to know what kind of electromagnetic technology is near you, or walking by? We know that hackers can swipe your credit card data, just by standing next to you in line, or passing near you in the grocery store—even with your cards hidden in your purse or wallet! Imagine how easy it will be hack your chip, duplicate the data onto their own, and effectively pass themselves off as you?

Frightening stuff. If the patent holders have their way, you will have your social credit system activated by human activity, thoughts, pulse and other body functions—supposedly monitored by sensors from "devices" outside the body. But we see the writing on the wall. The devices will be implanted. We have seen the implementation of embedded chips, tested on animals for decades now, being implanted in gleefully compliant human beings, who can't wait to be able to simply wave a hand to open a locked door or buy a Coke from the office vending machine. You will have injectable sensors that use tiny semiconducting crystals that read whether you or your child has been immunized with any and all the poisons they plan to inject you with, from now to forever. And you will have every bodily function, every neural response—possibly every thought—monitored, deciphered and stored by Big Brother, who, in turn, will allocate rewards for your good behavior and obedience.

If that doesn't sound like the Mark of the Beast to you, then tell me ... what does?

Dr. Carl Sanders figured it out, albeit too late.

Perhaps the very number of Microsoft's patent WO2020060606A1 can at least get people asking that question.

We recognize the beast.

What matters now is: What are we—the awakened, loving souls, spirit warriors, speakers of truth, system busters, lightworkers and sovereign beings—going to do about it?

Part Two
Light Upon Darkness

*"A visionary is one who can find his way by moonlight
and sees the dawn before the rest of the world . . . "*
—Oscar Wilde

Chapter 18

The Light Strings of the Universe

There is a reason I finally share a story I have not shared until now, and it ties in with the information I have presented throughout this book.

In 1996, in a farmer's field just across the road from Stonehenge, in Wiltshire, England, I laid down in my very first crop circle, the Julia Set, an event that would change the course of my life forever.

What a privilege to have been given access to that stairway to the stars.

I have since managed to enter hundreds of exquisite formations, year after year, either exploring on my own, or leading groups of seekers on my SoulQuest Journeys programs. From each site, I gleaned something new and unique from the geometry, the energetic anomalies and countless phenomena lain into the wheat or hovering overhead—but, never again, did I experience anything as mind-boggling and utterly unforgettable as what I received from the Julia Set.

How that formation catapulted me into the astral voyage of my life remains one of the greatest mysteries of a lifetime filled with extraordinary spiritual experiences. No other crop circle has ever provided a vehicle that could rocket me to the outer reaches of my "unconscious" connection to All-That-Exists, as that one did then. I am just so grateful that I was able to retain the memory of what happened there: where I was taken, and what I saw along the way. I know I was meant to understand and bring forward what I was being taught of the interconnectedness of all things, all time, and all space: **the DNA of the universe.**

I have been blessed at every juncture of this wondrous life path. Yet, no kundalini rising, no third eye explosion, no mystical journey . . . nothing before or since has ever compared (if comparisons are even necessary) to what I was allowed to see then. Not even my near-death experience at age seventeen, when rough waves threw me from a rocky promontory into the turbulent sea, and I drowned off a cliff at Davenport Beach in California, has had such an impact on my spirit. I was shown a glimpse of "heaven" then, when my soul went racing through a tube of light, into the brilliance. It was ecstatic, unconditional love that embraced me, such rapture that I did not want to come back, but, like so many who have had that same experience, I was told "it was not my time" and that I had an important mission to fulfill on Earth.

I saw my mother's despairing face, and felt her unbearable grief roll through me. I knew I could not leave her.

How I went from drowning in violent ocean waves to lying, bruised and bleeding, on the rocks remains one of the great mysteries of my life. A wave must have spit me out of the ocean, like a big piece of driftwood, and tossed me onto that cliff, impossible as that seems, or perhaps it was divine intervention that lifted me out of the sea.

When I opened my eyes, I was kissed by an angel, who then disappeared in thin air. I coughed up a gallon of sea water and came back to join the living.

As powerful as that was, dying and coming back, knowing God and eternity, it paled in significance to what happened that day—that one remarkable day—in the farmer's field just across the way from one of England's most revered sacred sites.

Whoever was meant to be there got there. Unfortunately, I have managed to speak to very few people whose paths led them to the Julia Set crop circle in 1996. I am certain that, for others like me, it was an appointment with destiny like no other. Like the bewildered characters in the film, *Close Encounters of the Third Kind,* magnetized to that enigmatic mountain monument, we were called into that field near Stonehenge to experience the immensity of what was lain into the wheat, the ethers, the air.

We came from the four directions of the Earth: Tibetan monks, Native American shamans, indigenous leaders, healers, priests and seekers from all over the physical world, to experience a reunion in the no-time of multidimensional consciousness. And in that sacred space, we were accompanied by beings from the non-physical worlds, with whom some, like me, were able to interact . . . somewhere between the dimensions, beyond time and space.

I cannot speak for anyone else, but it was my personal experience that I encountered and observed non-physical beings roaming about the circles, replete with strange phenomena from so many realms and dimensions. All I can say is that those who managed to be in the right time and place to get into that formation, as was I, were truly blessed.

How I would love, all these years later, to sit down with those fellow explorers to exchange experiences and perception. Imagine the stories we would share? Who knows if their lives were so immensely influenced as mine. Granted, no two experiences can ever be the same, but still, I cannot imagine anyone who accessed that field ever being the same again. Oh, to be offered a spin on a time machine! I would surely choose to go back to that moment in the Julia Set, to experience that life-changing cosmic juncture in time and space again, with all the innocence and wonder of that critical time in my spiritual evolution.

After spending so much time in the fields of England, year after year, it is my perception that multidimensional portals are not necessarily fixed to any specific coordinates on the time-space continuum, as some believe, although surely there are vortices on Earth and throughout the universe that hold a constant energetic frequency, or bandwidth, that allow for multidimensional anomalies to manifest. One of the most powerful of these is the Temple of Sety 1 in Abydos, built atop the far more ancient Osirion, where more than once I have experienced the whole structure undulating, spirits bleeding through the ethers, and found myself slipping into some strange parallel universe. Like the legendary British woman, Dorothy Eady (aka Omm Sety), whose extraordinary life (1904-1981) led her to becoming a draughtswoman for the Department of Egyptian Antiquities and eventually the caretaker of the Temple of Abydos years before I ever traveled there, I entered a mysterious chamber in the temple, an incongruous structure that did not fit with the history and art beyond its walls . . . and I lost time.

When I returned later in the day, after the scorching desert heat subsided, the chamber had vanished. I searched every space, wondering if I'd somehow gotten confused by the many columns and spaces in the temple, but it simply wasn't there. I soon realized that, like Omm Sety, I had slipped into another dimension or parallel universe, and was given a glimpse of what the other side of reality looks like: Ancient Egyptian style.

In the case of the Julia Set, something akin to a galactic whirlwind had clearly whipped down onto the wheat field, opening a temporary portal—a window on the Cosmos of Soul—that would later dissipate and disappear, as was meant to happen. No doubt that the energies of Stonehenge, just across the road, had something to do with the intensity of those otherworldly energies, and most likely they served to help manifest the opening of that portal.

Until this moment, I have never publicly shared, in any depth, what actually occurred to me then, when I was taken out of body to unite with six-dimensional, non-physical beings: where they took me, what I saw and experienced and, most importantly, what I learned. But it is relevant now that I am writing this book, and to the information I feel is so vital to our lives—present and future—and, because of that, I am prepared to shed some light upon the ultimate transformational experience in consciousness that I have ever known ... one that has set the pace of my journey every day since.

Several times, in interviews and talks, I have alluded to how I was taken out of my body almost instantly upon entering the Julia Set, but never have I revealed much more than to say that it was the "galactic joy ride" of my life. I choose to protect such very personal giant steps, taking care never to exalt my own process, or stroke my own ego, and knowing full well that some of our most sacred moments need to be held close to the heart, where **silence holds the power.**

I have been blessed with so many breakthrough moments in this journey called "life" that I cannot even recall them all, but I do remember everything about that particular out-of-body astral flight, which I can only call the "mother" of all experiences.

Twenty-five years later, every detail is still clear in my mind, like a freshly-etched tattoo. Now it is time to share it.

Immediately upon entering the formation, I felt someone, or something, pulling at my collar, drawing me in. I felt so dizzy, I nearly threw myself down to the ground in one of the 151 circles (lain in perfect Fibonacci sequence) that comprised the sacred geometrical design. Nauseated and weak, the dizziness had me spinning out immediately, while the earth shook beneath me. What a terrible feeling! Fortunately, I quickly lost awareness of my body, and began to experience myself as sound: a whirling vortex of high-pitched whistling and humming.

Like a rocket clearing the planet's atmosphere, I was thrust into space, watching Stonehenge, England and our beautiful blue Earth fade away behind me. Almost instantly, I was gifted with a brilliant display of what appeared to me to represent every light that ever shone across the entire universe. I could see how every single star, planet, moon, asteroids and meteors—all heavenly bodies—were connected by glowing, spiraling helices of light.

The Sirians have referred to these helices, in earlier works, as the "Gossamer Web of Light." Clearly, I was immersed in the DNA of the universe, in all its unfathomable glory.

I was given the extraordinary opportunity to travel the light strings of the Cosmos, as a spider navigates its own web, acutely aware of how my mere presence within and upon those holographic byways affected the structure itself. My consciousness traversing those spiraling light beams amplified the light: the mere act of observing it all affected it all—the entire network! I have been mesmerized by spiders and the gorgeous webs they weave ever since, seeing them as "showers of the way" of universal design, and it is always the case, when I observe a newly formed spider's web glistening in a gentle rain, that I have instant recall of that journey and all those ecstatic emotions.

As I danced the great highways of the universe, immersed in sacred geometric form and cosmic frequencies, I was exposed to the divine interconnectedness of all things in such a breathtakingly beautiful way that no learning, no knowledge nor prior experience could ever have shown me, before that moment, what I was brought to understand was the absolute essence of Creation.

I **was** the spider, plucking the strings of those sacred designs, playing the Music of the Spheres that I was capable of co-creating simply by being present, being aware and knowing, without question or doubt, that there is absolutely nothing haphazard about the Cosmos: no chaos . . . no separateness . . . no irrelevance. It all has its reason for being; it all serves a purpose. The Divine Blueprint of Creator's artistry and supreme wisdom is the underpinning of all existence; every layer has its unique DNA architecture, which sets the dynamic interaction between all things and all consciousness—even darkness.

No amount of spiritual training prepares you for something like that.

Mesmerized and resonating to the harmonics of the universe, I was gifted with the incredible opportunity to interact with the stars and planets as living, conscious beings, mutually aware of each and every being, as everything—all consciousness—played the symphony of Creation.

The immensity of that experience cannot be contained in words. Perhaps it is why I have never really tried to speak of it in any great detail.

I was blessed to have been given a glimpse of immense auric fields of planets teeming with life, craft traveling webs of light in deep space, colors, light explosions, clusters: so much light . . . so much life. And then, boom! The lights went out. I experienced obscurity so dark that not even a pinhole of light entered there and yet, I felt nothing: no fear, no curiosity, no wonder. I had reached the void, the state of absolute stillness, as close to non-existence as I can imagine, for I do not believe that any energy dies or disappears.

Had it not been shown to me that way, I would never have been able to conceptualize what a state of nothingness looks and feels like. I have no idea how long I floated there, in that state of detached awareness. I have never achieved it since, in any meditative state or astral journey. Nor do I wish to.

Jolted from that state of conscious unconsciousness, I saw myself traveling through my own body, shrinking . . . shrinking, staring at one of my own cells, shrinking smaller until I was so miniscule that I was able to step into the cell, without harming the cellular membrane. Smaller still, I observed so many unrecognizable bits and pieces: filaments, granules, mitochondria and then the nucleus, which appeared to me as the central headquarters of the structure. I shrank smaller, smaller until I found myself inside the nucleus, observing the DNA double helix, curled so tightly in its golden mean spiral. Everywhere were infinitely small bits and pieces, floating in and around my very own DNA structure, and somehow I knew I was being shown that this was what I had been brought to the far reaches of my multidimensional mind to see, and then to share with others.

Once again, every single bit of creation—every particle, every filament, every follicle—was connected by the Gossamer Web of Light; once again my mere observation of those aspects of consciousness affected their behavior. Their luminescence, activity and energy all became amplified, as I focused on each segment, with particular focus upon how the filaments of DNA connected consciously, in complex patterns of sacred geometry, reacting to each other's movements and pulse.

Through no conscious intention nor will of my own, as if some supreme wisdom had pre-designed every step of my voyage, I kept shrinking smaller, smaller than the minutia of a nucleus, until I found myself swimming around in the subatomic world—the microcosm— where atoms, protons and neutrons spun everywhere around me, in the most spectacular exhibition of perfected spatial relationship, form and vibration. There, too, every infinitesimal particle was connected by spiraling strings of light that permeated the infinite. Everything was connected in divine proportion, manifested through sacred geometry, sound and light.

Here again, these aspects—all the atomic elements—were just as aware of my watching and observing them, as I was of them. Wherever my focus went, the energy heated up and reacted to my awareness. It was clear we were dancing a cosmic ballet of consciousness together, choreographed by the Divine Maestro.

I was shown that from the immense macrocosmic display of the greater universe, to the vast microcosmic, subatomic world, there exists absolutely no difference whatsoever. What I had always understood intellectually was now imprinted on my soul! Between and within these two realms lies the physical realm, the coherence of light energy that forms what we perceive to be "matter." I understood, as I had never understood before, that we mortals are the coalesced light of such incredible divine planning and, like everything else that exists, every aspect of our being is woven together in sacred proportion, vibration, sound and light. All things are connected in this blueprint of pure love; all is in divine proportion, and all living things react to being observed, responding, in turn, to the energy of the observer.

Only that silent, dark vacuum remained obscure and unknowable. What had I been shown, and why? I knew it was important, but all I managed to glean from it was a sense of detachment and "nothingness." Was this the "void" transcendental meditation gurus strove for? Perhaps I was not meant to know it then, but looking back, I believe I was witnessing the "disconnect," a vibratory field so dense, so separate from the field of God light that it held nothing for me to see. Rather, it served as a mirror on my subconscious, where I could gaze with detachment into any residual fear of the dark unknown that I still held there.

I am well aware that fearlessness was a prerequisite to my being capacitated, on that very journey, to serve as a channel for these extraordinary light beings. Apparently, I passed the test.

I still do not fear the dark unknown, although I wonder what it is that lurks there, in opposition to Light, and whether something as sinister as synthetic intelligence is truly capable of separating souls from that love. Who knows what lies in that void, if anything at all? Some things are not meant to be analyzed with the rational mind. Surely the entirety of that cosmic journey through the wonder of all Creation defied the intellect and spoke directly to my heart and soul, and that is all that matters to me.

That is where I live.

It is how I breathe.

*

When at last I was thrust back into my body, which lay inert in that crop formation for over two hours, I could barely cope. The physical world was unrecognizable and I had a horrific time coming back to it. Everything looked, smelled and felt so different than when I had been jerked out of my body. It felt like forever before I was actually able to sit up, as things around me were spinning once again, almost out of control. I laid back down, waiting and hoping the dizziness and nausea would pass.

There was a smattering of people around, but night was falling and many were walking away, leaving the field. I can't say that I was capable of discerning which of those beings was physical, and which were spirits or apparitions from other dimensions. I remember an elderly woman, looking down at me with concern. I heard her ask me, telepathically, to move my fingers and hands. When I did, she disappeared, so I knew she was some sort of guide or angelic presence, helping me bridge back to the physical world.

My friend, Arthur, who had been kind enough to drive me there, appeared then. He said I had been "out cold" over two hours and that he'd been worried about me, but people told him to let me be and to not interrupt my process, so he had spent time at Stonehenge while I was traversing the universe. Thank God for those tuned-in people!

Once the spinning subsided and I managed to get grounded enough to stand up, I saw dozens of interdimensional beings combing the field, huge plasma balls hanging low in the air, and two Men in Black, close by, staring at me, menacingly. In that interim between the dimensions, coming back from the furthest reaches of what I can only describe as having consciously accessed the DNA of the quantum universe, I could see the gossamer web between them all, connecting all the pieces of our human and non-human experience. Slowly, as I came back to feeling fully present in body awareness, back into the illusion of separateness that defines our three-dimensional perception, it faded.

Walking back the long distance from the field to Arthur's parked car, I felt completely foreign to my own body. It took me the whole ride back to the town of Glastonbury before I was comfortable in my skin again.

And so began my work with extradimensional consciousness, and my life-long exploration of the Divine Blueprint—the God Code— laced throughout all Creation.

*

Upon return to my home in Rome, I began channeling the collective of Sirians with whom I had connected through the Julia Set, and from whom I am blessed, to this day, to continue to source information for humankind. Their messages, spanning over twenty-five years of my life, have, for the most part, been about awakening us to the interconnectedness of all Creation, the significance of geometry, light and sound as the "glue" that holds the strings of the universe together, and how these aspects can help us reassemble and heal the damaged and dormant DNA within and around us all. These interdimensional beings foretold of what we would be facing now, in the "desert days" of our time on Earth, and filled us with hope about what will follow, once we finally moved past this difficult phase of our transition.

Since the onset of those channeled sessions, when I first began the process of bringing forward their prophecies, I have been intent upon helping people around the world to accelerate that process. The work involves honoring the perfection of the light codes within our cellular memory and utilizing higher vibrational frequencies to help the body re-member its state of divine grace and wellness—and so, the spirit as well.

I have dedicated my life to scribing the wisdom of ancients, some of which we hold as karma in our own subconscious pools, some that we have gleaned from native peoples, who, despite the injustices committed against them, still manage to retain their innate ability to be in harmony with the earth, sky and waters. When we are clear and determined in our intent to enhance the biological being and honor all life in that process, we help to heal the broken pieces, right down to our very design—the cellular memory—and, as we are discovering, to awaken the dormant DNA (the "junk") that lies scrambled within us.

Never before has it been as important as it is now that we take absolute control over our sovereign experience of soul passing through the density of physical life on Planet Earth. We have a class of what appear to be alien invaders and AI robotoids, posing as humans they so despise, set upon the destruction of our entire species, and directing the mad scientists of their torturous laboratories to corral us, human fodder, into their transhumanist mind cages. Smugly anchored in their self-importance and manipulative powers, they cannot resist broadcasting that intention out to us.

Godless creatures, they believe that we are powerless against them. They are telling us outright that we have no recourse but to bow to them, because they now possess the nano-technology that they intend to forcibly implant within each and every one of us, to permanently mutate the human race, which they perceive as a herd of hackable animals. They are openly telling us that they are coming for our DNA, to replace the dilapidated version of our humanness—"human 1.0"—with their new model, a completely controllable, hackable one, utilizing "external" body sensors, RFID chip implants, glowing luciferin subcutaneous tattoos, DNA disrupters and God knows what other deviant tools we have yet to know. All of this is intended to turn us into their computerized, soulless version of our former selves: the "Human 2.0."

They intend to hack out the God Code, replace it with the 666, and to ritualistically steal the human soul, so that they can turn us over to their horned god.

Such is the nature of the Armageddon; such is the design of the Mark of the Beast.

But we, free-thinking human beings, are wild stallions on an open prairie. They may be able to corral some of us, but we will inevitably find a way to break loose. Our race to freedom is more important to us than life itself. It overrides the survival instinct, because life, without freedom, is not worth living.

We have experts in the right fields seeking ways to mitigate the damage of what has been injected into our brothers and sisters who acquiesced or were hypnotized into taking part in the "emergency experiment." We will find solutions. We must. Treatments, supplements, and new methodologies are becoming available to detox the poisons, and to extrude the graphene oxide and other horrors out of the body. Protocols are being developed to mitigate the damage inflicted upon the DNA. By the time this book goes to print, we may have already had a breakthrough.

In the meantime, we must remember that we are capable of altering every single cell of our being with our focused intent and thoughts, with the vibratory frequencies of light and sound, and with prayer, love and laughter. If we understand how to use absolute focused intent to affect matter, we will be capable of repairing what has been damaged. Surely, we can use mind-over-matter to cast out the invader. We can begin the process of activating some of the ninety-percent of our "non-coded" DNA, re-establishing the perfected, sacred geometry within us all. It is a matter of right thought, right word and right action, as we are taught in the Buddhist tradition; it is determined by our ability to focus the mind and set our intention. It is about achieving resonance with higher frequencies.

We need to question everything that challenges our freedom, our vision and our sovereign rights as human beings, and make choices that honor the soul's purpose.

We will need to be determined, vigilant, and more centered than we have ever been before, in order to navigate our way around the traps being laid into the forests of our minds.

So, protect your universe.

And always remember that they cannot take what you do not willingly give away.

Chapter 19

Manifestation and the Sovereign Spirit

Now that we have dirtied our hands in the soot of such dark doings as those we are up against, it is with an eye to the positive outcome that we must rinse ourselves off, and chart our course back to the incredible wonder of what it means to be alive, here and now.

Acknowledging evil's play has not weakened our resolve, nor has it brought us to resonate with the fear it wants to create within us all. Far from it. Rather, it has reminded us of our incredible determination. It has strengthened us, pushing us to face our fear and to move through it; it has cleared the runway, from a place so deep within, for what we know we came here to do. Now is the time we must push back against the omnipotent arbitrators of false power and move forward, piercing the shadow with our light sabers, and disabling their power with our clarity, our determination and, above all, with our love.

By writing this book and publishing it on my own, I avow to do just that.

For those who have received one or more of injections of the synthetic mRNA-DNA re-writing system, as well as for those who have refused it, this is the time when we must direct our energies towards mitigating any and all damage to the cellular memory, while accelerating re-assembly of the "non-coded" DNA. The answer is there, in those ten strands! We must use extraordinary focused intention to override the overwrite, if you will, and re-establish the integrity of the language of our Divine Blueprint.

I do absolutely believe the solution to the problem facing those who have accepted the invader lies in our activation of the "junk," whose true purpose will finally be revealed in this time—the hour of the Armageddon.

There are several forward-thinking doctors, researchers and scientists burning the night oil, searching for ways to treat the mounting numbers of adverse reactions incurred by those unfortunate people who trusted their governments, to neutralize that mRNA implant and flush it out of the system with supplements and herbs, but, personally, I do not think it is going to be that simple. There is no magic wand we can use, if you approach the problem from the use of supplements, nutrients and medications alone. I do not ascribe to the idea that you can take a few high-powered vitamins or parasite cleanses to "flush out" a synthetic nano-technology mechanism that has embedded itself into the DNA, spitting out new, destructive commands into the operating manual of your biological being and, utilizing the deposits of several injections worth of graphine oxide, building nano-computer systems within the blood and tissues that, it appears, are designed to respond to radio waves and other remote signals.

Bearing in mind that nothing has more power over our being and our ability to alter reality than the focused mind, we must now, with absolute clarity of intent and conscious integrity, dedicate our efforts to reversing all de-humanizing systems—those that are currently in progress, as well as agendas scheduled for the imminent future: to steal our souls, and turn us over to the techno-god of the reptilian domain.

Whether you have succumbed to the poison shots or not, and whether your focus is to repair the damage or to prevent it, now is the time, if you are ready, to exercise precision manifestation and visualization to clear yourself of any invasive thoughts, emotions or toxic matter, disrupt and disintegrate any and all non-consensual implants, and to reclaim your sovereignty against all authoritarian invaders.

Over twenty years ago, the Sirian High Council described this attempted coup to sabotage our DNA, with a very keen eye on the machinations that would be used to drive human evolution in the wrong direction, aborting our ascension trajectory. Their prediction of exactly what is unfolding now is described in the third book of the Sirian Revelations entitled: *No More Secrets, No More Lies*. In it, they warned us to confront the issues addressed in that material, and to take very serious, very urgent steps to reverse the course of events planned for our demise, by activating the dormant DNA within us . . . and healing what needed to be healed at the cellular level. They were calling us to refine our ability to exercise mind-over-matter, in order to manifest what we would need, and to overcome the adversities that we would be come up against—exactly where we are today.

From the chapter, DNA and the Crystalline Being[35], we read: "We have consistently driven home to you the need to be in center and to always set your sights upon the highest of intentions—that the All be served—in every aspect of your existence . . . and in your dedication to serve as warriors of light, healers and guides. This is of the utmost significance not only to your individual experience, or for the healing of Gaia, but for the soul patterns of the entire race . . . and outward, reverberating eternally and without limitation through the dimensions and across the no-time.

No universal law denies you the right to extend yourselves, reaching for that godly experience of altering matter. Indeed, that is every bit a part of your spiritual climb as is your desire to know Prime Creator and to understand the significance of all that exists everywhere around you. Know, however, that the realization of that quest will never be suc-

---

35   No More Secrets, No More Lies, Patricia Cori, 2022, pgs. 196-200

cessfully achieved in the tube and petri dish, the laboratory or operating room, where sovereignty is invaded—the soul essence being of no consequence or consideration—and where the sterility of the experimenter's mind is paramount to an "objective" outcome.

Rather, as we have shared with you throughout these works, the process of altering matter (disguised in the secret teachings of ancients as the "transmutation of lead into gold") is that exquisite transformation whereby heart-centered thought reaches resonance with the conscious vibration of matter, and then (through the focused intention that the highest good be served) the substance, raised to its exalted state of being, is either transmuted into new forms or disappears entirely!

The ultimate expression of your godliness occurs every time you raise the vibration of your own thoughts, those of the collective and matter of all densities and structures. Or when you simply come up to the perfection that is manifest in all the beauty that surrounds you: attuning to the scent of the rose, traveling the trill of the birdsong, journeying the rainbow bridge.

In those moments of supreme awareness, you are not merely "playing at" being godly. You are gods, gods of the earth kingdom, gods of the Universe, breathing your souls into the matrix, just as we have breathed into yours . . . just as Supreme Being breathes the All That Is into being.

The unbridled fervor of your genetic scientists and technicians to dissect and then rebuild the genome of every living being reflects the duality that prevails in your highly polarized world. On the one hand, your recognition of the mathematical foundations of chemistry and biology, Prime Creator's language, is the Secret Wisdom coming to light within you—

Noble Man rising to his innate gifts and intelligence. On the other, the desire of some to use the knowledge to bend reality in such ways that your race intervenes with the natural process, manipulating life and distorting it for any other purpose than the highest good of the All, is a reflection of humankind's ignorance . . . shiny and dark, like polished black onyx.

That is why it is so absolutely relevant that you, the awakening, become acutely aware of the architecture of life, the DNA, and the naturally occurring mutations that are beginning to manifest within the living of all planetary systems in Ra's embrace (for life does indeed proliferate upon other planets in your solar system), just as you are wise to investigate and consider the implications of the work that is taking place in the laboratories of dark design.

Fortunately, there exists a parallel scientific community, which is just as dedicated to understanding how spirit permeates and creates every aspect of reality, and it is uniting spirit and science in a way such that both intuitives and logic-based thinkers can embrace the wisdom that emerges from its discoveries. As these free scientists—the quantum physicists—bring forward the new paradigms of your 3D reality and the multidimensional Universe, more of you are capable of conceptually recognizing the true nature of all reality.

You are beginning to realize with what splendor and intricate cosmometry the intelligence of Creation—manifesting your soul intention and the genetic continuum of your inherited families, species, and race (and starseeded ancestry)—meticulously creates your physical forms. It is coded into the very fiber of your beings: human DNA. From the etheric essence to the densest aspects of your earthly bodies (if dense they can truly be defined), all is blueprinted with a most unfathomable precision, a superbly orchestrated numerical rhythm, and cosmometric proportion.

There are, as well, controlled genetic scientists who are funded and directed by the Power to unknowingly serve the Annunaki's plan for absolute dominion over the human race. Some, assigned the daunting task of cataloguing and preserving the DNA of all living earth forms, believe they are working for the good of humankind and the protection of other species, unaware that their dedicated life's work only receives government subsidies and financing to assure that the seed of all earth biology be transported to another host planet and to the moon station—the "holding zone" of the power elite.

Others, of a far darker persuasion, are willing specimen collectors for the Annunaki and their alien collaborators, who are ever intent upon gestating a perfected slave force for other worlds, in other space and time frameworks. Some of these government scientists are serving as laboratory assistants to the Zeta Reticulans, in that phase of their invasion of human sovereignty that involves collection of human sperm and ova from unwilling and terrified "abductees"—a program intent upon saving their own devolving race from extinction.

Others still, focused upon untold economic rewards, are at work "capitalizing" on the incredible stores of wisdom contained within the designs of Creation by seeking to create and perfect biomolecular DNA computer units that are so miniscule that they can fit, a trillion at a time, into a laboratory test tube.

The potential output capacity of a microscopic DNA computer (already past the preliminary stages of its biotechnological development) is the performance of well over sixty billion controlled computer operations per second. This, the command-triggered robotization of your innate intelligence from the molecular level of your human experience, is the cutting edge of their covert technology.

One cubic centimeter of your sophisticated DNA, in its limited expression—the double helix—can store more data than all that which can be recorded and stored on over nine hundred billion compact disks of your current data management technology. As you can well imagine, that is some highly exciting information for technology designers, who are intent upon computerizing human beings.

Each live cell, container of the DNA data management molecules, is being studied for its amazing capacities to manage and code unfathomable quantities of information. The double helix molecule, foundation of your existing DNA, records data based on four primary chemical platforms—currently identified by your scientists with the scripted letters: A, T, C, and G. This provides a monumental capacity for memory and a formula that can be developed into a most sophisticated biotechnological "language"—the likes of which the gene computer technicians have only begun to tap.

Their vision of living cells serving as complex biotechnological computers that can be programmed and commanded to function as information distribution networks represents the early stages of a left-brained approach to what we are intent upon helping you access from a right-brained experience the capacity of human awareness and focused mind to affect every molecular unit in the body, altering the make-up of the body, mind, and spirit.

Imagine, if you can, what twelve interactive DNA strands (four perfectly interfacing tetrahedrons of light) will be capable of computing? Imagine what the "junk" they told you had no recognizable function or purpose will be able to tell you, to create, to remember?

Imagine your enormous capacity, Homo sapiens.

And imagine, just imagine, with what majesty and light you were born into the Earth realm.

It is our intention to elaborate, in depth, the patterns of your evolving cellular consciousness and the light-encoded DNA that is operating now or lies dormant, awaiting reconnection, so that you can understand most succinctly what will occur as you re-bundle these light filaments: first creating triangulation, then the star tetrahedron, the Supraluminescence, and then the perfected cosmometrical Vortex of Light within every cell of your awakened light bodies."

*

In the activations and meditations that follow, I will call upon the Sirian High Council once again, to bring their extraordinary voice and vibrational signature to the work we commit to undertaking: reclaiming our sovereign right to freedom, healing, repairing the DNA and disengaging all interference therein, by reconstructing the sacred structure of two tetrahedral forms that correspond to the third, fourth, fifth and sixth strands of the ten that are dormant, calling the bits and pieces home, and setting the template for the additional two tetrahedrons (seventh to twelfth strands) to manifest at the appropriate time in the actualization of our personal and planetary vibrational ascension.

We will breathe the vibratory essence of Yahweh into the ethers, our auric fields, and into the DNA.

These meditations, in which I guide you through the activations utilizing Solfeggio frequency 528hertz to heal the DNA can be found on my on-line course, The Divine Blueprint; information can be found at the end of this book.

Please come to the work with no expectation; commit your absolute, focused intention to manifest your desired outcome to the experience.

Always remember, when you embark on any deep meditation or spirit work, to create sacred space around you. I use this prayer and declaration, whenever I embark upon any psychic work, in service to Spirit, and at night, when I lay myself down to rest:

"I call upon the Angel Warriors of Light,
asking to be encircled in an impenetrable blanket of golden white light.
Let it hold as a barrier against any energies that are not of the highest order,
and may it serve as a beacon
to Light Beings of the highest intention,
love, and Spirit."

Chapter 20

Reclaim Your Mind

Before you embark upon repairing any and all genetic disruption within your cellular matrix, and the activation of your "non-coded" DNA material, you are going to need to conduct a total *feng shui* of all electromagnetic interference that keeps you bound to the techno-grid. You will need to push yourself out of complacency, with regard to that interference, knowing that some of it is beyond your control, but that so much of its influence is a product of your own addiction to it.

Most people simply cannot recognize what this technology is doing to their lives, especially to the lives of their children, whose electromagnetic force fields are still in pastel, still manifesting energy in form.

You have to admit that, in order to be able to move beyond it. If you are already "there," good for you. You are one step closer to liberating yourself from the matrix than are most people on Planet Earth. If you are not ready to eschew technology, as it encroaches more and more on your daily life, that is a choice you are, of course, free to make. There is no one pushing you, and you do not need to judge yourself. Only you can decide if and when you are ready to break the chains that come from electronic entrainment and the mind-control that result from engaging these devices. You do, however, need to be aware of just what is being utilized against you, in order to make that call.

Only when you understand that television and other electronic devices have been designed by Big Tech not to entertain, but to entrain you and your loved ones, can you break free of that electronic addiction—hypnosis-inducing technology, electromagnetic radiation, and mind-altering frequencies and programming—that you allow to ooze into your psyche, day after day, for hours on end, with little or no safeguards whatsoever. They dull your intuition, distract you from everything unfolding around you, and direct your thoughts to skewed realities someone else—a stranger, or perhaps a robot—has designed for your mind.

That stranger reports to the military-industrial complex. Never forget that.

So, if you have already broken free of it, especially television programming, well done. You are one of a very small minority of people who have managed to see it for what it is and break free of its grasp. If you have not, and you are still addicted, but are determined to take back your freedom, then the time has come to change ... and change quickly.

Your release from its hold over you will have to involve a significant life-style adjustment—a permanent one—rather than putting yourself through a momentary exercise that you will later forget or sabotage. Everyone in your world, who is glued to the matrix, will do everything in their power to shut you down. You will have to be strong enough to hold your ground against their resistance, in order to become very clear about everything I have shared with you through this book, and realize what is happening in the hearts and minds of your family, your community and your world.

It is going to be the greatest detox you have ever embarked upon in your life.

You are going to need to find an inner strength you may never before have had to put to the test, before making the decision to release yourself from the induced addiction and hypnosis of technology.

You will regain control over your mind and your life by recognizing how much more clearly you can see what is happening around you, when your thoughts are not dictated by programming.

From the first appearance of black and white monitors in family rooms around the world, to the modern-day proliferation of all manner of high-tech gadgetry in our homes, offices, schools, clubs, stores, public squares, distraction pervades our private and communal lives. Everywhere, you'll find a television or cell phone screen, front and center. And who can walk down a street anymore without passing by people so fixated on their cell phones that they sometimes walk right into you? Oblivious to everything around them, these people have no idea how vulnerable that makes them in a world where violence is rising dramatically, and where children are being snatched off the sidewalk every single minute of the day.

I remember how, back when I was a child, my parents limited our viewing time in front of the TV screen, and how they made us sit a significant distance away from it. We still distrusted technology then, and I am grateful for that. Unfortunately, today's children do not enjoy such protection, because their post-boomer generation parents were not yet born when we were first confronted with television back in the mid-50's. People born after the 90s have no idea what life was like before computers, the Internet and the cell phone, which reared its ugly head soon after computers proliferated around the world. They do not seem to know or care about how dangerous these radiation-producing devices really are, and that is before we even begin to consider how addictive, especially on those still-forming neurons of a child's delicate brain.

So many of today's children have a cell phone, game console or laptop thrust into their hands by the time they are two-years-old. How crazy is that? Apparently these parents have not done their homework, or perhaps they just find it an easier "management tool" to entertain their babies with electromagnetic programming. They simply cannot fully understand what they are doing to their children, and how dangerous it all is on so many levels.

It is really criminal that this technology is marketed to anyone at all, particularly the young. Just remember that Steve Jobs and Bill Gates did not allow their children to go near it until a certain age. That should tell you everything you know about how dangerous it is. Unfortunately, for those who do not have the kind of influence to set their own standards over their lives and those of their children, and the wealth to back it up, being a protective parent, by denying "tools" other children have, can be perceived today as child abuse. We are all too well-aware of how eager and willing is the state to intervene between parents and their children, wherever it can stick its nose into a family's business . . . whatever excuse it can find to declare parents "unfit," so that it can take their children from them. Clearly, parental authority and the family unit are being usurped and deconstructed by an overreaching, increasingly unlawful state.

Depending on the statistics to which you ascribe, the estimated amount of time children spend glued to television, computer and cell phone screens today is reported to be over nine hours a day. That is more than half of their waking hours! That figure may even be a conservative, considering they are also working on computers at school, gaming—often into the wee hours—and taking their cell phones everywhere . . . even into the bathroom! That means that they are spending half of their conscious lives glued to a screen.

We are talking addiction, here.

The numbers are not much better for adults, estimated to be staring into screens for an average of seven hours a day. Seven hours of one's life . . . every day? What a waste of precious life.

What we have here, ladies and gentlemen, is a full-blown technology epidemic of the propaganda and mind-control varieties. Do you think this is by accident?

If so, you best think again.

*

Case in point: the work of Herbert E. Krugman, who served, from 1967-1983, as manager of Corporate Public Opinion Research, for the General Electric Corporation. He had also held the position of president of the American Association for Public Opinion Research, of the Division of Consumer Psychology of the American Psychological Association, and of the Market Research Council of New York.

Dr. Krugman received his Ph.D. from Columbia University in 1952, and his B.S.S. from The City College of New York in 1942. He served on the faculties of Yale, Princeton and Columbia Universities, and was a trustee of the Marketing Science Institute in Cambridge, a director of the Advertising Research Foundation and chairman of the Research Policy Committee of the Association of National Advertisers.

Interesting to note, isn't it, that an electric/electronics company like General Electric has people with such noteworthy credentials as his on its payroll, targeting psychology and the consumer. Keeping tabs on how people respond to advertising through television and other technologies must be pretty important to the bottom line. I can't help thinking that if it were only more important to the consumer, we would very possibly not find ourselves in the mess we're in today, and that we would certainly never have become such mindless consumers, as we have in our contemporary societies.

It has been thrust upon us through means that are truly insidious, immoral and, where we still have a functioning judicial system, outright illegal.

In 1969, Herbert Krugman carried out a clinical-studies experiment for G.E., conducted at the Neuropsychological Laboratory of the New York Medical School, for which he hooked up his test case, a twenty-one-year-old woman, to an EEG (an electroencephalogram.) Within sixty seconds of watching the television screen, her brainwaves switched from active, alert thought, to a receptive, passive state, which favors the conscious and subconscious minds to absorb whatever input the subject is receiving: from Beta to Alpha or low Alpha, within sixty seconds of sitting in front of the television screen.

What emerged from that study, heralded by the Advertising Research Foundation he directed, was that advertisers did not even need to plant subliminal messages in their advertisements (although they do), because the brain goes into a state of receptivity to suggestion within seconds of turning on the set.

Imagine what is being dumped into a receptive brain that is glued to multiple screens seven hours or more a day?

Consider that what you've understood as contributing to a healthier life style, until now, by reducing or eliminating electronic addiction, entrainment and electromagnetic radiation, is now a matter of life or death.

More is coming.

Much much more is coming.

You are going to need to make a choice between freedom and entrapment. Television, computers, and cell phones—all electronic screens—are designed to take you into a hypnotic trance state within seconds, without your ever being aware of how you are being entrained by the frequencies being used against you. They all are mind-control devices that manipulate your psyche, dumping programming of every sort into your present and future memory.

Those memories can be triggered later on. That means that whatever has been dumped into your subconscious reservoir can be called upon by the ones doing the dumping, at will. And that, my friends, is mind-control, pure and simple.

The screen flicker in television is designed to facilitate exactly that. It is no accident. It lowers brainwaves from beta to alpha state by inducing a trance state; this has been proven in test after test. The subconscious receives and absorbs those messages, and the "programming" then gets deposited in the deep well of your subconscious mind, reflecting back up to you what they want you to think, to fear and to desire.

All this you may already know. But did you know that US Patent 650506158B2, entitled, "Nervous System Manipulation by Electromagnetic Fields From Monitors," was filed in 2001 by a certain Hendricus G. Loos (is that even a real name?) that proposes, as the title states, a method to manipulate a subject, near monitors utilizing pulsed electromagnetic fields, to "excite a sensory resonance?" This takes the flicker from the television set to a whole other level, and this reason alone is why we need to turn off our screens and detox from any and all addiction to electronics.

Technology that has, as its objective, the manipulation of your energy fields, entraining you and "exciting" a desired response to that manipulation, was patented twenty years ago.

From the white paper[36] provided in Mr. Loos's patent application, we read:

"Physiological effects have been observed in a human subject in response to stimulation of the skin with weak electromagnetic fields that are pulsed with certain frequencies near ½ Hz or 2.4 Hz, such as to excite a sensory resonance. Many computer monitors and TV tubes, when displaying pulsed images, emit pulsed electromagnetic fields of sufficient amplitudes to cause such excitation. It is therefore possible to manipulate the nervous system of a subject by pulsing images displayed on a nearby computer monitor or TV set. For the latter, the

---

36   https://patents.google.com/patent/US6506148

image pulsing may be imbedded in the program material, or it may be overlaid by modulating a video stream, either as an RF signal or as a video signal. The image displayed on a computer monitor may be pulsed effectively by a simple computer program. For certain monitors, pulsed electromagnetic fields capable of exciting sensory resonances in nearby subjects may be generated even as the displayed images are pulsed with subliminal intensity.

CLAIMS:

- A method for manipulating the nervous system of a subject located near a monitor, the monitor emitting an electromagnetic field when displaying an image by virtue of the physical display process, the subject having a sensory resonance frequency, the method comprising: creating a video signal for displaying an image on the monitor, the image having an intensity; modulating the video signal for pulsing the image intensity with a frequency in the range 0.1 Hz to 15 Hz; and setting the pulse frequency to the resonance frequency.

- A computer program for manipulating the nervous system of a subject located near a monitor, the monitor emitting an electromagnetic field when displaying an image by virtue of the physical display process, the subject having cutaneous nerves that fire spontaneously and have spiking patterns, the computer program comprising: a display routine for displaying an image on the monitor, the image having an intensity; a pulse routine for pulsing the image intensity with a frequency in the range 0.1 Hz to 15 Hz; and a frequency routine that can be internally controlled by the subject, for setting the frequency; whereby the emitted electromagnetic field is pulsed, the cutaneous nerves are exposed to the pulsed electromagnetic field, and the spiking patterns of the nerves acquire a frequency modulation.

- A source of video stream for manipulating the nervous system of a subject located near a monitor, the monitor emitting an electromagnetic field when displaying an image by virtue of the physical display process, the subject having cutaneous nerves that fire spontaneously and have spiking patterns, the source of video stream comprising: means for defining an image on the monitor, the image having an intensity; and means for subliminally pulsing the image intensity with a frequency in the range 0.1 Hz to 15 Hz; whereby the emitted electromagnetic field is pulsed, the cutaneous nerves are exposed to the pulsed electromagnetic field, and the spiking patterns of the nerves acquire a frequency modulation.

SUMMARY:

Computer monitors and TV monitors can be made to emit weak low-frequency electromagnetic fields merely by pulsing the intensity of displayed images. Experiments have shown that the ½ Hz sensory resonance can be excited in this manner in a subject near the monitor. The 2.4 Hz sensory resonance can also be excited in this fashion. Hence, a TV monitor or computer monitor can be used to manipulate the nervous system of nearby people.

The implementations of the invention are adapted to the source of video stream that drives the monitor, be it a computer program, a TV broadcast, a video tape or a digital video disc (DVD).

For a computer monitor, the image pulses can be produced by a suitable computer program. The pulse frequency may be controlled through keyboard input, so that the subject can tune to an individual sensory resonance frequency. The pulse amplitude can be controlled as well in this manner. A program written in Visual Basic(R) is particularly suitable for use on computers that run the Windows 95(R) or Windows 98(R) operating system. The structure of such a program is described. Production of periodic pulses requires an accurate timing procedure. Such a procedure is constructed from the GetTimeCount function available in the Application Program Interface (API) of the Windows operating system, together with an extrapolation procedure that improves the timing accuracy.

Pulse variability can be introduced through software, for the purpose of thwarting habituation of the nervous system to the field stimulation, or when the precise resonance frequency is not known. The variability may be a pseudo-random variation within a narrow interval, or it can take the form of a frequency or amplitude sweep in time. The pulse variability may be under control of the subject.

The program that causes a monitor to display a pulsing image may be run on a remote computer that is connected to the user computer by a link; the latter may partly belong to a network, which may be the Internet.

For a TV monitor, the image pulsing may be inherent in the video stream as it flows from the video source, or else the stream may be modulated such as to overlay the pulsing. In the first case, a live TV broadcast can be arranged to have the feature imbedded simply by slightly pulsing the illumination of the scene that is being broadcast. This method can of course also be used in making movies and recording video tapes and DVDs.

Video tapes can be edited such as to overlay the pulsing by means of modulating hardware. A simple modulator is discussed wherein the luminance signal of composite video is pulsed without affecting the chroma signal. The same effect may be introduced at the consumer end, by modulating the video stream that is produced by the video source. A DVD can be edited through software, by introducing pulse-like variations in the digital RGB signals. Image intensity pulses can be overlaid onto the analog component video output of a DVD player by modulating the luminance signal component. Before entering the TV set, a television signal can be modulated such as to cause pulsing of the image intensity by means of a variable delay line that is connected to a pulse generator.

Certain monitors can emit electromagnetic field pulses that excite a sensory resonance in a nearby subject, through image pulses that are so weak as to be subliminal. This is unfortunate since it opens a way for mischievous application of the invention, whereby people are exposed unknowingly to manipulation of their nervous systems for someone else's purposes. Such application would be unethical and is of course not advocated. It is mentioned here in order to alert the public to the possibility of covert abuse that may occur while being online, or while watching TV, a video, or a DVD."

Yes, indeed, such application would be unethical to say the least, and thank you for the warning, Dr. Krugman. Unfortunately, most of the public never got your message.

As for the covert abuse to which he alluded, they are definitely upping the game at this time. 5G radiation is coming into play in cities around the world, frying birds in flight and burning nearby trees and foliage. Imagine what it will do to human beings, holding the not-so-smart phone to their ear, hours on end? And how will it be interacting with all that nano-technology within the body?

Computer software is far more invasive now. It will not be long before your biometric profile will be required to get into your own computer or phone. And the neural system programming pouring out of your television set is oceans more dangerous than when the good doctor was still alive. Add a little 5G super radiation charge to that and, oh my God, what a nightmare.

If you truly wish to break free from entrapment from the ubiquitous technology matrix, it is my sincere hope that, having read this information, you will have gleaned enough of the science to convince you to remove (as much as you possibly can) all devices upon which you have been made to feel dependent, since their inception.

If you do not want to fall prey to the agenda, you will have to make a commitment to completely alter your dependency on the viewing screen. I do understand how difficult it will be to make a complete lifestyle change; remember that the more difficult it is, the more you are addicted to it. It may feel nearly impossible to wean yourself and your family off the programming that is being beamed into the manipulated brain, deliberately.

I know. I experienced it first-hand.

I removed television from my life over twenty-five years ago. I gave away my iPad. I have greatly reduced my on-line activity and participation in social media, and when I am on the computer, I actually set a timer to break me out of the trance, unless I am writing, in which case there are no time limits at all. I leave the cell phone outside the front door, in a metal box, only checking it once or twice a day for phone calls, or if I need to transact on-line.

Please understand. I am not suggesting that we deny ourselves entertainment provided through these media and communication instruments, or that we go back to a Victorian age of sitting around a candle at night, reciting poetry or sharing ghost stories. Of course not. There is still wonderful content being created in film, TV programming, sports . . . whatever genre you love. It is more than abundantly available, and we are entitled to the pleasure we receive from laughing at a great comedy, or being intrigued by the plot of a great movie or TV show—even the high of watching a favorite sport play out. There is a wealth of great content available on YouTube and other channels, to be sure. And of course, we are facilitated in our ability to communicate with people anywhere in the world.

I am merely suggesting that when the screen becomes an addiction, and you cannot live without it, then it is time to reconsider how prevalent it is in your life and how deeply it is penetrating your consciousness. You want to be in control of your mind, rather than being mind-controlled, by people we know all too well have set up the technology industry to do just that.

Your liberation from the technicians, who want to turn you into a brain-dead robot, requires that you take this situation in hand with firm resolution. You will need to address the following four primary sources of disruption:

1. *Television:* This is the ultimate entrainment mechanism, second to electronic gaming, which is not as widespread—not yet, that is—and you are going to need to remove it. Yes, you read that right: **remove it.** If you can't get your family to go along with it, which is most likely the case, then you need to rearrange your house, if you can, so that you personally have no exposure when your family is glued to it, hour after precious hour.

You cannot take on their addictions at this point. You are the one who is ready, and you can only decide for yourself. For now, at least.

People balk at this idea. I have had friends tell me it is too drastic—"overkill"—and that they do not need to completely eliminate television in order to limit its influence, in which case, I cannot help but notice, they usually do not. Never mind the science. They refuse to believe that technology has been designed into the equipment to alter the mind electronically, and through persuasive programming, and, of course, via subliminal inlays in those programs and non-stop advertising. If you are one of these people, and hear doubt creeping into your mind, the kind that says: "There's no way our own government would allow the tech industry to do anything like that to us," make sure you re-read the information provided in US Patent US5606148B2. Or, if you do understand it, but still cannot get your head around why so many people are so insanely addicted to the programming, remind yourself that the techno-maniacs are admitting to "manipulating the nervous system." That should be enough to help you pursue a determined course that will allow you to release from your television addiction, and move past "step one."

No matter how much resistance you get from family and housemates, demand that the television be turned off during meals. Cell phones, too. There is so little opportunity these days to share with loved ones, and that is deliberate. Government is stripping from us our desire to interact with each other, destroying the family unit. So, the dinner table is a great place to reclaim it! Be present, and demand that your family do the same. You are providing sustenance and love through the food you prepare and that needs to be honored, and the love needs to be reciprocated.

You will get resistance, no doubt, but do it anyway. Take your children back.

Do you have a television in the bedroom? You may not be aware that it is most likely watching you through that little red light you think is simply a sensor for the remote control. So I was told, fifteen years ago, by a senior engineer who worked for Sony. He told me then that one in ten sets had cameras built into them, and that within ten years they would all be equipped with the technology to spy on unsuspecting viewers.

Particularly dangerous is the "smart" TV, which any savvy IT security expert will tell you can be easily hacked, allowing the prying eye of a stranger to access your private uploaded videos, to access the camera in the set, to spy on you in what you thought was the privacy of your own home, and to manipulate what you are watching. That includes broadcasting dangerous programming to your children.

Let the bedroom be a place of intimacy and restfulness, and be sure you shut the AI system, and prying eyes, out. Needless-to-say, that would include "Alexa" and that whole line of AI intrusive listening devices that people think are so innocuous. They aren't. They are spying on you.

2. *Cell Phone:* Big Tech is ramping up the electromagnetic pulse and radiation on these devices deliberately. Their radiation is getting much stronger, especially now that we are seeing 5G being turned on and interactive programming becoming more prevalent and more invasive. Soon, you will not even be able to access your cell phone without passing facial recognition ID system requirements. It can track your every move and anticipate your thoughts and response to targeted adverts. The fact that people have their cell phones on their bodies, in their

hands, up to their ears for hours on end makes it harmful not only to the individual, but to others in near proximity.

I do not allow people to come into my home with their cell phone. The metal box is for visitors as well.

It is time to realize that the phone is an absolute control device. Bear in mind, your smart phone is never "off," no matter whether you think you've shut it down, or not. You have not. Be wary. People are listening, screening and storing your voice and your conversations . . . every single word you utter.

3. *Computers:* I know how hard it is to limit the amount of time we spend at the computer, especially for those who sit in front of it, at work, for eight hours a day. Children are learning from computers in school, or through home school on-line programs. Do what you can to set limits to your exposure. Try setting a timer, as I do. It helps remind me how much time I'm really losing, and how much radiation I am absorbing, staring into the screen, and it reminds me to walk away every two hours, to give my eyes, mind and energy fields a rest.

Covid lockdowns the last two years (and counting) have made us so much more dependent upon the Internet for social interaction, entertainment, work and all forms of communication. We need to break free of the conditions set for us through this never-ending emergency drama, and disengage, as much as we can. So important is our time in nature: walking through a forest, swimming in the ocean, or hiking a trail to where it meets the sky. Why would anyone choose simulated reality from a screen over that?

4. *Gaming:* What we are learning about damage done to people who get hooked on high-tech gaming, particularly children, would fill a book in itself. This is high-level mind control,

much more addictive than a lot of illicit drugs. If you haven't started gaming, do not. And if you have, consider that, for the entire time you are plugged into the "game" of virtual reality, your body hormones, your emotions and mind are being manipulated by the program, which keeps you in that state I mentioned earlier of "fight or flight" adrenal stress.

Get your kids off of them. They are sucking the life force out of all who engage and programming all who "play" that virtual reality is far more exciting, entertaining and pleasurable than the world into which they were born. Set limits, and save your children.

Technology is designed to isolate us from one another, to groom us for what lies ahead in the transhumanists' simulated world. They want us entrained, hypnotized, addicted and, finally, implanted with hardware that will allow them remote access to the workings of our bodies and minds.

We do not have to subscribe.

We can say no, and take our power back.

To prepare for the work of restoring and heightening the sacred language of light that is written within you, removing the implants and subliminal codes and all the horrific invasion of our sovereignty through mind control, by means of electronic manipulation and subliminal programming, you are first going to have to release from the entrainment and brain-altering pulses that come from those monitors and screens, designed and patented to disrupt all neurological processes and distorting your perception of reality.

Now is the time to make that choice. You "take the blue pill," ask no questions, and stay embroiled in the matrix, or you take a metaphorical hammer to the screens and break free from their "nervous system manipulation" forever. Reject invasion of your body electric and you will avoid simulated reality. That is what it boils down to, and that is the decision you will have to make, if you are truly ready to take back your power.

Your liberation begins here. Remember: if you believe you cannot do without it, you're addicted. What you decide to do about that is your choice to make, as it is for your young children and those whose lives matter to you.

Exercise discernment: for you, for the people you love, and for the collective unconscious to which you contribute as a unit of the greater whole.

For the highest good of all concerned, I pray that you will defy the architects of control, and choose freedom.

Chapter 21

Sacred Designs, Perfect Ratios

From the subatomic to the densest matter, the dance of life subscribes to a universal language of mathematical proportion, and its artistic and spatial expression to endless displays of geometric form. We speak of "sacred" geometry, as if there could be any other kind, for all geometry is a matter of divine proportion, frequency and vibration, organized into layers upon layers of exquisite templates—planes and multidimensional constructs—that are interconnected and mutually relevant.

All is sacred.

It is the universal language of all Creation: the order, the structure, and the palette of all that exists. It is the quintessential template from which all things are designed, elaborated and breathed into being by the Master Artist: Prime Creator. Geometry holds within its forms the interconnectedness of vibration-imprinting-matter, and of the plane where space seems to intersect with a perception of time: the time-space continuum. It is the microcosm; it is the macrocosm. It communicates number, ratio, vibration, frequency, certain mathematical precepts and the conscious intention of Prime Creator to build, from a seed thought, entire universes of manifest beauty and awareness.

One often hears asked the existential question: "If a tree fell in the woods, and no one was there to hear it, would it really have happened?"

A bigger question challenging the metaphysical philosopher, and one that begs answering is: "If everything in the universe is a perpetual unfolding of geometric form and sacred ratios, but no one within it is able to grasp the entirety of that design, then, does it really exist?" The answer to both of these philosophical conundrums, especially for those who acknowledge a Prime Creator, is "Yes, without question. Creation is not dependent upon who or what can perceive its existence, or why." But oh, how much richer and vastly more fulfilling is one's appreciation of life and the magnificence of Creation, when we can recognize the patterns and dynamic relationships—the rhythm and pace—that fill the endless worlds and infinite possibilities that lie somewhere between the ocean waves, the clouds, and the swaying motions of a wheat field, when the wind blows.

We are blessed with microcosmic forms of the greater whole, everywhere around and within us. When we stop to observe a bee in motion, we see patterns in its flight, in its interaction with the flower, and with others of its hive who are busy there, too, gathering nectar . . . working in unison. Its body is an extraordinary design of sacred form and intricate patterns, head to stinger. In that act of really paying attention, we become involved, triggering our own nervous system's reaction to the scents, the sounds, and the frequencies emanating from different phases of the bee's activity. Even if we are not consciously aware of the geometric proportions of all those aspects, as that dance of life unfolds, we perceive those spatial dynamics and input from our senses.

We perceive sacred geometry because we **are** sacred geometry.

Through the work of Hans Jenny, who brought us the field of Cymatics, the study of how vibration and sound affect matter, and later, from the renowned Dr. Masaru Emoto, who showed us how water molecules perpetually seek to achieve perfection of their innate form, and how they respond to thought, sound and emotion, we have learned much about how our thoughts, and the vibration that emanates from them, determine the quality of form, structure and the essence of matter. We have had proven for us, over and over again, how vibrational waves of energy can alter matter, and how thought can affect the geometric design of a single molecule, frozen in time.

Surely, we can apply those same principles to the question of how our thoughts affect our DNA, and how we can use our focused intention to bring our genetic blueprint back to its ultimate form—the God light within—no matter what invasive mechanisms have been introduced into our system to disconnect us.

The Sirians foretold of what was coming. They guided me from the very beginning to address the question of DNA, and the quality of our cellular memory, determined by what we feed into our body electric, in the way of thoughts, nourishment and the very words we speak. They foresaw the invasive intervention in our DNA, and guided us as to how we could manage to maintain its perfect health and accelerated activation. They warned us off all electronic devices, knowing how they would all be used to lull us into complacency when this injection agenda would be rolled out against the human race.

In the book, No More Secrets, No More Lies[37], they explained:
"No matter how discordant and energetically shattered are the water molecules of your environmentally bombarded bodies, it is the nature of life and consciousness to eventually achieve perfection—to climb the spiral, seeking full illumination. So is every molecule of your being intent upon that soul purpose from which it was designed—to reclaim the pattern of cosmometric proportion and beauty and to resonate that vibration through the Universe of Being.

Whether you are determined to consciously effect change at the cellular level or whether you choose to ignore the spiritual nature of your molecular composition, we ask that you always bear in mind that every unit of consciousness (from

---

37   No More Secrets, No More Lies, Patricia Cori, 2022 edition, pgs. 203-204

the sub-atomic particle to the galaxy . . . to the most expansive of universes that exist in the Cosmos of Soul) strives for greatness. Each beats with its own rhythm . . . each is a divine product of the environment and the supreme consciousness that permeate its inner and outer space.

To ignore the consciousness of every single cell is to relinquish your ability to command these micro-units of your being to perform in perfect harmony, to create excellent health of body, mind, and spirit, and to alter any dysfunction that has occurred in your process of living in the often conflict-ridden and disturbing times through which you are now passing in body.

Indeed, ignoring that the cell is a receptive unit of the body electric means that you are utterly unaware of your own make- up and of the power that you have over all aspects of your physical manifestation.

The receptive quality of a cosmometrically aligned hexagonal water molecule is identified in the molecule's capacity to reverberate at those specific resonant frequencies that create the ideal vibrational field into which the third strand of DNA, the first etheric strand to be reintegrated into the double helix, can be eventually crystallized and ultimately anchored as a material reality—first at the molecular level of awareness, then at the cellular level, and so on.

The integration of the third strand is the most important progression of all that will follow, for it weaves into your essence the consciousness of all the celestial bodies of your solar system, the intent of the extradimensional beings who served you at the seeding, and the higher consciousness of your souls—creating triangulation within every cell of your being. Correctly executed, the process of the stranding instantaneously activates the thymus—the master gland and central control tower of your light bodies—like the flick of a wall switch floods a dark room with light."

If what we have learned about mind-over-matter and manifestation is indeed capable of empowering us to such an extent that we can focus our minds to alter the material realm, or to bring into form that which has yet to coalesce as matter, then it can certainly be applied to the important task of repairing whatever has occurred at the DNA level of the body's cellular make-up.

Anyone capable of acute focus and unwavering intent to isolate and remove the synthetic messenger RNA and the nano-technologies being constructed with graphene and other elements introduced through those needles, should, theoretically, be able to deconstruct and remove those invasive elements from their being.

Bear in mind that the human brain is estimated to process around forty quadrillion calculations per second. No super computer exists, nor will it ever, that can compete with your mind power.

We can call the shattered fragments back into the light, reconstructing the sacred geometry of our stellar design, and remove all pernicious codes, data and signals from the entire organism: mind, body and soul. We can utilize powerful sound frequencies to heal DNA and vocalize the God code, Yahweh, into the restructuring of our cellular memory. We must never forget that, although artificial intelligence is powerful, and in many ways formidable, it is nothing compared to our innate intelligence and everything that the human mind is capable of visualizing and bringing to form. If we truly understand this principle, we cannot help but surmise that we are capable, through the power of focused intent and visualization, to deconstruct the invasive messenger, and dissolve whatever it was sent to deliver, and whatever it was designed to take away.

Remember: *"Every molecule of your being {is} intent upon that soul purpose from which it was designed—to reclaim the pattern of cosmometric proportion and beauty and to resonate that vibration through the Universe of Being."*

Let us commit to that process.

Chapter 22

The "Shattered Glass"

Always holding in our awareness that we are electromagnetic, biological units of consciousness, manifest in form and boundless energy, and that everything in the universe is vibration, we can only assume that certain sounds, and the frequencies that any and all vibrations emit, are going to affect us on many levels: negatively, as is the case with raucous, unharmonious music, and positively, with certain tones, melodies and rhythms that are sympathetic with our energy systems.

Indeed, sacred sounds and highly vibrational tools, such as Tibetan bowls, tuning forks, crystal bowls and other, more modern devices—emitters of frequency—have been proven to affect molecules, cells, and the entire being on all levels: mind/body/spirit. So do other sounds that we take for granted, such as the purr of a cat, the cooing of a baby, the bird song and many manifestations of vibrational music, to include classical works, which are like sacred geometry frozen in space and time, and Solfeggio frequencies, utilized by ancient Gregorian monks in their sacred chants.

The capacity of sound to alter matter has been demonstrated effectively through the exercise of an opera singer shattering a crystal wine glass through the frequency emitted by her voice. When it reaches resonance with the intrinsic energy of the glass—which vibrates at a certain frequency by nature of its material essence—and she holds that note long enough to excite the vibrational field within the molecular structure of the glass, it shatters.

You may be aware of the Rife Machine, radio-frequency technology developed in the 1930s by Royal Rife—an absolute genius of his time. His immense contribution to the field of vibrational science taught that very principle of sympathetic resonance, and how objects in a field will begin to vibrate to the same frequency. A device that generates energy in the form of radio waves, the machine is designed to tune into the body and search out extremely low frequencies, using the principle of reaching resonance. The concept behind it is that when you find the frequency of a pathogenic micro-organism within the body, and transmit a powerful load of that frequency into it, it will be disrupted—or explode, just like the crystal glass—and then die, without creating any residual harm to the otherwise healthy organism.

It stands to reason that once the disharmonies that have been injected into human beings have been openly admitted to and made known to the population, the team of electronic engineers, technical designers, software developers and Rife practitioners will inevitably be bringing forward invaluable solutions to the issue at hand: shattering the imposed, unnatural and low-frequency matter delivered to human subjects of the "experiment," and bringing the body back into balance. **That can only mean healing the DNA as well.**

In a universe that is held together by frequency and vibration, so is the organic, biological body representative of that cohesion.

What we have been learning, and remembering from ancient wisdom keepers, is that certain sounds and frequencies can be utilized for specific outcomes, which improve and heal disharmonies in the body and, at the same time, activate and repair the DNA.

As science merges with spirit, genius minds are applying the "up" side of technology (for there is an "up" side to everything) particularly as regards vibrational healing, to the discovery and application of specific frequencies for cellular repair and body healing, which appear to have very significant effects on both the conscious and subconscious mind.

Another genius in the field of bioelectricity is researcher and physician, Dr. Joseph Puleo, who rediscovered Solfeggio frequencies, over fifty years ago, and who was instrumental in bringing the healing benefits of this musical scale back to public awareness. In his vast body of work, researching frequency and mathematical vibration, he correlated the six Solfeggio frequencies to the Pythagorean method of reducing numbers to a base number (as we do in numerology). You can find more about it by investigating Dr. Puleo and the "Pythagorean method," for it is too deep and complex to illustrate in this text. What is important to extract from his contribution to our rediscovery of Solfeggio is that his research identified six distinct tones, electromagnetic frequencies, which he dedicated to discovering what potential benefit each contributed to healing the body, repairing the DNA, and promoting well-being.

Solfeggio Frequencies

174 Hz – Reduce pain, alleviate stresses
285 Hz – Influence Energy, Rejuvenation
396 Hz – Liberating Guilt and Fear
417 Hz – Facilitating Change
528 Hz – Transformation and Miracles: DNA Repair
639 Hz – Connecting/Relationships

Using the Pythagorean method of number and vibration, and bearing in mind his emphasis on the numbers three, six and nine, Dr. Puleo found that the six original Solfeggio frequencies, in fact, reduce to those base numbers: 1+7+4=12=**3**; 2+8+5=15=**6**, etc. I find this ex-

279

tremely fascinating with regard to my own work with DNA activation, which, as opposed to all the circulating information that proposes reactivating two strands of DNA at a time, bases the structure of our eventual twelve-stranded DNA on the creation of sacred tetrahedral forms within it: three, six and nine, interwoven to form, when one reaches that point of ascension, the dodecahedral DNA structure of Christ consciousness!

Researchers of sacred sound and sound healing believe the original Solfeggio frequencies, of the ancient musical scale, were utilized by Gregorian monks, imbuing powerful spiritual blessings and healing upon the people during religious ceremonies. Mysteriously, they disappeared around 1050 AD, and were replaced with our modern musical scale, which is slightly "off" energetically from the sacred tones. Experts even go so far as to declare that our music today is actually atonal in comparison to these amazing Solfeggio tones, and that it is literally causing dis-ease within the human body.

The contemporary musical scale, they have found, resonates to a 440 hertz frequency, which was changed in the early 1900s from the frequency of 417 hertz, the Solfeggio frequency, whose effect on the human body, it is believed, is to **facilitate change**. Isn't that interesting? And have we been manipulated, by the deliberate subversion of music itself, into obedience and acceptance of the status quo?

The Solfeggio scale shapes and transforms matter and, according to some texts, it was used to heal disease and exorcise demonic spirits. Today, so much of the pop music we hear actually invokes those spirits, and creates all manner of dis-ease in the listener. So, be selective when you turn on the radio. Whatever you are listening to is coming into your body at every level, and much of it is disrupting the natural harmonics of the body electric, right down to the cellular level . . . and that means right into the DNA.

Fortunately, we are rediscovering Solfeggio and many are the healers, practitioners and musicians who have reverted back to those sacred tones in their work.

Scientists and spiritualists alike have taken the torch, and gone on to develop a new, revitalized understanding of how these frequencies actually do evoke very powerful, positive effects on human consciousness, and the workings of our mental, emotional and physical beings.

Dr. Glen Rein received his Ph.D. from the University of London in Bio(neuro)-chemistry in 1983. In 1984 he became a professor at Mt. Sinai Hospital, where he researched the very exciting field of bio-electromagnetics. Beginning in 1987, he studied psychoneuroimmunology at Stanford University Medical Center. He is the director of the Quantum Biology Research Lab in New York, and a devoted research scientist.

Here's where things get exciting.

According to noted researcher, Celeste Solum, around 1998 (the same time I was bringing DNA information through from the Sirian High Council), Dr. Rein was performing experiments on in vitro DNA, using different forms of music, converting them into scalar audio waves and then playing them to the test tubes. The absorption of UV light within one hour of receiving those audio waves served as the measure to determine what effect the music was having, if any, on the DNA. The experiment showed that various forms of music can resonate with DNA, but it was Solfeggio frequencies that caused a significant spike in the absorption of light at the DNA level. It is not a giant leap to consider that if genes can be affected by sound and audio waves in the laboratory, so can DNA within the body.

Sacred geometry experts describe 528 hertz as essential to the structure and restructuring of the geometric designs of DNA. I utilize it in my Divine Blueprint meditations, available on my website: www.patriciacori.com. It is considered the "miracle" tone of the entire scale of six, each with its vibrational importance ... each with its healing properties. Although we still cannot prove it, it seems a natural conclusion that it can help repair damage to our DNA, to restore whatever has been interfered with, energetically, and to remove whatever has been implanted, which—if the rules of resonance apply—can be shattered with the right frequencies, like the proverbial glass.

I love the idea that sound brings light into the DNA, particularly Solfeggio frequencies, and **that**, along with the meditative state it puts me into, is why I listen to it every day.

In my contemplation of what I have shared earlier regarding the vocalization of "Yahweh" into the DNA, I knew it would be most effective if integrated into a 528 hertz background.

You cannot imagine my excitement, when researching this possibility, to find that the master of sound, Jonathan Goldman, an internationally recognized authority on sound healing and vibrational harmonics, was doing that precise work . . . and clearly had reached the same conclusion as I!

To my breathtaking surprise, Jonathan is chanting Yahweh exactly as I described it should be done earlier, perfectly the same in tone and phonetics, and breathing the God Code back into the DNA. I am sure we both received that information from a higher source, and celebrate how we are being gifted with such vital information, when we need it most.

You can observe Jonathan perform this extraordinary chant, which surely utilizes the 528 hertz as background, in a video[38] he has posted to YouTube. It demonstrates exceptional auric amplification through use of aura photography, and, most importantly, it shows us exactly how to chant the word, the name . . . the God Code, back into the DNA.

---

38   https://www.youtube.com/watch?v=0vXOFcwJz3s

How miraculous that we are all finding our way back to this wisdom: back to God . . . back to Source . . . back to sovereignty.

And aren't "miracles" what 528 hertz is all about?

Visualization
Clearing the Pathways

You are going to go inward now, so you will need to remove all distraction. If you have not already cleared your home of electronic interference, take the time now to unplug the television, remove the cell phone and other electronic devices, and find a quiet place where you can be free of noise, distractions, and the daily business of your life—all those perturbations that hold you in a perpetual state of mental and emotional imbalance, and inquietude.

If this is not a good time, come back to it when you are free, and unfettered.

Do what you can to assure there will be no interruptions, for this is intended to be a moment of gentle introspection, peaceful observance, and reflection . . . to make yours now, and forever.

Take this moment to breathe deeply. Consciously. We take breathing for granted, never stopping to think that, just seconds without air to the lungs, the body short-circuits and soon expires. We can go weeks without food, and days without water, but only seconds without air. If ever you have held a thought or feeling of being alone and separate from the world around you, just remember that, on levels you may still not understand, you are interacting with the forces of the entire multidimensional universe every time you inhale, drawing energy through your body electric, and sending a part of yourself back out, into the quantum field, every time you exhale.

Pay attention. Be aware of how good it feels to breathe in, and breathe out, following the oxygen and prana as they move through you, filling the lungs, and back out again, and just repeat the "in and out"—slow and easy—until you realize how really good you are feeling in your body. When you take time to follow the life force moving through you, you quickly become more relaxed, and centered . . . more present. You feel the calm that comes from focusing your mind on the process of conscious breathing, inhaling peace and serenity, and exhaling whatever does not serve you, and which you are ready now to release.

The cells of your body retain full memory of every thought you have ever thought, every word you have ever spoken or that has been uttered to you, every experience and every emotion that has surged from all of that input, within the sacred waters contained in their membranous walls. From those conscious pools, in turn, you reflect and emit vibrational currents that define your state of mind and emotion into every tissue, organ, and hormonal system of your body temple. All body systems—every cell, the blood, the lymph, the hormones, the organs, the chakric energy byways—respond to every thought you pack into the house of your soul-manifesting-biological-life on Earth.

So, be aware of your thoughts, because your body never stops listening, even when you sleep.

Your analytical mind, the left brain, loves to play tricks on the right brain. Always programmed to analyze situational data and question perceptivity, it has been trained by your life experience to override the intuitive mind—if you let it—and that can interfere with your ability to manifest. It may rear its head as "ego consciousness," and tell you, "I don't need to do this. I already know all of this," and you do. Of course you do. Many of us know how to meditate effectively, and some are better than others at manifesting . . . but we all know how to breathe. You don't have to think about it.

But today, you do. Today, like no other day before this, you are going to reclaim your power and communicate your strength and re-solve to all aspects of your being, starting with your conscious breath.

Begin by declaring your commitment to every cell in your body that it is your intention to release all that does not serve you, as is for the highest good for the entire body organism. Let it go out into ethers, and ask that it be diffused and healed in the light of infinite love. State your intention that you are seeing the sheath that encircles you—the auric field—fill with a vibrant reflection of your loving, empowered spirit, and know that nothing can ever penetrate that shield, unless you pull it back in close to you, out of fear or a feeling of separateness.

Be careful not to abuse substance; that too can weaken the auric sheath, creating a fissure through which marauding, low-energy spirits can slip into you.

Remember that you are abundant, the quantum field is pulsating energy through you and you possess all the love of universe. You are glowing, radiant . . . pure brilliance.

Within and around you, and beyond your immediate sphere, where you are free to draw from and contribute to the wisdom of the Cosmos, let the message be heard: you are reclaiming your sovereignty. Send your declaration out, into the astral layers that interface with your ener-gy field, that any intended interference be sent back to its source, for it will no longer find resonance in the space you occupy, nor in the energy with which you interact and draw sustenance. You send out the com-mand to the universe that no interference against your sovereign rights will be allowed from this point forward. The universe will respond, in kind.

You have to own all of this entirely. You have to breathe it, walk it, live it, in order to re-establish, wherever needed, your divine, God-given rights over all meddling and misdirection from the outer world.

How important is it to be aware of your thoughts and how you resonate to the energies coming into you? It is everything; it is the core of your accumulated experience from this and many other lifetimes, for it is wound, around and around, in your karmic sac, like a ball of the finest angel hair, filaments you have gathered from everything upon which your soul has chosen to focus and to carry along, upon its journey. Whether you choose to unravel it in this lifetime, or to hold onto it, for whatever lessons will still need to be learned, further along, is your free will to determine. Those are the choices that can catapult you forward, up the ascension spiral, or keep you tethered, spinning on the tedious wheel of reincarnation, until finally you understand and deal with whatever was meant to be learned, forgiven, and healed, so that you are free to take the next giant leaps in your soul's progression back to Source.

You are going to commit today to holding on to those memories that nourish you and bring you happiness and joy, and to letting go of whatever makes you uncomfortable or stirs disharmony within.

When you silence your mind long enough to follow your life breath in and out, in and out ... letting go, letting God, it is that simple. It is your commitment to freeing yourself of disruptive thoughts and to be seated in the soft light of inner peace that makes it so.

Your body is an extension of the Akashic Record: an extraordinary library—a hall of mirrors—endlessly bouncing all the information you feed into it ... throughout the tiniest aspects of your being, into your auric energy field, and then out, through the ethers, to other life forms and aspects of consciousness that engage with you, on levels of which you may not even hold awareness.

Like a stone tossed into a placid lake, you ripple across the waves of the Cosmos of Soul.

It is so important that you finally understand that it is not the information that you access that is in question, nor the experience you accumulate, that sculpts your perception of reality. Remember that you are walking through a field of illusion, no matter how "real" it appears to be. Rather, it is how you absorb and process all that input, and what you choose to make yours, knowing that it will bounce around in the deep waters of your being for as long as you do not rewrite it with other instructions and commands, that is at stake here.

If you are ready and determined to reclaim your sovereignty and clear the fields of disharmony within your being—all the angst, the dread, the worry—you will want to start here, in the right now of this moment. You will set the intention that you release all judgment that has come before now—all self-incrimination, regret, fear and doubt—to come to that place of neutrality from whence you can reclaim that truly primordial experience of yourself as a sovereign being: an immortal, eternal being of God's Creation.

Could you have made better decisions along the way? Absolutely. We all are in a condition where we win and lose throughout any given lifetime. We didn't come in as Masters. What would have been the point? We came as newcomers into this particular university of higher education. Let us never allow the ego to fool us into believing we have nothing to learn from our passing here. We do the best we can with what we have to work with, and from where we are, on our conscious journey, in every moment: whether we understand it at the time, or come to realize it later on.

Does what you've done in the past, things you wish you could wipe off your karmic slate, matter now? Yes, it does. Everything matters. Everything adds to the tapestry of our passing, lifetime to lifetime.

Just remember that you need your mistakes to grow.

You need to fall; it teaches you how to stand strong and resolute. You need to know your weaknesses to celebrate your strengths. Those are the greatest lessons life offers; those are the signs that you do still have free will to choose and accept the consequences of the choices you make, and to survive the missteps and "accidents" that befall you along the way. We most always learn, down the road, why they happen and what they are meant to teach us, do we not?

Who wouldn't willingly go back in time to erase a bad decision, or to resolve a painful circumstance? We all make mistakes and it is so easy to misinterpret the options that lie before us in any given moment. Understanding those moments as opportunities now, rather than regrets that cannot be undone later, starts the process of burning their karmic imprint on the soul's flight home.

What matters is that you focus on what you can do to repair the damage, heal the suffering and move forward, from a place of non-judgment and self-acceptance, and from whence you may even reach a place of gratitude, when you can look back and recognize how every decision, and every choice, has propelled you forward on your journey of awakening.

Be reminded, with every breath, that the past is behind you. The future is an elusive field of possibilities that you continuously affect, directly and indirectly, as a unit of the greater whole, and as a contributor to the collective. The perpetual present is your only operative template, and that is where you want your thoughts focused.

The now is everything.

You breathe peace into the cellular structure of your body organism, and the cells respond. They instantly realign themselves with the vibratory frequencies you send into your inner and outer being. They reflect that state of balance, trust and knowing throughout the organism, all body systems, all energy byways. The whole becomes instantly aware that you are transmuting fear, doubt and anxiety into trust, and that at the center of your being is only love and the joy that emanates from it. You know that everything is in divine order in the universe, and that peace can only ever be derived from a state of mind, not from the state of the world.

You speak to your DNA, telling it that you are aligned with the design of Creation, and that you can read the God Code. It is pure, it is untainted, it is intact. You tell the body: "I am a child of the Universe. Nothing can deter my mission. I am a spark of Divine Light. I am **sovereign**."

You tell the body again and again and again. "I read the God Code within me. It is pure, it is untainted, it is intact."

You recognize the glue of the matrix that surrounds you for what it is and you observe it with detachment. It wants you . . . but it cannot have you.

Holding to anxiety and trepidation of what has been, or worrying about what may or may not come, keeps you in a state of perpetual dissatisfaction and suffering. Your true power lies in your ability to understand the forces that involve you in this experience of present, and to choose the best actions for the highest outcome. Your acutely focused intent is what brings you back to center, where you can feel peace and joy in every experience, letting the outer world fall away, knowing you are holding your ground—in the heart, and in your power.

We spirit beings came to have a human experience and, by God, what a journey we have set our sights on here, in this lifetime of Earth's crazy revolution, traversing two Great Ages of cosmic no-time, on a planet passing from one dimension to another.

You are a heroic soul to do that. Never forget it.

This is a lifetime you chose because you wanted to be in the thick of it, whether standing in the front lines, or watching from a front-row seat the turning of such gargantuan wheels of the universe.

Let this be your mantra:

"I embody the love of Spirit.

I choose to experience everything I continue to co-create in this lifetime. I release fear and judgment and all energies that attempt to deter me.

And I stand in my beauty, my truth, my power, for I am the manifestation and the light and the glory of Divine Creation.

I am the universe unfolding. ***I am sovereign.****"*

Visualization

Scanning the Double Helix

Prepare yourself to take a sacred journey into the deep within. Call upon the Angel Warriors of Light, and your spirit guides, asking that you be encircled in an impenetrable sphere of golden white light, where loving light beings are welcomed, and where any energies that are not of the highest intention are bounced back to their source.

Let us give thanks for the miracle of Spirit, in all its brilliance and manifestations.

Let the business of your mind slow to the rhythm of your heartbeat, as you move to the inner sounds of your being. You move your mind through your body, listening to your breath, slowing more and more as you relax and allow yourself to become at one with the flow of energies moving through you. Breathing deeply, releasing, breathing deeply, releasing, letting go of the outer world, as you attune to all that which is your sensate experience, listening to the sounds of all the music that emanates from the temple of your soul.

As you yield to the steady beating of your heart and the long, rhythmic breathing, you feel your mind beginning to drift in a state of dreamy abandon, at peace with all that surrounds you. Let yourself follow the breeze, your thoughts floating in space, your heart filling with a sense of warmth, light and contentment.

Let go of any expectation.

Let go of need and of desire.

Let go of all thoughts that do not serve your highest good.

You breathe in all that is right about the world, focused on the beauty and all the love, and you breathe away all that is inharmonious. With every breath, you feel yourself going deeper and deeper, to the very core of your being—the flame of light that is your very essence. You go to your center. With each cyclical breath, see that flame expanding, its light moving upward, into your head, down into your toes and everywhere throughout your being. Let its light expand outwards, into the space that surrounds you, and inwards, filling every cell, so that your entire body, and the auric shield are filled with light.

Once you are aglow in the brilliance of Spirit, send this light beyond your immediate being, reaching out to the star beings and guides who work with you and who are part of your circle of light. Spread your light to them as well. This brilliant circle of light reaches out to all the light beings that hover around you, and others, who travel the web of golden light that is woven through the One Soul. Send the love of all that you are, that you have ever been and that forever you will be outward, into the cosmic sea, and throughout the waters of your being—into the DNA itself—and know that in this moment, you are in resonance with the love of all Creation.

Draw your attention to the crown chakra. Can you see it? If you cannot, believe, imagine it fully activated, luminous, connected to Source. Slowly open the crown chakra, folding back the petals of the lotus, and extending a beam of light from your head to serve as a beacon to all the light ones of Creation. Ask them to connect with you, to assist in the evaluation of your cellular condition. They will. They will come when you call out to them. Can you feel them? Take time to sit with that experience, a feeling of being at one with all the light beings of the universe and beyond . . . a sense of **knowing** Creator.

Imagine, visualize, feel the light of so many beings fill you with their brilliance, and send that light through the crown, traversing the spinal cord, as it washes over the chakric energy system and descending deep inside the earth, where you will anchor it.

Now that you have turned on the flood lights, you are free to observe all body systems and all body functions, as you scan your organism, with detachment and non-judgmental observation of anything that appears to be out of place, or foreign to your sacred temple. You are going to run a scan of your entire organism, head to toe, from the dense organs, tissues, blood, cellular waters and the double helix of your divine blueprint. You will be free to observe any attachment, hook, cord or foreign body that appears to your mind's scanning procedure, examining your lungs, heart, digestive system, your bones and all tissues that comprise the dense structure of your physical structure. You make note of anything that appears in your scanning screen as anomalous, or invasive, and then move deeper, past the organs, observing the blood.

Your blood is the fuel of your entire organism: your vital life force. How does it appear to you? Observe the texture, the color, the flow of the blood through the miles and miles of its arterial and venal highways and through the heart, pumping life to every inch of your being. Is there any peculiarity that you need to make note of? You do not have to know what you are looking for, for you are not a scientist. You are simply observing, and asking that you be shown what you need to see.

Spirit knows exactly what to do.

You move your consciousness through the blood, into a cell. Is the light still brilliant? You can call upon those who have come to assist you and ask that it be turned up brighter, for you are going to be examining the workings of every cell, the sacred geometry in its waters, and the nucleus, where you will scan the DNA. What do you see? Can you make out patterns of geometric design in the waters of the cell? Are they crystalline or opaque? Can you hear words that have been held there, reverberating, for who knows how long?

Again, there is nothing to feel, no judgment or emotion. You are detached from it all, simply observing. Recording. Breathing.

You move your conscious awareness into the nucleus now. Magnifying the minutia of the DNA coil, you are free to see the double helix. We all have at least two strands of DNA lit up within us. You are scanning the spiral ladder looking for fragments, tears or anomalies that do not fit there. There are many factors that can disrupt the DNA, and you are free to see them now. You may see swarms of bits and pieces swimming in and around the coil, you may see a third strand of DNA woven into the helix. Or more. Trust what you see, and know that this is what you have come to observe.

Breathe your light into the blueprint of your soul.

Utter the God Code into your divine blueprint.

Yahweh . . . Yahweh . . . Yahweh . . .

Vocalize the God Code, sounding its harmonics as "yah-oooo-oh-eh," the same way you use your voice to chant "Om."

Sound it out gently, no more than a whisper, and then louder, establishing that point of rich resonance where you can feel the sound reverberating through your body.

Do you see the coil light up even brighter?

Take your time. You are at the very core of what you came to find and you want to stay with this until you receive what you came for, even if you did not know what that is when you set out to scan and observe your body template.

Whatever you visualize, see, or imagine is right. There is nothing to feel, to fear; there is no right answer . . . no way you need to react.

Ask to see what you need to see, to make yours . . . to forgive and to heal. There will be time for that. For now, just see, observe, and bring to the foreground what is needed.

When you are confident that you have gathered all the images and information you need, you will slowly redirect your awareness to return from the nucleus, out of the cell, through the blood, the organs, the tissues, all body fluids and outside of the physical body, into the auric field. You have imprinted your scanning mechanism with all observations that need your attention, and you are free to see them now.

This is a vital moment and you need to give yourself all the time you need to observe and record what you have brought into the light of your conscious awareness.

Breathe deeply, knowing that the highest good will prevail. Call upon the Angels of Light to assist you, as you slowly imagine the beam of light from your crown retracting and closing the crown center. Draw up the light from the earth as well.

Soon all you will see is a tiny point of light and then . . . it disappears.

When you are ready to take the next step, you will be able to examine the scanned information and go on to healing, repairing and liberating the cellular memory, so that you can move ahead to the process of healing the double helix, activating a third strand of your dormant DNA, and re-weaving the sacred that is your birthright.

Meditation
The Primary Tetrahedron

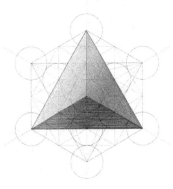

*"The harmonics of the heightened cellular communication
manifesting with the integration of the third strand,
forming triangulation in the entire network
of your intelligence communities of DNA and cellular units,
creates within your microcosmic bodies
a universal vibrational "template" of intelligent light coding.
Around this cardinal matrix,
the remaining three triad formations of etheric DNA
will coalesce in three succinct stages of your passage,
which you will experience as immeasurable leaps in consciousness
and your progressive release from the entrainment
of all three-dimensional illusion—
freeing you from the grip with which it holds you locked in the
polarities
of your journey through the Desert Days of Earth's transition."*
—The Sirian High Council

Create whatever you need to assure that you are comfortable and un-interrupted. Remove as best you can all electromagnetic devices from your environment. If you have television and computers nearby, be sure they are unplugged from the wall socket and be sure the cell phone is not only turned off, it should be out of the house entirely. You want to be very aware of how your electromagnetic biological unit runs energy, and that nothing interferes with that flow at this time.

You may wish to record this meditation, and play it back for yourself, as your guide through this meditational journey. It will help you go deeper, to let go of "process" and simply allow you to "experience."

Call upon the Angel Warriors of Light, asking to be encircled in an impenetrable sphere of golden white light, and ask that it hold as a barrier to any energies that are not of the highest intent. Let them be bounced back to their source, and dealt with as is appropriate to their karmic destiny. There is nothing to feel about it, nothing to be concerned about. When you state your intention to the universe, it knows exactly what to do.

It's all about intention.

Lie, or sit quietly. Breathe deeply and rhythmically, eyes closed, letting the sensate world slowly fall away from you ... slipping into a place of calm and deep relaxation. With every breath, feel yourself becoming more centered and peaceful, and the body lighter and lighter ... so light, you feel like a feather in a soft breeze.

You're going to visualize the crown chakra opening, by peeling back the petals of the lotus, one at a time, and as you do, you call in the light of Spirit—pure light—to enter through this sacred center and to pass, like a golden cord, through your spinal column. Imagine a golden anchor at the end of this cord of light, as you send it down through the skull, around the back of your head, through your neck and passing, one vertebra at a time, down ... down ... down, through the root chakra, and out of your physical body—moving through the floor, the foundation ... the soil. Send it down deep into the cool of Mother Earth's embrace, until you reach a place where you can hook your anchor to the rocks of the inner earth. You ground yourself there, feeling how powerful is your connection to Gaia, and knowing that nothing can ever blow you away again, as you long as you are grounded.

Observe as your entire being fills with light. Direct it through the energy wheels of your chakric system, to every organ, every body system, the blood, the lymph, every cell, every aspect of your being. The auric field becomes brighter, bigger, pulsating with the vibratory essence of this great light moving through you.

Draw your attention back to the crown. You may not be visual—do not let that deter you. It does not matter if you feel you have been interfered with in any way. You can let that go. You are going to release it. Just imagine, visualize, feel, believe that appearing in the space above your crown is a golden tetrahedron, manifesting in the sacred geometric template that underlies all physical reality. Feel the light shimmering through you, as this golden tetrahedron slowly spins overhead, reflecting golden white light everywhere around and within you.

Once you have anchored this rotating form clearly in your vision, draw it into the crown and place it directly over the pineal gland, which sits at the epicenter of your head, just behind the bridge of your nose. The pineal gland will be perfectly centered within the tetrahedron, if you ask that it be so. As it activates, the golden tetrahedron will start to spin, showering more light within and around you. Feel that golden white light bathe the lighthouse of your soul, a sense that will be new to you . . . just as it will be a sense of remembering.

Positioned at the gateway of your emerging consciousness, the golden tetrahedron serves as the matrix from which you will weave the third strand of DNA into your conscious awareness.

Show yourself the double helix formation of your DNA codex, intelligent architect upon which you have constructed your physical being. You can ask now that you be shown the information you gleaned from the scan you performed earlier. The light of your higher consciousness is directed by Higher Beings to scan this form, to know it, to examine any areas where there may be tears, rips, pieces missing. Ask that you be shown anything that is extraneous to your natural order, and that it be brought into the bright light, where now it will be released and carried away, back to its source.

Take stock of everything you see. Where are those broken pieces? You are free to see everything that disturbs or disrupts the divine blueprint within you, and to command all conscious units within to re-assemble, reunite and repair the fragments and disruption within the sacred language of the Divine Blueprint. Like a software engineer re-writes code, you will now overwrite any interfering or menacing data, signature or frequencies with the sacred God Code within you, pro-nouncing the name of Creator:

"Yahweh . . . Yahweh . . . Ya-ooo-oh-eh . . ."

You may be able to see the DNA changing, re-assembling the bro-ken or tattered pieces . . . becoming more luminous. Sometimes, you can hear or feel vibrational shifts when you connect with your Source code in this way. It does not matter if you are not visual, or capable of perceiving it that way. The DNA hears you, and responds to your com-mands. It hears you calling out the sacred utterance that will reactivate any part of the God Code that has been in any way hidden or shad-owed by any interfering entity, attachment, hook or mechanism.

Sing it again: Ya-ooo-oh-eh, imagining its vibrational impact upon the waters of your being, rippling through you.

Breathe deep, release. Breathe, release. Let go of any emotion at-tached to this moment and know that you are initiating a process that will continue long after you shift your awareness elsewhere. There may be many bridges that need to be rebuilt, and that can happen in an in-stant, or over some time—even in your sleep. What is important is that you have begun the process and that any and all disruption will repair.

See it, feel it, believe that it is so, and so it will be.

Let us move forward. Visualize, believe, imagine that from this immense field of Light within you, you are sending a laser beam into the sea of particles of scattered DNA. Let is serve as a magnet for those fragments that have forgotten their purpose and reason for being there. You are imprinting the waters of every cell of your body with the etheric form of a third DNA thread, calling the fragments home. As you send this brilliant ray of light into the sea of your cellular waters, certain fragments hear the call. They recognize the vibrational sequencing and are drawn to it. They know who they are, and they respond to the lighthouse of your mind. They move into the geometric template that has begun to take form, in and around this beam of light, and align to the frequencies of its resonant field.

A third DNA thread, a single strand of illuminated DNA, is now taking form.

Take time with this. Give yourself time to breathe it into being.

You are going to command this thread to weave itself into the double helix, re-creating the tetrahedral form that has been positioned over the pineal in the three-stranded geometric design of your activated DNA . . . creating triangulation within every cell of your body. Every cell reflects back to you the perfect symmetry of the sacred triangulation, taking form within the DNA, reflecting God light through every part of you and every aspect of your being.

Three, the resolution of duality, is now being imprinted upon the sacred designs coalescing within you. It overwrites any disruptive signature, code or vibration with the love and perfection of the God Code.

Know that within every cell of your body a new dynamic—your higher vibration—has begun to manifest, and will that it be so forever. State your intention to every part of your being – every organ, every cell, every subatomic particle, and every unit of consciousness that breathes as you breathe – that you intend that the etheric strands of DNA now crystallize within you, as is appropriate to your spirit journey.

They are your birthright.

This is a returning . . .

An arrival and a departure: the multidimensional journey.

The golden tetrahedron is still positioned around the pineal gland. If you are comfortable that it remain there, you can command that it be so. If not, and you prefer to release it, breathe it out through the crown chakra, and return it to the light, in gratitude.

And now, before you return to body consciousness, and only when you are ready to do so, fold in the petals of the lotus, blessing the Light Ones who have assisted you here . . . taking as much time as you need to integrate the new that is being birthed within you.

Taking all the time you need to integrate this experience.

You will return to your body now. Feel your fingers, move your toes. Get the blood circulating.

Lie still, taking all the time you need to come completely back to the room, the space in which you find yourself.

Taking all the time you need.

Taking all the time you need . . . to come home.

Meditation
The Star Tetrahedron

*The activation and synthesis of the fourth, fifth, and sixth strands,
will be achieved not as a sequential process,
whereby you acquire one strand after another but simultaneously—
a perfect triad of light strings resonating as one major chord
in the symphony of light playing through you.
Once integrated into the matrix, this exquisite light unit,
the higher dimensional reflection of the primary triangulation, will
send enormous frequencies coursing through the nuclei of all the cells
of your body
and pulsate (first through you and then from the nuclear mind)
the intricate rhythms and proportions of a complex star tetrahedron,
which you are learning is the cosmometric model
of the merkaba energy fields that surround you.
Its complex structure represents the unity of the principles of form,
purpose, and order with those of space, force, and duration.*
—The Sirian High Council

Let pass several days before you proceed to the activation of the second tetrahedron. There is much to integrate, and it is important to sit with the experience of the first activation, to feel the shift within you. It may be subtle, it may be immense. As always, there is no right way to feel, to be, to experience.

When you are ready, and when you have made all the preparations that involve creating an amenable environment around you, lie or sit quietly, following your breathing, until you reach a place of quiet reflection.

You begin by asking to see the scanned images you have brought to the foreground of your consciousness prior to this moment. What do you see there? Let that information be brought forward, to be transformed in the light of your accelerated DNA template: into the God light.

Call upon the elemental spirits of fire, water, air and earth, the spirit guides, the light teams of all higher realms, the power animals, Ascended Masters, and Christed extraterrestrials to encircle you in a sphere of golden white light, to hold as a barrier against any energies that are not of the highest intention. Let them be bounced back to their source and be dealt with according to their karmic destiny. Ask to be shown a vehicle of white light that will serve to encapsulate any energies of any form or presence that are not resonant with the light of Spirit, one that you can utilize to assist in their transmutation and release back to their source, as is appropriate to their evolutionary pace.

Breathe in. Breathe out. Breathe in the love of unconditional love, and breathe out anything that still holds you in disharmony and concern. You can simply breathe out and away all those tensions, stress and fears that deter you, and watch them dissipate in the light of All-That-Is. You are accelerating the flow of prana by breathing deeply and rhythmically, in and out . . . breathing in peace and acceptance. On the outbreath, you release expectation and all desire that you may still have attached to this experience. You breathe in and out—calm in, stress out—until you feel that you are in a beautifully neutral, harmonious, "now" moment.

Draw your attention to the pineal gland and the space that surrounds it.

Do you still see, feel, intuit the golden tetrahedron there? If not, draw it in now, and position it as before, perfectly centered around the gland. You do not have to think about where that is, or what it would look like. The body responds to your command that it be so, and Spirit does the rest.

We're going to set the tetrahedron in motion. Ask that it start to rotate, so that it is spinning slowly around the gland in a clockwise direction. As it does, shimmering golden white light bathes your skull, all body systems, the cells, right down to the DNA within them. The light gets brighter and brighter still, so luminous now that you can see the coiled DNA. Do you have two strands illuminated? Or three?

Remember that if you are not visual it does not matter. Feel it, intuit, imagine it.

Check to see if you have two or three strands of DNA illuminated. In this bright light, you are able to "see" if there is still anything there that is not of the highest vibration, and you are free now to remove those energies. They are no longer allowed access. You are going to send them into that light vehicle to be taken away . . . forever. Take time to see any residue, shadow, anything at all that you know is not meant to be there—any foreign aspect—and send it into that bubble of light.

Breathing . . . breathing . . . being sure to gather every last bit of it, and now sending it into the bubble, sealing it tight, and sending it up . . . up . . . and away. As you let go, you breathe in the lightness of being, the light flowing in, and the weight of what has been before lifting as you watch it float away.

See, feel, imagine the tetrahedral form of the triple helix within your DNA. The pineal gland is activating very powerfully now, as the golden tetrahedron spins around it, re-connecting the third strand into the master seed—a work in progress.

Holding that sacred geometric form in your conscious awareness, you are now going to send out the call to those fragments that constitute the fourth, fifth and sixth strands of your DNA. They resonate to the template—the primary triangulation—and like the water crystal as it responds to thought and energy, they strive to re-assemble their godly form. Joined by all the light beings who have come to assist you, you send a powerful beam of light into the nucleus of every cell, into the coil of your DNA, a beacon to call those fragments of DNA back into the sacred resonance of their geometric memory.

The particles and bits of DNA begin to take form. The second triangulation is being re-assembled. We are going to activate these structures with the Divine Light frequencies, the cosmometry of infinite love, the light of all divine beings, the fire letters and the God Code: "Ya-ooo-oh-eh," whispered into the waters, again and again.

And when that moment comes when you know, see, feel, imagine that the second tetrahedron has taken form, you are going to set it spinning counterclockwise (the magnetic field), while the first tetrahedron will be in a clockwise spin (the electric) and observe as they are drawn to each other, and finally merge into each other as one.

Within the DNA of every cell of your being, you have now formed the merkaba, the star tetrahedron, the sacred form and geometry of six-stranded DNA awareness.

Always remember that it is not important if this experience is not a visual one—if it is not visceral or explosive in its breadth. Know that energy follows thought and thought follows intention, and so, set your intention that, from this moment forward, this brilliant golden white energy that emanates from the merkaba within your DNA will continue to shine so brightly that only the highest vibrations will be attracted to you . . . to the temple of light that you are.

Take time to recognize the wonder of your being here, in the epicenter of your evolutionary journey, from one state of awareness to another, climbing higher with every step. The outer world is irrelevant; it is only a screen on possible realities that you will create with every thought, every breath you take.

You breathe love and acceptance into your fear for Earth's process, for the lives of all those you love, and for humanity everywhere. And you let it go.

You breathe love and acceptance into any remaining sense of lack or limitation.

And you trust that, this day, you have released yourself from any and all energies that have yet to understand that you hold a space between the earth and sky, a perfected template of the God light: the Divine Blueprint.

You are the commander of your own destiny, a free-will being, and so you will remain, until you leave this mortal coil behind you and return to the Light.

Nothing and no one can ever take that away.

Remember that you are the star, the cosmic storm; you are the grain of sand, the wave; you are the exquisite love laced throughout every moment of Creator's master plan.

Above all, remember that you are a sovereign being, moving through the eternal wonder of Be-ing.

"You are a child of the universe,
no less than the trees and the stars;
you have a right to be here.
And whether or not it is clear to you,
no doubt the universe is unfolding as it should.
Therefore, be at peace with God,
whatever you conceive Him to be,
and whatever your labors and aspirations,
in the noisy confusion of life keep peace with your soul.
With all its sham, drudgery, and broken dreams,
it is still a beautiful world.
Be cheerful.
Strive to be happy."
Excerpt from The Desiderata
—Max Ehrmann

Epilogue

So many years ago, the Council said, "How we wish you could know with certainty that what you dream for the future is the reality, and that what appears to be so terrifyingly real now is only a dream of the collective unconscious."[39]

It is not a good dream, this, and we want to wake up from it—we need to. And we need to in a hurry, all doing our part to imprint the collective with visions of humanity, rising.

It feels like we have gone through the looking glass and landed in an insane and freakish upside-down world. The world of matter and things looks pretty much the same, but the vibrational frequencies of Planet Earth have shifted beyond our wildest imaginings—out to both extremes of the poles. At the societal level, everything feels disproportionate and grotesque, because we are facing the clashing karma of all existence on this planet, all at once—here, and now. Societal values, behaviors, and dialogue are so unfamiliar to us, in these uncharted waters. At a scale we perceive as the world-at-large, we are mostly living in a dissonant, destructive hologram that keeps pulling at the lower vibrational chords of our existence, dragging us down.

At the opposite pole, we are witnessing, and taking part in, the Great Awakening. The veils are lifting, people are shaking off the dream spell, and we know that an exceptional uprising, from those of the light vision, is unstoppable and gaining ground.

Those of us who are fortunate and determined enough to resonate with the vibration of Spirit, walking in the God light, recognize the im-

---

39   No More Secrets, No More Lies, Patricia Cori, 2022 edition, pg. 249-250

mense opportunities this frenzy brings, to burn ancient karma, so that, if the intention is to step off this wheel, and complete our reincarnation cycle, we can be free to travel the ascension spiral to higher ground.

Those who are determined to resist and free the Earth of the dark force understand that these growing pains are necessary initiations that precede our giant steps, those magnificent moments when we grow by "leaps and bounds," and that **is** ascension. We will step off the wheel of reincarnation and move up the spiral, closer to Source than we have been for such a very, very long time.

That is the reality of which the blessed Ascended Masters speak.

We strive for the halcyon days of peace and contentment we believe we lived sometime before, somewhere else—in the stars, and God knows we, loving souls, have earned them. But, first, we have this small matter of pushing back the dark cloak of evil here on our planet, to restore peace, right here on Earth, within and outside of ourselves, and by God, that is what we are going to do.

We, the awakened, know that from this intense turmoil and suffering, we shall emerge glorious and victorious, to see evil vanquished and Earth reborn. It may not look that way now, but peace will come. And peace shall prevail.

At long last, peace shall prevail.

We are settling into the fourth dimension now and it is does not look or feel like anything we imagined or were told a "higher" dimension would be. Nothing about this battle feels "higher" at all! Most people don't even have an idea of multidimensional reality whatsoever, so they will most likely be bounced around at the outer limits of their mutating awareness, until finally they realize what this insanity is all about, and where they will land, once they are tossed out of this cosmic wind tunnel.

The farther one strays from Source, the deeper the trauma and pain.

The celestial bodies within our solar system and our central star are experiencing immense galactic upheaval, as I have described earlier in this work. All of this continues to challenge our existence, as these cosmic forces and their influence on all life on our planet shake us to the core. World events threaten our 3D world with every imaginable form of destruction. By the time you will be reading this, we will have survived the immediate threat of nuclear war, emanating from the contrived conflict in Ukraine, the financial system as we knew it will be teetering on collapse and the world will continue to find itself in terrible social upheaval. No doubt, many will die before their time, as tragic as that is, and as painful it is for me to verbalize it. It is not because I wish to project such thoughts; it is because I am well aware of what has been put in place to create that reality.

Yet, our higher perception of reality allows us to recognize how necessary it is that the old be broken down, dissected, and allowed to disintegrate, so that the new can coalesce, take form and build a new framework for our evolving world. We fantasized an ascension paradigm based on our imaginations—that somehow "beyond 3D" meant higher, lighter, freer, but very few visionaries gave any thought to our passing through 4D first—a virtual quagmire of karmic retribution for the individual and the collective.

Like *Dante's Inferno*, *The Egyptian Book of The Dead* and *The Tibetan Book of Dead*, there exists a recurring theme: a difficult, treacherous point of passage. Religions define it as the soul passing from life, through stages of a form of purgatory, where it must surmount its demons, before it can progress to heaven, however that is represented in each belief system.

Isn't that the fourth dimension? And aren't we now in a state of initiation, or "purgatory?" The Sirians have always told us that we pass through the fourth dimension, a place where we are faced with our individual and collective karma, on our way to less dense vibrational realms, that we call the higher dimensions. It sure looks like purgatory to me.

May our passing through it be swift and painless.

*

We will see amazing things in these next years: amazingly dark, amazingly light.

We will understand more, because we will **be** more.

As we anchor the star tetrahedron of our six-stranded DNA within us, re-activating the God Code wherever it has been disabled, we will beam more light into the communal memory, and we will know so much more about who we really are, and who we are becoming: not as mechanical, soulless zombies of the transhumanists' dream, but as vibrant, God-loving souls, traversing this tiny dot in the Cosmos of Soul—on our way to the next miracle.

They will never dim the God light within us, or deter our Spirit Eternal, for as long as we do not bow to the dark master.

I, Patricia Cori, know I never will. And I know that is the way of my beloved family of lightworkers.

And that, my dear and loving friends, is what sovereignty is all about.

About the Channel

A native of the San Francisco Bay Area, Patricia Cori has been immersed in the Spirit Movement since its inception there in the early 1970s. She has utilized her clairvoyant abilities in healing and support work throughout her life, which has been dedicated in great part to the study of mysticism and philosophy, ancient civilizations, metaphysical healing, spirituality, and extraterrestrial life.

A world teacher, Patricia is helping many realize their natural healing abilities, release the blockages of unresolved emotions and limitation, attuning to the higher vibrations of our ascending celestial realm. She is a pioneer in the work of preparing the awakening in the healing and activation of DNA, so vital for souls to retain their sovereign, godly design – the God Code.

Patricia immigrated to Rome in 1983, knowing that she had to take part in a mission . . . as she was instructed by her guides that she would have to help "burn a hole in the lead dome." She currently resides in the Azores Islands, Portugal, which she understands are remnants of the Ancient Land of Atlantis.

She is a prominent figure in the Spirit and Truther communities, well-known on the lecture circuit, offering courses, seminars, and workshops internationally, which reflect her conscious awareness of the Higher Knowledge and the empowering guidance of the light beings working through her.

She has been actively channeling the Speakers of the Sirian High Council since her first visitation to the crop circles in 1996, and continues to lecture and transcribe their messages for all those who seek the wisdom.

The Divine Blueprint –
On-Line Course in DNA Activation

Patricia Cori offers her comprehensive DNA activation course on-line, with deep meditations utilizing the healing properties of Solfeggio frequencies, as directed by the healing teams of the Sirian High Council.

DNA Activation

This eight-part intensive course facilitated by Sirian Light Beings focuses on opening the energy byways, drawing from the multidimensional self the innate abilities that will accelerate your preparation for ascension. Guided by Light Beings from many dimensions, you will be shown the way to the new horizons upon the path of your spiritual and emotional experience—preparing the way for the activation of the third strand of DNA and the awakening of the light body.

Activation of the new crystalline matrix that is forming in your evolving being (the integration of the third strand of DNA), creates triangulation within the consciousness of every cell of your physical body—the trinity of divine awareness.

The entire energy body, the chakras and their corresponding glandular systems (particularly the pineal gland) the *Ida and Pingala* energy byways, the auric body—every aspect of existence in the world of matter is about to change and as one of the awakening, you are eager to accelerate that process.

Those of you who have come in to serve as guides and healers in the process of Gaia's evolution are called to Initiation: the activation of the third strand; chakric clearing; cellular regeneration; resonance with the higher frequencies; connection with the Galactic Family of Light Beings.

Participants are guided through specific techniques and procedures to heal and activate the DNA. They will learn to construct the cosmometric cellular geometries and to raise the vibratory frequencies that will prepare the way for activation of the 4th, 5th, and 6th strands, triggering pineal illumination and strengthening their link with the higher beings who are serving in the process. This process is offered in deep meditations provided in the course.

As we draw upon the patterns of all cosmic consciousness, we will also ground ourselves to Gaia, for this is our celestial home—as it will be for those who choose to ascend into the higher dimensions: the New Frontier. This, in absolute integrity, honesty, and conviction—for we are past the time when we can distract ourselves with imaginings, posturing, and spiritual rhetoric. We must clear away the distractions and be prepared to walk in the light of Absolute Truth—at peace in our souls as we climb the spiral of Return.

The intensive course, facilitated by Sirian Light Beings, is created and offered in this format in conjunction with Patricia's spirit journeys of initiation at the sacred sites of the world's power points.

For additional information about her courses, private clairvoyant readings and future SoulQuest™ Journeys guided by Patricia Cori, please consult her website:

www.patriciacori.com

CPSIA information can be obtained
at www.ICGtesting.com
Printed in the USA
LVHW022224151122
732907LV00008B/266